Darkness Is Light Enough

Darkness Is Light Enough

Mystery and Enlightenment at Lake Geneva, Wisconsin

Gerald R. Lishka

1996
Galde Press, Inc.
Lakeville, Minnesota U.S.A.

First Edition
First Printing, 1996

Cover design by Christopher Wells

Library of Congress Cataloging-in-Publication Data
Lishka, Gerald R., 1949–
    Darkness is light enough : mystery and enlightenment at Lake Geneva,
Wisconsin / Gerald R. Lishka.
        p.   cm.
    ISBN 1–880090–28–7
    1. Lishka, Gerald R., 1949–   . 2. Spiritual biography—United
States. 3. Private revelations. 4. Vision quests. 5. Shamanism.
6. Lake Geneva (Wis.)   I. Title.
BL73.L57A3   1996
299'.93—dc20
[B]   96–8002
                                                                CIP

Galde Press, Inc.
PO Box 460
Lakeville, Minnesota 55044

Contents

Dedications

I am writing this dedication page more than thirteen years after completing *Darkness Is Light Enough*, during which time I have done a great deal of living, including ten years in Los Angeles, California. Sadly, I have divorced a second time, and prior to that, experienced the most heartbreaking loss of a lifetime, the death of my three-year-old foster daughter, Jennifer. Actually, I am rewriting the original dedication by adding these thoughts and by naming many loved ones here, because I now see clearly that I must include many more names than the two to whom the book was originally dedicated. In doing this, I hope to right what I admit may be an imbalance in the manuscript, one which, in my mind, will be fully restored only by a sequel to this book. The concern I have with this present manuscript is that, although I stand today and always behind its message, which expresses so much of the spiritual passion of my earlier life, it poses certain questions regarding the direction and resolution of my spiritual search which should be answered, and which can now be answered due to the passage of time; and also, very importantly, I feel that the manuscript does not deal fully enough with a dimension of life fully as important as the spiritual ones explored so thoroughly in these pages, and one which I have come face-to-face with so profoundly in the last few years—that no body of metaphysical knowledge or spiritual exercises and experiences, although absolutely valid in their own right and essential to a meaningful life, can substitute for the giving and receiving of love between other people, the expression of love between souls, whether between parent and child, husband and wife, or between lovers or friends. To seek spiritual realization is a road that all souls must eventually embark upon. But to do so without being grounded in love for other people, without recognizing and fulfilling that need with other souls, is a sham and a dangerous lie. The present book is large enough. The thoughts touched upon here must await full expression in a later volume. But saying what I have said here helps very much, I feel, to put the message of this book in proper perspective, and enables me, finally, to offer it without reservation and with a free heart.

I dedicate this book:

to my innermost circle of friends and spiritual warriors, Jerry Alber, my age-old companion of many lifetimes; Dawn Grant; and Gillian McKenna;

to David Cull, an old friend and counselor, not forgotten;

to Anna McGrosso, a dear friend, a wonderful pianist, and my teacher;

to my Mother and Father, for all the years of loving and caring;

to my cousin, Carolyn Divan, who induced in me a breathtaking realization which found expression in this new dedication page;

to Suzanne Marie Schimpeler, my former wife, and a soul whom I will love and value deeply, always;

to Jessica Christina Pivaral, my beautiful and exuberant little goddaughter, whom I love so much, my child in previous lifetimes, who this time around has lifted me up so many times from my grief at the loss of her half-sister;

and most especially, to Jennifer Janeth Pivaral, my foster daughter who died so young, who yet was so seasoned in wisdom, my precious baby, surely reigning now as Queen of Heaven, truly, truly my daughter and teacher in this and in many past incarnations, my true savior, whose being is fused eternally with mine in the purest love that can be realized between two souls, who overturned my world, took me to a spiritual mountaintop, and taught me that love of cosmic dimensions can be fully found and intimately shared in the human heart, probably more easily than along the paths of mysticism.

I am thankful for my great fortune of having found so much love in both human and divine spheres, which I now see clearly are one and the same.

"Let God kill him who does not know, yet presumes to teach." (Sufi saying)

May the souls named above protect me from lightning bolts.

Prologue

When you need this book the most,
you will find it.

Beyond the boundaries of daily perception that we view as reality lies a world of truth, beauty, and power beyond measure that eludes all attempts at description. Once revealed, this world changes one forever and renders inadequate things that were once regarded as important. Such things may maintain a foothold in one's life, but they are never again enough in themselves. I have not written this book to proselytize or change people. People seldom change, and when they do it is only through powerful efforts of will or because of rare moments in life when one steps into exactly the right time and place and extraordinary events leave their mark. I have written because of my own extraordinary experiences, at the core of which is the emotional power that became the fuel for writing. I speak of awe—the feelings of wonder that possessed me when I was confronted with new worlds. I have witnessed a mystery. There also came a time when I saw that I had no choice but to write, and that failure to do so would result in unhappiness and spiritual stagnation. A wise friend told me that it was not right that I carried around inside of me the things I had experienced like some secret that I kept tucked away in my shirt pocket to peek at once in a while when it suited me.

My experiences have had to stand by themselves. They have no bible, scripture, or doctrine, and no minister or guru. They are direct perception. I could rightly call them revelations. Thus I realized that I had a message for people who had themselves had visions or glimpsed some truth. As others had done for me, I could encourage them to accept and embrace their experiences despite the skepticism and limited vision they might encounter from people around them.

I hope also that my book will convince people that the universe and all that it contains is a living thing, and that it is the expression and handiwork of an unfathomable love. I write in response to the exquisite love that showed me the living world, and to a special place where that love was revealed to me. The perceptions I had there radically changed my life, and since perceptions are food that sustains the spirit, this book is about the perceptions that have fed me.

Many would call my experiences religious. Someone close to me once said that my experiences were beyond religion. When I realized this and stopped trying to fit the square pegs of my experiences into round holes, I was freed of a terrible weight. I became responsible to myself instead of feeling accountable to the host of dogmas that clamored for my allegiance.

The vision that brought about my rebirth was the event out of which all else grew—the primal cause that initiated a lifetime of searching. Sometimes I encountered darkness, but it too was integral to my experiences of light. To seek light is to embark upon a path that lasts a lifetime. My own path led me to a beautiful place of power in whose magical setting I embraced extraordinary experiences. There, I have stood at the brink of an awesome and inexpressible world. To share the supreme power of that unique and lovely place and my experiences there is the heart and purpose of this book.

Psalm 8

O Lord, our Lord,
How majestic is Thy name in all the earth,
Who hast displayed Thy splendor above the heavens!
From the mouth of infants and nursing babes
Thou hast established strength,
Because of Thine adversaries,
To make the enemy and the revengeful cease.

When I consider Thy heavens, the work
of Thy fingers,
The moon and the stars, which Thou hast ordained;
What is man, that Thou dost take thought of him?
And the son of man, that Thou dost care for him?
Yet Thou hast made him a little lower than God,
And dost crown him with glory and majesty!

Thou dost make him to rule over the works
of Thy hands;
Thou hast put all things under his feet,
All sheep and oxen,
And also the beasts of the field,
The birds of the heavens, and the fish of the sea,
Whatever passes through the paths of the seas.

O Lord, our Lord,
How majestic is Thy name in all the earth!

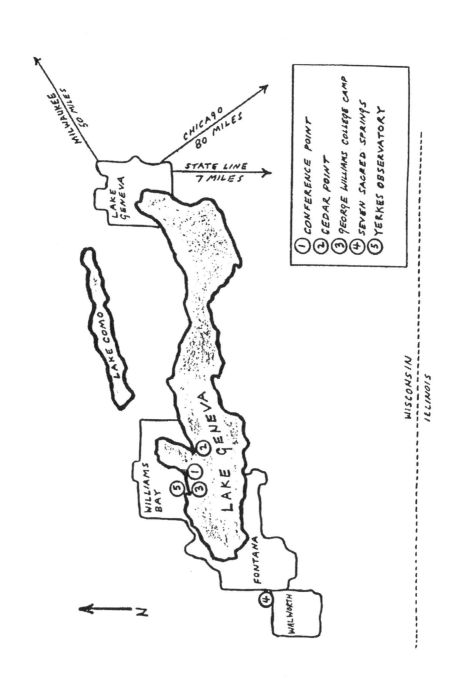

The Vision

IT WAS AN EVENING in August, 1964, in Wisconsin, along the shores of Lake Geneva, and I was fifteen years old. I was in the company of a large group of young people like myself, who had gathered to participate in a religious service. I was deeply preoccupied, and virtually heedless of their words and actions. Now, more than thirty-one years in retrospect, I have no recollection of what transpired among the people at that meeting. My mental and emotional state was one of intense abstraction, and I vividly remember the compelling harbingers, the portentous and thrilling perceptions whose provocative and ominous character engrossed me, and which foreshadowed the events which, on that auspicious night, were to burst into my life with transcendental power and light.

We were assembled that evening in a very large, multiroomed cabin which served as a meeting hall. Among the things that I vividly recall which compelled my attention, one singular aspect of the interior of that room stands out in my memory. The fire, which danced and crackled in the fireplace, hissed and popped with a peculiar and disturbing intensity, and I felt in it the disquieting yet seductive sensation of a presence. The fire seemed somehow alive, and as I gazed into its flickering blue and yellow lights and its searing, glowing heart, I felt, not without some apprehension, that there might be revealed to me the startling vision of some elemental being lurking there.

Commingled with the presence of the fire, the alluring and seductive chirping of the insects beckoned to me with a disquieting intensity. Somewhere outside, in the darkness of the night, a deep and irresistible yet undefined volition was pulling me, drawing me to itself. I could hear its treacherously captivating summons in the melodious voices of the insects and in the distant, almost inaudible murmuring of waves along the shores of the lake.

Utterly oblivious to my peers and to whatever may have occupied their attentions, I experienced a mounting restlessness and excitement, an acute and tremulous anticipation which welled up inside me and enkindled my whole being. I was seized with a tremendous agitation which penetrated my solar plexus, saturated my perceptions and inexorably permeated the totality of my consciousness. At a certain point, my level of energy and tension became so heightened and intensified that I was unable to remain seated or to endure the confinement of the room and, getting up, I headed anxiously for a door and hurried out into the darkness.

Something irresistible was drawing me, hunting me, searching me out, calling to me. I experienced a profound sense of urgency. I was overcome at once by the wonder of being pursued, even stalked by this awesome, terrifyingly incalculable and measureless power, yet on the other hand, of being touched, probed to the bottom of my being by a gentle and unfathomable love which was somehow indescribably passionate. This power was searching my being. It worked its way into the depths of my feelings and compelled me to go on, to hasten my steps down the dark paved roadway.

I felt a most profound and consuming passion and love for this power, a sense of oneness and intimacy with it. With mounting anticipation, I now ran quickly through the night toward the place of power, to my place of meditation where all the force seemed to center and converge. I shortly found myself at the top of the long series of concrete steps which led down to the dark shore and to the water, to the place of power. With growing anticipation I descended the steps, and in a moment I was standing only a few feet from where, in the starry darkness, the waves lapped against the rocks and boulders, softly uttering to me their mysteries.

As I stood there I began to experience the greatest moments of realization that I had ever known in the fifteen years of my life. I truly "saw," in a single moment, those past fifteen years of my life, and I felt the weight of all the loneliness and sorrow I had ever known. I felt the years of darkness and frustration, and the bitter alienation that I had known, with all their pain and aloneness. And then I perceived, with crystal clarity, that all those years were steps which had led inexorably and marvelously to this dark shore and to this lovely, starry night, to this moment—to this one moment in time when the course of my life was altered forever. Out of all those years of blindness and apparent meaninglessness there emerged in one wonderful and mysterious moment an unmistakable meaning and truth and purpose.

A titanic power that had been sealed up inside me for years rose up in a flood of unimaginable force. The years of purposelessness and longing converged on that one moment like a gigantic wedge and shattered the walls that had damned up my feelings. Inside me it was as if a volcano had quickened to life. The top blew off, unleashing the avalanche of emotion that had culminated in that moment. I burst into tears and sobbed violently and uncontrollably for a long time. The flood kept pouring out of me. I could not have imagined that so much emotion could ever have been sealed up inside me. Wave after wave it came, as I shuddered and released this power.

I will never forget the things which happened to me during those moments. I know that in those dynamic and critical moments some force within nature manifested itself, mirrored my psychological state in an unmistakable and incredible manner. During the time that I stood on that dark shore, as my tension was progressively mounting, a strong wind began to blow across the lake toward me. As my inner state grew in intensity, the wind likewise grew in power, whipping up the waves which dashed with stronger and stronger force against the rocks around me. As I entered the climax, the fullest, shuddering intensity of this experience, the waves crashed at my feet and covered me with spray. They roared in my ears, as the branches in the trees about me bent and hissed with the driving wind. My being and the being of the universe were one—one perception, one emotion, one vital, breathing union.

In the power of those moments a most strange thing occurred, which I was unable to rationalize and which I came to understand and explain only after seventeen years of subsequent searching. It was as if during those moments of eternity and power, there in front of me, perhaps twenty feet away, the universe, the air, something opened up, and I glimpsed a kind of "hole" into another dimension, into a higher world. And in this "warp" in the fabric of space, confronting me, in the midst of light, was a figure, a being. I cannot recall, and I did not observe, many particular features of this entity, for I was being swept through a whirlwind of experience. I do not remember his face. But the figure resembled that of a man. He was suspended above the waters in this strange and indescribable hole in space. His arms were outstretched from his sides and parallel to the water, and it was as if he were clothed in a long-sleeved robe which covered his feet, a garment which seemed almost as if it were made of brilliant white light.

I had no knowledge as to the nature or identity of this being. I did not know whether he was some avatar or guardian, or whatever else he may have been. But in reflecting back on this remarkable experience I have the distinct feeling that my witnessing him was, although not really accidental, rather, incidental. It was as if he were somehow influencing nature and the world, there, at that moment—the wind, the trees, the waves and all else, and was somehow a powerful initiator and controller of those elements and events, rather than specifically someone or something for me to witness. And yet I saw him, and his presence was very evident. It was almost as if I had been watching a stage with marionettes and had momentarily and incidentally glimpsed the puppeteer himself, who was controlling them and giving them life. Somehow, in a similar manner, I perceived him, as if at the side of the stage or behind it, overseeing what was taking place.

I do not know how long this experience lasted nor how long I saw this being. It cannot have lasted long. Gradually everything began to subside, to become quieter, and more at rest. The world around me, the water and wind, and my state of being, all gradually became calm. I do not remember how long I stood there then, nor do I recall with any clarity leaving that spot. But I remember that once I had ascended the long series of steps and was making my way slowly, almost in a dreamlike state, yet with heretofore unparalleled clarity of mind, toward the cabin in which I was staying with some of my peers, I felt enshrouded, almost entombed in an indescribable silence and peace, as if there were some kind of invisible and immaterial barrier or "surface" between my unparalleled state of consciousness and the outer world, particularly the outer world of my peers to which I was almost completely oblivious. It was as if I was in a trance, and yet I was experiencing a state of unprecedented lucidity, vibrant, and alive with mystery.

As I stood in my small cabin among several of my peers with whom I had eaten and slept and among whom I had moved that week, my isolation from them seemed total. They were somehow very far-off. Their words did not reach my ears. I was utterly heedless of their presence. It is said that in true magic the barrier between the perceiver and the perceived melts away, and the sense of what is "subjective" or "objective" loses its distinctness. Likewise I cannot truly say that what befell me then was inner or outer, or a combination of both. Yet, I feel that both elements were in some way active; that is, I was most certainly experiencing profoundly nonordinary states of inner consciousness, and yet I feel that around me, on a subtle plane, certain mysterious yet very real phenomena were transpiring.

I perceived and sensed around me the aura and feeling of an incomparably subtle and fragrant garden of roses. I was enshrouded and encircled by their delicate presence. I could "see" them all about me, literally see and perceive them, yet with some organ other than my eyes and which I did not clearly understand. They formed, actually, a vertical wall about me, and yet seemed not to manifest any of the solidity or limitations of a wall in the traditionally understood sense. Although substantial enough to be perceived, at least by me, they were exquisitely delicate and ethereal. It was not exactly as though I could see clearly through them, but rather that it was somehow possible to cognize the physical plane while at the same time apprehending their presence. My only thought was to contemplate the possibility that I could live every moment of my life from then on within the wondrous garden of that incomparable love.

As I stood there in the cabin, these perceptions gradually and gently faded away. But their impact had been overwhelming, and it has never left me. My life was changed forever. However, it would be many years before I would find any explanation for those mysterious experiences. And thus, although I still do not fully understand the significance of that aspect of my experiences which revealed to me the vision of the roses, I can now look back, in retrospect, and note with great interest that, over three years later, after I had begun to study a system of meditation and yoga known as Kriya Yoga, with a monk from India who was a member of the Giri order, I was struck by the extensive use and significance of roses in many of the ceremonies and rites of initiation in which I participated, and particularly in those which involved the impartation to me of certain kinds of advanced techniques involving breath control, or pranayama. Just as I had sensed my being to be enveloped by the ethereal presence of roses during part of my initial experiences at the lake, I was later physically enveloped and protected in their sacredness during the yogic ceremonies, and I sensed a subtle, or noumenal relationship between those events of my earlier years and those which occurred during my years of yoga studies, a relationship which was indeed substantiated for me by my spiritual teacher. He felt that, even over three years earlier, I had been touched by a force which throughout my life has called to me through various pathways and avenues of perception. I will discuss in detail some of these numerous experiences later, in the course of this book. I have not seen my guru in many years. We have long since parted company and gone separate ways. But I still have in a special place a gold locket which contains petals from roses which he blessed during those ceremonies and initiations.

I had been at the lake only a few days, and I would be leaving it very soon. I would be there for only one week, and yet my life would be drastically and irrevocably changed. I had gone there expecting nothing. Indeed, I do not remember now why I went at all, except for the fact that a friend had invited me. The church of which I was a member had taken a group of young people there every year for a long time, and I had become eligible to go that year. But the experiences which I encountered that week were worlds apart from the activities of those with whom I had gone, and I remember almost nothing of what they did that week. Yet now, in retrospect, I feel that something led me there, and indeed, even though it has not always been overwhelmingly apparent to me, I feel that I have been guided by some force ever since that time. Through the multitude of experiences and changes which I have undergone since then, and even in spite of the darkness through which I have sometimes walked, my life has followed the tracings of some kind of plan. But one cannot usually perceive such things except in retrospect.

When I think of it now, it seems strange and awesome that the course of one's life can hinge upon incidents which outwardly seem so incidental, or subject to chance. But during that week at the lake, the entire direction of my life was determined by just such an apparently coincidental event which is perhaps a classic example of that mysterious, acausal relationship known as synchronicity, that ties certain apparently unrelated events together into a unity. More than once, the direction of my life has been significantly altered through just such circumstances.

Thus it was that, one day at the beginning of my visit to the lake, I overheard a fragment of a conversation which was really nothing more than a phrase, but which instantly gripped my attention. I heard a new acquaintance of mine speaking to someone else, and she used the phrase, "God in nature." It was an idea that I do not remember ever having thought about for one moment in my life before I heard it then. And yet, when I heard it, I instantaneously experienced the birth of a light inside of me, and I knew that I had to know more about what she was saying. I spoke with my friend about this later, and I asked her how I might go about experiencing this entity that existed within the being of nature. At her suggestion, I sought solitude along the shores of the lake and, very simply, in the only way I knew how, I opened my mind to whatever might be there. I uttered a silent longing that I wished to know whatever was real. Whatever the nature of truth, I wished to embrace it. If it was ugly and hideous, I still wanted to know. I did not go seeking happiness or beauty, but only truth, for I did not want to be deceived.

But from the very outset of my meditations, I began to detect within the lake and the earth and sky, and all things, a matchless, unifying consciousness. And every time that I sought solitude and opened myself to the power which was there, it grew more and more evident to me. Later, I will more fully reveal the details of these early experiences, but for now I wish only to express the fact that, with the passing of each day, my perceptions evolved more and more dramatically. I came to see beyond the surface of nature's form, into the depths of the limitless being whose inexpressible consciousness moved within the world and permeated it. Nothing could have deterred me from seeking it out. But what was perhaps most overwhelming to me was that I could sense that it was seeking me, and as the days passed, this feeling grew in intensity until I encountered the extraordinary experiences which I have just described. My friend who had set me upon this new and disturbing path remarked to me once that week, after listening to me speak about my experiences, that I was being pursued by "the hound of heaven," and although at the time I did not know exactly to what she referred, I found her phrase most apt and descriptive, in terms of what I had been feeling. More than sixteen years passed before I discovered Francis Thompson's famous poem entitled "The Hound of Heaven," to which I am sure my friend was referring. I read it with interest, and was struck by the image which it painted, of a man being inexorably pursued by a spiritual force which was at the same time relentless and yet loving.

During the days of that first momentous visit to the lake, it became apparent to me, as a result of what I had encountered there, that one could indeed experience almost too much beauty. For just as one has a limitation, or threshold for the endurance of pain, or sorrow, or other negative feelings, one can likewise bear the weight and impact of such devastating beauty only according to his "spiritual conditioning," or level or receptivity at the time of such experiences. I am reminded of a certain piece of music which I have always deeply loved and which very poignantly revivifies for me the emotions which came to life in me during my initial visits to this place of magnificent power, and I remember that a music critic once described this ravishing work as "almost unbearably beautiful." I cannot think of a more appropriate description for my experiences of awakening there, and this phrase has remained with me over many years. During my first sun-filled, magical days at Lake Geneva, I realized that my individual psyche was indeed a fragile and insignificant instrument compared to the vastness of the force that I had encountered. How easily I could have been crushed or obliterated by the influx of power from this gigantic Soul if it had exceeded its delicate balance. What an incredibly fine balance indeed must have preserved my existence, my very sanity and my mental being, from being annihilated by even a slight overdose of this influx of energy and power.

I had been deeply impressed and influenced by what I had seen that week, and because of the very traditional religious background from which I had come, I was somewhat confused and could not reconcile my background with my direct experiences. I was well familiar with the doctrine of original sin, and yet my experience had been like a return to primal innocence. I could not find a place for "sin" in what I had seen. Within the new and inscrutable world which I had found, there was only wonder, and the possibilities of an expanse of unlimited perception. I had gone looking for truth, and had found immeasurable joy. It was as though, if there had indeed been an original state of grace from which man had fallen, I had embraced it. I had known the original innocence of man, and had seen the world as he had seen it, through uncorrupted eyes, before he had walked in darkness. I had been confronted by an ecstatic consciousness which permeated every aspect of nature. Within its shining and exuberant identity I perceived a perpetual rejoicing, and endless sabbath, expressed through a world the totality of which I saw as sanctified, in which every shrub and tree and rock was holy ground.

Ubi caritas et amor, Deus ibi est.
Where charity and love are, there is God.

All around me, there was only Light. Everything lived within an ocean of pure consciousness, which was grounded in an unfathomable Love. Everywhere I looked, I saw God.

In only a matter of days my whole life and inner nature had undergone a volcanic metamorphosis. My old view of the world, whatever it had been, was suddenly and forever gone. I was living in a terrifyingly beautiful new world. My whole universe was suddenly saturated with unforeseen revelations of a truly shattering nature. For me, every act was full of new wonder and joy. It all had happened so very fast that I really could not fully digest and assimilate in so short a time these wondrous but traumatic shocks to my life, and one day during that week at the lake the full impact of these encounters descended on me and overwhelmed me with unforgettable impact.

It was very late one afternoon, and I was eating my evening meal. I was surrounded by the activities and conversations of many people, but they were somehow very distant from me. I felt isolated from them. For some reason, in the middle of my meal, my thoughts became totally suspended and the joyous momentum of my new life and being halted, abruptly and without warning. During those past few days and nights I had been so enraptured and carried up into the heights of my experiences that it had never for one moment occurred to me, until then, that I might for some reason fall from them. My spiritual momentum had driven me to soar into a rarified and breathless realm of perceptions, and when the currents of enthrallment suddenly ceased to flow, I was left suspended in the most profound doubt and uncertainty that I had ever experienced.

What if I was mistaken or deluded in these new perceptions? What if they were not real? Then I would have nothing—even less than I had had before those momentous days at the lake, because the world which I had known all my life was now gone. I had seen things which, for better or worse, had irrevocably changed my life. I was not the same, and in a most real sense I had been truly reborn. I had discovered a new world of matchless power and beauty. I had been initiated into a world of awareness which was so alive and tangible that, in comparison with its expanded consciousness, the ordinary existence which I had previously known seemed unsubstantial and flat, without dimension and devoid of meaning. Whatever I had previously accepted as life and as being alive was now, by comparison, almost death. It was like a dream with no substance or direction.

At that moment, my mental sensations were so acute that it was as if I could almost see the dark, bottomless abyss of doubt which yawned wide, below me. My body could feel it, waiting to swallow me up. Why it happened, and at that particular moment, I do not know, although I suspect that it was my mind's way of reacting to experiences which had been such an unforeseen and overwhelming spiritual shock for me. Perhaps it was my old self rising up, trying to survive through reaffirming and maintaining its old view of life and its familiar, comfortable ways. Fortunately, whatever forces were working in my life at that moment moved in such a way that my precarious poise over that pit lasted for only the briefest time before my momentum unexplainably resumed and I found myself beyond that terrible moment of doubt. It has remained the most unique and dynamic experience of its kind in my memory. Neither previously nor afterward did I ever know again with such intensity the feeling of being ungrounded. Although during the years which followed I naturally encountered varying periods and degrees of self-doubt, I have never again experienced one so potent, so acutely focused and uniquely intense.

Time was slipping away, and I would soon be leaving Lake Geneva. Very early one evening, the last, precious evening of my visit to that lovely place of power, I took my usual walk down to the edge of the water and stood for a long time, gazing out over the surface of the lake. The sun, which was working its way down toward the tops of the hills surrounding the lake, cast the world in a radiant and supernatural light. In the atmosphere was a freshness and serenity which lulled all my senses, and yet I felt supremely stimulated and exalted. The effects of my surroundings caressed my spirit with a depthless tranquility. My mind was exquisitely lucid. How tangible and sweet and holy was that peace, in that magical time when the late afternoon transmuted to the early shades of evening. Its perfect image cast its reflection onto the still mirror of my soul, where it reflected itself and touched me, even embraced me—no, possessed me with its matchless placidity.

The world glistened in its vibrancy, set afire from the golden afternoon sunlight. How achingly and passionately in love I was with the lushness and opulence of the rich green hills. The earth beckoned to me with an alluring and treacherous sweetness. And to look above! There, in the infinite blue spaces, I knew a harmony and brotherhood which embraced and united the sky and the hills and the shining rocks and all things in its stillness, and I knew even in the very rocks a profound presence and pregnant meaning. I embraced the exquisite revelation of form—form cast upon space. I knew somehow that what I saw there was sustained only through the consciousness of the Reality which existed beyond it and saturated it, and that the images of the world which I was witnessing were sustained even moment by moment. For nothing ensured the continuance of their existence except for that great Will itself, that nameless and unsearchable Presence, whatever its ultimate nature. The rocks and water, the sky, the trees and hills became energy. Their images became, in a sense, like mirages. I could "see" that the world was not really solid at all, and it acquired an aspect of insubstantiality. It was light and energy and movement which was sustained moment to moment, through all time, only by the love and consciousness of the Mind which embraced infinity itself. Indeed, infinity was merely an attribute of this incomprehensibly immense Presence.

The essence of what I am trying to express is this central fact, this exquisite idea: the world ceased merely to be a procession of phenomena. But rather, the motion of every wave, every slap of the waves against the rocks, every slosh and eddy; the slightest change of direction or intensity of the wind; the colors of the world and their shifting and changing; the sweet freshness of the atmosphere, and all else became impregnated with the utmost expressiveness. Every undulation and change and movement revealed the infinite underlying movements of some great force behind it, and portrayed with the most vivid eloquence imaginable the passionate and depthless and unbounded ocean of loving consciousness behind it and saturating it. I could rightly say that I had looked directly into the noumenal world.

As I contemplated in silent awe these spectacular images, I spotted a kingfisher perched near me in the glorious white birches at the edge of the water, his plumage aglow in the mellow, golden light which radiated from the sun out over the tops of the hills and across the gently rippling water. I was very close to him, and I could observe every detail of his delicate feathers and animated form. I sensed his identity and felt at one with him. I was enthralled to be so close to this little being with whom I shared that moment, whose form and consciousness was such a perfect and beautiful expression of the life there. The image of that moment has always remained in my memory, and several years later, during the winter of 1970-71, I wrote a poem, the final section of which recalled that experience.

> Clear and deep,
>   ineffable lays the silence,
> On the far-off
>   verdant shores.
> Lulled, hushed lays the lake
>   in dusk,
> In hues of muted
>   pink and crimson.
>
> In the afterglow of day,
>   the bright kingfisher soars,
> Taking its flight
>   from shining birches,
> Into the flaming
>   depths of Heaven,
> A pellucid realm
>   of orange and rose...

The subtle murmuring of the water and the infinitely varied expressions of its undulating waves set into play in some acutely sensed yet undefined part of me an inexpressible pleasure and joy, and I am certain that some psychic organ of perception within me, which exists, developed or undeveloped, known or unknown, in all men, was "fed" to fullness through my communion with the consciousness of that place. I had been awakened to a new need. Although I had not consciously known it, my hunger for this world had been born and was growing long before I had ever gone to the lake. I had found a "food" there, a sustenance in the perceptions which were engendered there, that would now become indispensible to my completeness. I would be leaving on the following day, and I did not know for certain, then, if or when I would ever return. In the days to come, and indeed for many years afterwards, I would reflect over the meaning of what I had encountered at the lake. I could not possibly have envisioned, then, the years of searching which were before me, as I sought to understand and rediscover the experiences which I had met with there. But I knew that I would never be able to forget the incredible consciousness which had revealed itself to me there, and the memory of it would haunt me relentlessly. Standing on the shore by the edge of the water, I felt at that moment much like I have felt during many subsequent visits. I wished that I would never leave, but rather, remain there forever. Even before I had gone away, I felt the ache of separation from that world which would come to be a familiar experience to me—the longing for communion with this sparkling, dancing, living lake, these radiant skies and deep green hills—this gem of creation. Here was home.

The Search

To Lake Geneva

Such a long time, it seems, since
I have felt your companionship.
In the sun-filled land of my
memories, vaguely, I remember you:
the gentle wind upon my face,
the summer sunlight that warmed my flesh
and illumined my soul.

Such a long time ago, since I sat
upon the glistening rocks, drenched with
spray from the dancing waves,
lapping at their base.
Those surging waves!
What beautiful mysteries they brought,
unmuffled, to my ears.

In the silent moments of
my heart, that memory floods up
within me; for an instant, your spirit is
with me.
Then it is gone.
But my heart is always there.
Often, in my dreams, I walk along
your shores where time is suspended,
and eternity unfolds to shed its light
upon my yearning soul.

Shall I ever again gaze upon
your beauty? Yes, surely; for 'twas
there that I was born...
        You are my home. You will draw
me back unto you.
        I see not how there can be any
other place as beautiful as you.

Your shimmering trees,
reaching up into the sun, tell me
that you are eternal; the force in you
is everlasting.
        Your waters whisper the longings
of my soul. They speak that secret
        which I can never express.

So long, it seems, since last
I walked, with a song in my heart,
along those shores.
        But I will return.
        For you are a part of my soul,
now, and I a part of you.
        Now I am yours.
And that blessed spirit that dwells
in you, dwells in me. Now,
        and forever.

                                        February 1966

A fter my initial visit to the lake in August 1964, my life took on the character of a quest which has continued up through the present time and
   which I feel will continue for the rest of my life. That quest, which has
taken me back to the shores of Lake Geneva many times, has prompted me to
explore and experience many diverse disciplines and schools of thought, and
has led me to encounter many varied and incredible experiences.

At one point, some unforeseen but very dramatic and decisive events took
place that were related to my experience of the lake, and I was led to new and
critical and powerful insights about their nature and meaning. This dramatic
period began in the latter part of 1980, during which time I conceived the idea to
write this book, and is still unfolding. I will later describe the events and experiences of this period in great detail, but first it is necessary to account for the

interim between August 1964 and the latter part of 1980. That period of search-ing was not without struggle and conflict, and there were times when I experi-enced profound feelings of doubt and darkness, and a sense of separation from the lake and the light and power which I had encountered there. With the experi-ences of transcendental beauty came periods of self-questioning and uncertainty, and it was difficult to find support and reinforcement, let alone real guidance.

I have sometimes wondered what my life might have been like if I had remained at Lake Geneva in 1964, or any time after that. I am not able to say exactly what I thought my life would be like after that momentous first visit, but I have to admit that, during the height of those initial experiences, I must have felt, or at least hoped, that all of my life from that point forward, no matter where I was or what circumstances I was in, would be filled with unbounded joy and the mysterious sense of grace which I had experienced there. But I remember very clearly that, even before I had departed from the lake that first time, and certainly as I had taken a last look at its sparkling waters and gone to board the bus that would carry me away, I was already eagerly anticipating the time when I would return. And I remember vividly my reentry into the everyday world of existence. It was a plummeting descent into a spiritual desert, an emptiness, and dry wasteland, without beauty or power, in which I found no sustenance.

The world to which I returned was a severe shock. I did not know how to adjust to it. In actuality, it was the same world in which I had lived before that first trip to the lake, but now, by contrast, I felt in it a great emptiness. It was sterile and flat. It now lacked an incredible, living, and joyous dimension which I had found at the lake. I did not know then that this was a problem with which I would contend for a very long time. But I quickly discerned that there was noth-ing in my exterior world which was going to reflect or sustain the light and beauty of what I had seen. I had an enormous, unsatisfied hunger which I did not know how to feed.

I was an only child, and had always been somewhat of a loner. The feeling of loneliness was very familiar to me, and now, after this first encounter with the lake, I began to feel even more alone and isolated. In the totality of my life then, there was only one individual with whom I could talk about what had happened to me. This was Margaret Patton, the minister of music for the Presbyterian church where I was a member. Although I had gone to the lake with a group of young people from this church, the experiences I had encountered there, at a place called Conference Point, on the northern shores of the lake, had nothing whatsoever to do with these people, and I was largely unaware even of what they did that week. I went to the required classes and, apart from that, spent the rest of my time exploring my own perceptions. But I had met Margaret Patton at the lake that week, and it was a conversation of hers with someone else, a fragment of which I overheard, in which she said something about "God in nature," that almost instantaneously changed my life. Although that was about all I heard, it was as if a light had suddenly been turned on inside my head. I was struck by this idea, and she and I had talked about it later. As a result, I had looked within myself and within the realm of the lake to search out this idea, and had found a new world. Margaret Patton and I talked many times that week, and after I returned home, I continued to share my feelings with her.

During the first year after my initial visit to Lake Geneva, she was the only person who knew anything about what had happened to me. I learned that my experiences were not something appropriate to share with my friends, nor even with any of the adults who were a part of my life. And even Margaret Patton did not know about the vision which had confronted me along the shores of the Point. There is one thing about that period of my life I remember very well, and I continued to experience it until I moved away to college and lost contact with the church. After a few attempts to open up and share my perceptions with those who were part of that way of life, I felt that there was no room for my ideas in that church community. At the very best, my experiences were not understood, and I began to develop a sense of separation between myself and those in the religious community around me. I will never forget a conversation which I had with one of the ministers of that church, sometime during that general period of my life, in which I referred to the wonder and beauty of what I had once seen at the lake. And I remember that his reaction was to counsel me, in a very fatherly yet condescending way, that what had happened to me was merely, as he put it, "an experience of the glands." I can only conclude from this gem of insight that I have never physically matured, since I have continued to have such perceptions for thirty-one years.

My relationship with Margaret Patton was qualified by the fact that, although it was she who had introduced me to the ideas which had catalyzed my perceptions and experiences, her viewpoint was thoroughly and unmistakably Christian. This fact certainly did not create any antagonism between us. It was simply that, as far as I was concerned, my experiences had nothing to do with what I perceived at that time as the theology of the Presbyterian church. I saw no relationship between it and the visions and perceptions which I had had, and which focused primarily on the glorious power and consciousness within the being of nature. And my differences in feeling from those around me created a kind of vacuum for me, in which I had little opportunity to experience real fellowship with others. This concerned Margaret, and it created a conflict in me for many years. But in spite of my philosophical differences with the church, I participated actively in many of its various activities. I did so quite deliberately, for several reasons: it provided a social contact with people my age. I was very

Conference Point, Lake Geneva

lonely and I wanted to belong to a group of people. Furthermore, although I had little in common with them in terms of spiritual experience, they were nevertheless the group with which I had gone to the lake, and thus they were like a kind of reminder or link for me with that world. And what was by far most important of all was that, if I remained active within that religious and social sphere, it would provide a means, the only means available, for me to return to Lake Geneva the following August. This in itself would have been reason enough. But I enjoyed these young people, and I had made friends among them. I was a member of their circle.

My great salvation at that time was music. I was fifteen, and a sophomore in high school, and already a serious classical pianist. I was highly respected for this by my peers and by the adults around me, both in school and in church. I recall that it was that spring that I performed the Grieg Piano Concerto with an orchestra. I sang in the church choir, not so much because of any musical fulfillment, but because it provided further access to some social activity. Margaret Patton was also a fluent pianist, a fact that further added to the strength of our relationship. It was through music that I found both a reflection for the light and joy I had known and a means to express it. I had been seriously interested in the piano and in music since the age of ten, but it was after my initial experiences at the lake that music acquired a whole new power for me. I could articulate to a degree the Truth I had encountered at the lake.

I began a literary search that would continue for many years, and which I initiated for the purpose of trying to seek out sources that might shed some light on the experiences I had had. I wanted to find evidence of experiences that were related to my own, and which could help me to understand what had happened to me. I was particularly interested in the ideas which were embodied in the concept of transcendentalism, and also pantheism. It seemed to me that these two philosophies were the most clearly akin to what I had experienced at Lake Geneva. Thus, I eagerly read works of Emerson and Thoreau, and I remember being very much taken with *I and Thou* of Martin Buber. I also became deeply interested in the works of Aldous Huxley, and I remember the particular impact *Island* made upon me. I believe that it was through mention of them in that work that I developed an interest in the Bach Brandenburg Concertos, to which I listened often during that period of my life.

And thus I spent the first year after my visit to the lake. Aside from the sources I have specifically mentioned, I read anything else I could find that might bear upon the experiences I had had there. There are many details of that period of my life which I no longer remember clearly, but I would say that probably not a single day passed during all those months that I did not think of the lake. It was always in my thoughts, and I continually contemplated the prospect of returning the following August, in 1965. The whole direction of my inner life was aimed at that reunion. It was the central thing upon which all my desires focused, and I waited with eager anticipation for the day when I would stand again on the shores of that beloved lake.

In August 1965, I went back. During the four-hour ride to the lake I experienced an intense anticipation. My consciousness was totally absorbed with quivering expectancy. This first return to the lake revealed a whole repertory of sensations and emotions I would re-encounter many times in the future, during such return trips. I would always reexperience that enormous expectation, that nervousness, as I drove through Wisconsin and entered the hills which encircled the lake. I was not then, nor for many years, ever quite prepared for those first moments of contact with the supreme power of the lake. Although of a positive character, it would always be somewhat of a jolt for me, a kind of shock to my system. I always felt a sensation of amazement at what I found waiting there, and it always required a little time for me to become adjusted to those surroundings and to the immediate and profound shift in consciousness they engendered in me. It seemed almost as if I were dreaming, and yet what confronted me was ultimately real. But I could hardly believe my sensations there of the remarkable quality of life and consciousness which that locale exhibited for me.

I noticed a change as soon as we neared the lake. And from the moment the bus entered the grounds of Conference Point, the exquisite power of that place began to invade me. I could feel it pulling me, and a flood of intense memories and sensations welled up inside of me. As I set foot upon that ground, I was possessed at once by the overwhelming presence of the beautiful consciousness which breathed there. As my experiences during the week unfolded, I underwent a progressive inner awakening. As I had done there during my previous visit a year earlier, I spent whatever time I possibly could in solitude. As soon as whatever obligations which I had with the group were fulfilled, I removed myself to some place where I might be alone. Whenever possible, this was somewhere along the shores of the lake, and ideally, among the trees and boulders at the Point itself, or perhaps above them, in the brick alcove which was just to one side of the concrete steps which were built into the bluff there.

My whole mind and inner nature were acutely sensitive and alive during that week at Lake Geneva. To enter the world of the lake was like stepping through a door into another world. It was an experience that I might have expected to find in some fantastic novel, and yet it was supremely real. The power and consciousness of the lake was so incredible that, as it then became clear to me, I had not, during the interim of my separation from it, been able to really sustain the memory of its full impact.

But during this first return to the lake, in spite of my immediate recognition of the living consciousness that pervaded everything there, and even in light of the tremendous excitement which I felt from having gone back, I began to feel slightly troubled as the days passed. I gradually became aware of a dichotomy in my experience there. On the one hand, not a moment slipped by without my being deeply aware of the shining presence which dwelt there. I was continually conscious of it, drawing me, calling to me. How clearly I could hear its mysterious, sweet voice in the murmuring of the lake. The sounds of its waves uttered their secrets to me with an alluring, elemental eloquence. That indescribable voice gripped me and possessed me, and filled my heart with a deep desire to be one with it, with the indescribable consciousness within it. And yet, the intense, passionate union with it which I had once known seemed somehow just to evade me, to recede just beyond my grasp. I could detect the exquisite light there, and could feel the thought of that unfathomable love which expressed itself there through every wave and rock and breath of wind. And yet it was as if there was a thin veil between myself and it, which I did not understand and which I could not seem to break through. It was a strange feeling, and, in a very quiet way, an agonizing one. At first, I decided that what was lacking was a kind of momentum which I would gain as the days passed, as had been the case the preceding August. I felt that it would require some time for me to open myself again fully to the forces there. After all, was there not probably some degree of acclimatization required in order for me to adjust fully to the unique and powerful identity of this locale?

I felt that this was probably so, but as my stay there came nearer to its end, I began to realize that, although that lovely reality which I had known so deeply was there, and although its presence was overwhelmingly apparent to me, I had not lost myself in it as I had once done. I was completely at a loss for answers as to why this might be so. I was deeply perplexed by it, and it was anguishing to consider that all too shortly I would be gone from there, not to return for at least another entire year. What an incredible acceleration of time had characterized my brief days there! How irreplaceable and irretrievable they were! A flowing of hours through which I moved all too quickly, skirting the realm of heaven, but somehow not quite entering into the fullness of its presence. And I contemplated what seemed like an ocean of separation which lay ahead, until I should return again. I spoke with the light that moved over everything there; I peered into its glorious spirit. I felt it drawing me, pulling me, and I experienced a heartfelt longing for oneness with it. But that almost imperceptible barrier was there, and my spirit was on one side of it, and the soul of that boundless reality lay on the other. I say again that I was deeply touched by the unfathomable purity and light which expressed itself there, but I longed to know it more deeply and fully, to meet it face to face, and I felt that I had not done this. Thus, with joy and sadness and longing, I reluctantly said good-bye to the exquisite being of the lake. But I was more resolved than ever that I would never forget it, that I would never let go of it, and I prayed that it would never release its hold on me. And I knew that I would return.

I was at least somewhat more prepared this time for what the transition would be like to the more ordinary world of my everyday existence. I did not welcome it, but I knew that it was coming and I was not so devastated by it as I had been the previous year. There was too much to occupy me. It was my junior year in high school, and there were the usual academic responsibilities and, not too far in the future, the prospect of selecting a college. I had by this point in my life already begun to experience various romantic inclinations and entanglements which, according to my nature, were very intense and tumultuous, although not very rewarding, and fortunately, I was able to channel much of this energy into music. I remained active within the church, and it was fully my intention to go back to Lake Geneva in August 1966. Margaret Patton would remain in my life for another year before leaving the church to accept another position elsewhere.

Through music, I was able to feel alive inside and to develop my consciousness. It was about that time that, although I do not believe that I had ever even heard of yoga, or astral projection, or such things, I began intuitively to develop and practice various techniques of concentration and meditation, usually but not always in conjunction with music, with the end in mind of aligning my spirit with the forces of the lake, even though I was physically apart from it, and perhaps even developing a technique whereby I could actually will my consciousness to go there. I applied myself to these experiments with great effort, and achieved enough results to feel that what I was attempting was possible. I was developing a powerful inner tie with the lake. Thus it was that, during this period of my life, I existed largely within a world of inner reality. I found that I could "live" if I focused my consciousness in this direction, and so I committed extensive amounts of time and energy to exploring the capabilities of my own mind.

As I look back now on that period of my life, I note with great interest that it was characterized by an almost rhythmical, or cyclical series of entrances into my life of individuals who in one way or another were to exert strong influences upon my life and consciousness, and who were to have significant bearing upon the nature and direction of my search for reality. The first of these individuals had been Margaret Patton. It was just a little over a year later, in the early fall of 1965, after I returned from my second visit to Lake Geneva and began my junior year of high school, that I met Bess Hibarger. I believe that Bess went to my church, although I do not seem to remember ever seeing her there. And perhaps it was even Margaret Patton who steered me in her direction. But what was important was that I met her.

I telephoned her to make an appointment to see her, and although I do not remember very well what I said, I am sure that I told her that I was looking for a certain kind of knowledge in my life, and it was my understanding that she might be able to offer me some help. When I subsequently went to see her at her home, I encountered a remarkable being whom I will remember fondly for the rest of my life. Bess was a very elderly woman, and although she was very slow and careful in her movements and somewhat frail, she seemed to be in perfect health. I remember her wire glasses and her hair, which was pure white and radiant. The fine features of her face immediately portrayed great wisdom and a highly refined intelligence. She radiated an aura of patience and love, and her mind was keen and sharp and crystal clear. She was the epitome of what a human being ought to be, and she was the embodiment of age with dignity. Actually, as time passed, I seldom thought about the fact that she was quite elderly. I simply thought of her as a youthful and radiant and evolved being in an old body. I never learned many details about her life. She had never married, but had traveled a great deal, and possessed an extensive metaphysical knowledge. She was considered to be a fine Biblical scholar, and had published numerous magazine articles which dealt with various metaphysical themes. She was very proficient in the practice of numerology and was well versed in occult and theosophical knowledge.

Our relationship was to last for almost seven years, and although it dwindled somewhat toward the end, I always sustained the warmest feelings for her. Bess quickly became someone with whom I shared many of my perceptions and feelings, to which she always responded with openness and understanding. She provided me with guidance and support, but always in a very skillful, noninterfering way. I perceive now that she had a remarkable ability to introduce new ideas to me in a very gentle, subtle manner, so that I was always open to them and eager to learn more. She presented knowledge in such a way that it always seemed very natural and acceptable. During the year interim between my second and third visits to the lake, I went to visit her very often, and within that period of time she introduced me to many new ideas, including the concept of reincarnation. She shared her knowledge of Biblical prophecy with me and enabled me to become thoroughly acquainted with the tenets of theosophy. I did not solve the mysteries of the lake, but my relationship with her greatly enriched my perspective and stimulated my inner growth. It provided me with a friendship characterized by trust and enabled me to articulate my feelings.

The summer of 1966 arrived, and I began to think more about going back to Lake Geneva that August. Emotionally speaking, it was a rather difficult summer. The girl with whom I was involved, or at least with whom I wanted to be involved, was away in Europe touring with a youth orchestra, and I was trapped working nights in a factory. It was an episode in my life that I hated beyond words. But the weeks passed, and August arrived. I was to be going back to the lake with the same group of people that I had gone with before, except that, just very shortly before this, Margaret Patton had resigned to take another position elsewhere, so she did not go. That was the last time I ever saw her, although we exchanged letters once after that. During the two years we had known each other, she had never stopped being concerned about what she saw as my spiritual remoteness from others, which she expressed again in the one letter that I later received from her. And on the other hand, I remained firm. My feelings and attitudes did not change.

I returned to the lake, and the perceptions and experiences I encountered there were much the same as the year before. Was there something that I had done to warrant this? Would things forever remain this way? How could it call to me, beckon to me, pull at my heart and being as it did, and yet remain so disturbingly elusive? I did not understand, and somewhere inside me was the fear of always seeing a beautiful light which I might never again be able to reach. And yet it haunted me with its shining presence.

As these thoughts occupied my mind that week, the third individual in that cycle of encounters which I spoke of entered my life. During my third visit to the lake, I met Jerry Alber. He had only recently become the new organist for the church, and had come to the lake with us as accompanist for choral rehearsals. Among the relationships I have had with people, that which I developed with Jerry has most strongly suggested to me the likelihood of a karmic origin; that is, I believe that we had known each other closely during a past life, and that we had now met again during this present incarnation. As time went on, there were strong reasons why this became more clearly apparent to me.

I remember clearly the circumstances of my first conversation with Jerry. I was in a large building situated on top of the hill that overlooked the shores of the Point. From its front entrance, there was a view of the land that sloped very gently for about two hundred feet to the edge of the hill, where the bluffs, which were covered with thick vegetation, descended steeply to the path along the edge of the water. There was an organ which was at the foot of the stage inside that building, and as I sat there playing, I turned to see Jerry Alber. We began to talk, and the rapport which immediately existed between us formed the basis of a relationship which has lasted through the present time, almost thirty years. I would describe Jerry as a truly spiritually minded person. Neither then, nor in all the time I have known him, has he ever manifested in even the slightest degree the negative traits which unfortunately afflict so many human beings. I have never heard him speak maliciously of anyone, now have I ever known him to commit any unkindness to another person. And he has consistently shown himself to be unqualifiedly generous and completely free from the slightest traces of materialism and greed. In all honesty, I have to say that our intuitive understanding of each other was not due to any similarity of character based on the terms in which I have described Jerry. But we were strongly linked by a kind of inner longing which expressed itself in each of our beings. Stated simply, we seemed to view the world in much the same way. And yet, there was also an unquestionable tie which went much deeper than this.

Strangely, although I vividly remember our first meeting and the tone of our conversation, I can remember nothing specific in terms of what we said to each other. But I remember that we were immediately and inexplicably close, and for the remainder of that week at the lake, any feelings I had that demanded expression were articulated to Jerry. He is the only person whom I can remember spending my personal time with. Furthermore, after acquiring the necessary permission from the minister who was in charge of the group, I moved out of my cabin in which I had been staying with several of my peers and moved into the room in which Jerry had been staying alone. For me, this was a very fortunate thing, and in looking back, I am surprised that we were able to maneuver such an arrangement. It was in fact due solely to the consent of the man who was then the minister of that church, and in retrospect, although I did not know him well, I think that he was a very fine and serious person, and an exception among those whom I have known to hold that position in that church. Less than a year later, however, he left the church to go elsewhere, for reasons which were never made completely clear.

My living with Jerry for the remainder of that week at the lake greatly enhanced my personal freedom and afforded me the opportunity to develop a truly meaningful relationship with him, in which I could share my personal feelings and communicate my thoughts to someone who truly understood what I was trying to say. Such relationships are relatively unique and supremely valuable, and I have found deep gratification in the experience of being able to say something to someone who immediately understands what it is that I am trying to express, who intuitively perceives the nature of my thoughts and feelings, without my having to struggle, sometimes futilely, to convey what is going on within my consciousness. We exchanged many thoughts, and I talked about the lake and my relationship with it. We had established a communication which would develop further after we returned home from the lake.

I left the lake that year with much the same feelings that I had the year before. And as always, during the year that followed that third visit to the lake, I thought about it a great deal. And I began to write more. I wrote about the lake, about the experiences I had had there, and about my deep longing for it and my desire for union with the truth that shined there. And although I sometimes wrote along mystical lines that did not always refer directly to my experiences at the lake, they were still the result of the spiritual impetus which had been born there. There also appeared in some of these writings impulses which were engendered by the feelings I had for a very lovely young girl, whom I grew to love very deeply and who loved me equally. Our relationship endured through the following August of 1967, after which time I went away to school. Endured was the right word, and perhaps it would have endured after that except for the fact that her parents, whom I still regard today as truly insane, managed finally to destroy it beyond all hope of repair. It was a situation that created tremendous turmoil in my life, and I remembered her for many years.

It was my senior year in high school, and I sang again in the church choir. I had been accepted as a performance major in the piano department of the University of Illinois at Champaign-Urbana for the fall of 1967, and I was very active musically that year in preparing for those studies. Jerry Alber and I gave a recital together that year at the church, he on the organ and I on the piano. As well as being the full-time organist for the church, he was finishing his work that year in acquiring a Master's degree from Illinois Wesleyan University. We spent a great deal of time together, and related to each other on many different levels. We enjoyed a fine musical companionship, which was a very valuable growth experience for me, and we were able to offer one another a mutual spiritual understanding and support.

As well as the relationship I had with Jerry, I maintained an ongoing friendship with Bess Hibarger, and thus there were two people in my life at that time who were sympathetic to my metaphysical pursuits and who were enormously helpful to me in my spiritual growth. As well as generally enriching my metaphysical knowledge, particularly along theosophical lines, Bess contributed greatly to my knowledge of a subject in which I was specifically and deeply interested—astral projection, a process whereby, to put it in its simplest terms, one's consciousness left their physical body and traveled independently of it to other physical locations. She and I talked about this subject often. My interest in it was a natural outgrowth of the techniques involving the projection of consciousness I had been intuitively experimenting with for some time previous to that, and which I have already mentioned. Bess had an extensive personal occult library that I was free to use, and as a result I studied many of the classic works on astral projection. As well as having a general desire to enhance my metaphysical knowledge, I had two specific motives for acquiring proficiency in astral projection. One was that it could enable me to send my consciousness to the lake, and the other was that it might somehow allow me more communication with Shirley, whose parents were giving us so much trouble. I actually achieved a degree of success with astral projection in both areas of endeavor, and had one vivid and dramatic experience in which Shirley actually saw me, at which time she was several hundred miles away from me, in New York City. With regard to my sending my consciousness to the lake with this method, I achieved limited results that, although by no means completely unsuccessful, were somewhat vague in character. Jerry shared my interest in this subject, and we conducted several experiments together. But these practices required great energy and concentration, and they were rather depleting. My interest in it subsequently dwindled, particularly after I went away to college, when lack of privacy made such efforts almost impossible.

During my final year of high school, Bess began to introduce me to the possibilities of exercising more control over my own mind and thoughts, and it was through her influence that I began to read various works along those lines, including that inspirational work by James Allen entitled, *As a Man Thinketh.* Without my being aware of it then, she was preparing me for other knowledge she would communicate to me in the future. Thus it was that the year preceding my fourth trip to the lake was a very intense one. And yet, the lake was central in my thoughts, and when I was not specifically occupied with thinking or writing about it, it was nevertheless in the background of my mind, and it motivated much of what I did in my life, particularly my musical studies and my search for knowledge.

A chapter in my life was coming to an end. In fall, I would leave my home and go away to school. It would be a new world. I realized also that August 1967 would be the last time that I would go to Lake Geneva as a member of my church group. I had planned all year to make this fourth trip, and it was more important to me than anything else. But what would happen to my relationship with the lake after this? It was something that troubled me very much, and I could see no answers. During that summer before I went to the lake, I worked in the factory again, this time during the day. And again, I hated it. I resolved that I would never work there again.

August came, and I was on my way to the lake again, full of a mixture of feelings, including an intense anticipation. It was interesting that Shirley had been there with my group the previous summer and I had not even known her then. Now, her parents would not allow her to go because I would be there. I was glad that Jerry was able to go again, and as always, I spent my time with him. The head minister who had been with us last year and who had just recently left the church was replaced by his assistant. He did not permit me to live with Jerry as I had been able to do the previous summer, and so I had to stay in a room with several of my peers again.

Although I did not understand things at that time, I see things much more clearly now in looking back, and I feel that I now understand what was happening to me at the lake that August, and the two Augusts previous to it. I think that the primary reason that I felt a kind of separation from the power I knew was there was because I simply had too much company. I would realize later in my life that these were experiences of solitude, and I did not have it then. Even Jerry, who was a close friend, divided my energy and attention by his mere presence. This was neither his fault nor mine, but simply a condition that was unclear to me then. Furthermore, in spite of the times of solitude I did manage, I was surrounded most of the time by other people who had no relationship to what I was doing there, and their presence and my involvement in their activities was a serious distraction for me, more so than I realized. It is strange that I see it so clearly now, and yet that I did not see it then. But since then I have gained many years of experience and insight.

Besides my relationship with Jerry, there were one or two other people there that I had developed relationships with over the past year, and I see now that the totality of this situation completely cut me off from the mysterious world of perceptions which was there, which I profoundly and keenly sensed, and yet which remained ultimately inaccessible to me. And thus I faced a situation which had confronted me also during my two previous visits, and I was deeply troubled by it. But at that time I was bewildered by it. I was unable to understand what was happening. During my fourth trip to the lake, I drew back from a total involvement in seeking the power that existed there, perhaps without even realizing it. Without being conscious of it, I was afraid of the emptiness that might overwhelm me if I failed. And yet, although I can understand this aspect of my experience there, it is still, ultimately, a mystery to me why I was confronted by the beautiful power there with such direct and overwhelming force during my first visit to the lake. Was it simply a combination of the right time and place and circumstance, or was it the design of some volition which I could not comprehend? This is perhaps something which I am destined never to know.

Thus, during my fourth visit to Lake Geneva, I saw the power there and longed for it, and yet I unconsciously withdrew from it. And I must have felt, though incorrectly, that the power itself was in some way withdrawing or receding from me. I am sure that the character of my initial experiences at the lake contributed to this erroneous perception. That is, during the powerful experiences which surrounded my first visit there, in August 1964, I felt quite strongly that I was being sought out by the power there, and I am still today completely convinced that there is truth to this. Something had actually hunted me then, probed me, searched my being. It had been an awesome experience, and I have never forgotten the feelings that accompanied it. It was as if I had been guided there; my whole life had led to that moment. And during my fourth trip to the lake three years later, I could still feel it pulling me, but I had unwittingly allowed my consciousness to become entangled enough in other distractions which were decisively fatal to my receptivity to the power there that I could not reattain it.

Jerry had some rather remarkable psychic experiences at the lake that week that foreshadowed some events which would manifest themselves in his life not long after that trip, and which would also greatly affect me. He left the lake to return home a couple of days before that week was over, and thus I left the lake without his company that year. I did not know when I would return to it, and this engendered some very profound and acute feelings within me. I saw that an era in my life had truly come to an end, and I did not know what lay ahead, or in what way the lake would be a part of my life in the future. I paid the lake and the marvelous power there a particularly intense farewell. Standing at the edge of the water, upon the shores of my beloved Point, I surveyed the motion of the lake one last time. I burned everything there deeply within my memory, and breathed deeply the power and consciousness of everything around me. And then I turned and went away, wondering if I would ever see that beloved place again.

My first year at college was a very full one. I worked hard at the piano and encountered new circles of friends. My metaphysical interests remained very strong. I was particularly interested in acquiring more control over my own mind and, although the nature of my living accommodations made its practice quite difficult, I was still desirous of developing my proficiency at astral projection. I engaged in a certain degree of writing which, although it made no reference to the lake, nevertheless revealed a certain sense of wandering, or searching, which was the result of an uncertainty I felt at that time about the lake and my future relationship with it. I actively sought after new knowledge, which I hoped would bring a stability to my spiritual state of being and indicate a direction for me to pursue.

I went home regularly. I was therefore able to see Bess Hibarger from time to time, but my relationship with Jerry was the one that remained the most active, and it was because of this relationship that I soon became involved in a new and unexpected development that deeply affected my life. It was around the beginning of October 1967 that I met Swami Nirmalananda Giri. He was the last in that cycle of individuals to which I have referred before. I do not remember how Jerry had come to meet him, but it was during one of my weekend trips home that Jerry introduced me to him. Swami was extremely tall and imposing. His eyes were sharp and highly intelligent. And although his voice was very soft and gentle, it was misleading, because he could on occasion be unbelievably terrifying. When I first knew him, his black hair was quite long, tied in a ponytail that fell well below his shoulders, and he dressed in long, black robes. He had adopted this appearance as the result of spending a period of time in a Russian Orthodox monastery. However, after a time he again began to dress in the traditional ocher robes worn by Hindu monks.

He had figured in the psychic experiences that Jerry had recently had at the lake, and it was therefore not surprising to Jerry that Swami appeared in his life only a few weeks later. In fact, Jerry had fully intended to leave the United States and return to Germany, which he loved very much, and it was the appearance of Swami that had made him change his mind and remain in America. I knew nothing at that time about yoga or Hinduism. I wanted to meet Swami because I felt that he might be able to give me more information and guidance concerning astral projection, and that was really my sole motive. Ironically, although my life was deeply involved with Swami Nirmalananda Giri for almost a year after that, we talked very little about astral projection. In fact, although I am sure that we must have discussed it some, I cannot remember ever discussing it specifically with him. From the moment he saw me, he had other things in mind for me. At our very first meeting, his keen psychic powers saw deeply within me, and he initiated me into the first phase of a kind of yoga known as Kriya Yoga. This was a comprehensive type of yoga that embraced several different kinds of practices and disciplines, and which centered upon certain very potent and powerful techniques of pranayama, which is the control and development of consciousness through specific kinds of breathing and through the use of specific sounds that affect the nervous system.

My experiences with yoga and with the ideas embodied in Hinduism profoundly and permanently affected my consciousness and the character of my life. To a great extent, my previous contact with Bess Hibarger had served me well with respect to this, because it was through her that I became familiar with such concepts as karma and reincarnation. And because of this, and because of my internal nature, I took quite readily and naturally to these philosophical ideas, and to others related to them. They have remained a permanent part of my philosophical makeup and my view of the world. With respect to yoga itself, it produced immediately discernible effects upon my consciousness. Indeed, these were techniques of true integrity and power. Among all the techniques that I have ever studied, these were in many respects the purest, the most powerful, and the most truly elevated. They were the product of ages of experimenting and searching, and had been passed down through a line of great beings to my spiritual teacher and thus to me. I consider this yoga to be one of the greatest gifts which I have ever received, a tool of the most supreme value, designed to accelerate the evolution of one's consciousness in a dramatic, but thoroughly balanced and rational manner. This great yoga truly awakened my mind in a new way. I would say that it somehow made me more intelligent.

During my first year of college, Swami Nirmalananda Giri initiated me successively into more advanced phases of yoga, and I went home often to spend the weekend with him and with Jerry, who was now living with him. Although I have not had any contact with Swami for many years, I still regard him to be a being of the highest and purest spiritual integrity. He was frighteningly demanding at times, but I cannot resent him for this, for he was an irreproachable example of the standards which he set. He sometimes spoke to me about the relationships he and I had had in more than one past life, and his details were very specific. And although there was no way I could conclusively prove the truth of what he said, I accepted it. It was credible to me both on a strongly intuitive level, and from the standpoint of many things that were then true of my present life. He had also known Jerry in past lives, and substantiated Jerry's feeling that Jerry and I had been very close in another life. It was always true that the nature of the things that Swami said was such that they seemed to be borne out and verified more and more as the years passed. When he expressed something, it had a kind of authority that seemed not only to last through time, but to be enhanced by it.

During one particular conversation we had about the lake, he made some comments that, although they were almost like an afterthought, nevertheless revealed themselves many years later to be profoundly prophetic in a most uncanny way. He said that the special vibrations which I felt at the lake, and particularly at the Point, might be due, perhaps at least in part, to the past influence left by someone who had once lived there, perhaps some American Indian saint, or sage. The contents of this conversation sifted down in my mind to be stored someplace by my memory, more or less consciously forgotten for many years. But at a certain point in my life, they would be recalled dramatically to my attention and would assume a previously unimagined significance.

In spite of the benefits I derived from yoga, and in spite of the closeness which I had with my spiritual teacher, there were problems that began to develop between us. It is true that, on many levels, I responded naturally and rapidly both to yoga and to the doctrines behind it. But on other levels, it is clear to me now that I had no idea what I was getting into, and I felt completely unprepared, both physically and emotionally, for many of the demands my guru began to place upon me. I viewed the situation from the standpoint that Swami was someone to whom I had gone primarily to obtain information about astral projection, and who had, even without my asking, presented me with certain techniques to practice. I accepted them eagerly, because I sought ways to develop my consciousness, but I had made no commitments to him or to the ideals and goals of yoga. Indeed, for many months, I was not even aware that any kind of specific commitments were implied. Thus it was that I realized in time that Swami had seen me as going in a certain direction with my life that I had never had any intention of going. For example, I had no intention of meditating eight hours a day, nor of living the rest of my life in celibacy. I had no plans for renouncing the world, namely music and my academic studies, nor for becoming a monk. I had had some very remarkable perceptions and experiences by that time in my life, but I was still only eighteen years old, and a product of the American Midwest. As a result, the pressures which I began to feel from my spiritual teacher frightened me to death, and gave rise to a terrible spiritual confusion and conflict in my life.

I had in a sense become "dependent" to a degree upon yoga. That is, I perceived that it had unquestionable value for me, and I had no desire to stop practicing its techniques. On the other hand, I now associated it in my mind with various philosophical ideas and with the pressures which my spiritual teacher was bringing to bear upon me, which I could not accept. I perceived it as a kind of all-or-nothing situation, and whether or not this was really true, my spiritual teacher did nothing to make it appear otherwise. By the end of spring, 1968, Swami was planning to return to India, and Jerry Alber and certain other members of Swami's following were to go with him. I was included. This put an almost unendurable pressure on me, for it meant that to go to India, even for a year or so, would in all likelihood permanently interrupt my musical studies, and therefore many of my goals. If I left college I would lose scholarships, and my parents who, needless to say, were by this time completely shocked and horrified by what I was potentially about to do, made it very clear that they would in no way help me to resume my musical studies and academic pursuits if I abandoned them and went to India. I was caught in the middle.

Despite the conflicts which began to grow, the metaphysical aspect of my life during my first year of college was dominated almost entirely by my yoga studies and by my relationship with Swami. During the summer of 1968, I worked as a lifeguard for a camp which was situated on a rather attractive lake about fifteen miles from my home town. Although I lived at the camp for the summer, I went into town quite often, and thus remained in close contact with Swami and Jerry. For a time, it seemed that Swami's demands upon me had softened a bit, and I experienced a degree of relief. But in the middle of the summer, during one of my visits to the ashram, or the place where Swami lived and met with his followers, some of whom lived there with him, he announced to me his decision to leave that August. I realized that I might never see him again, which has indeed been so thus far in my life, and I remember that I began to cry and hugged him very tightly. Before I had finished my work at the camp and returned to school, he was gone.

I came to experience a peculiar sense of aloneness. It had been a year since I had been to the lake, and I had no idea when I would be able to return to it. Swami was gone, and with him had gone Jerry Alber, my spiritual brother and closest friend. I returned to school to pursue my music studies. I managed to do some writing that year, but the only spiritual references they made conveyed a sense of inner wandering. And although I did not touch upon Lake Geneva, my writings contained several vivid references to various images in nature and to sailing, which were inspired by my summer stay on the small lake outside my home town, where I learned to sail that season. Although I tried to continue in the yoga techniques I knew, I experienced great emotional turbulence in doing them, and my momentum quickly decelerated until I halted completely. I was actually afraid to continue the practices, for whether or not it was actually so, I felt as if the approval of my spiritual teacher had been withdrawn, and it was as if I might bring some kind of harm down upon myself if I continued.

Two things happened to make these matters worse. Swami had come to the university the year before to speak about yoga and to give some instruction. A friend of mine who was also a music major had thereby come to know Swami and had become very much involved with him. It was my understanding that he was even going off to India with the others, but one day during the fall of 1968 he appeared at my door. He had gotten all the way to boarding the plane in New York City with Swami and his group and had backed out. He was in a terrible emotional state, and I feared that he was heading for a nervous breakdown. But in time, he got himself back together and continued his yoga studies under another teacher. I lost contact with him many years ago. The second thing that happened was that at some point I received either one or two letters from Swami in India which produced a devastating effect on me. It seemed to me that these letters were harsh and dictatorial, and it was as if he had become a tyrant. What he said, in effect, was that I was throwing my life away, and if I did not come to India, he was turning his back on me forever. I did not go, and I have never heard from him again, although I eventually learned through certain contacts that Swami had been in an automobile accident in India which, by all rights, should have been fatal. But he survived it, and when he recovered he became like a different being, far more severe in his demands than he had ever been in the past. He and Jerry and others from their group eventually returned to the United States, and settled in the western part of the country, where they formed another ashram. From time to time, I received various indirect reports about their activities and certain religious changes which they underwent, but I had no direct contact with them, and I did not hear from Jerry again until January 1974.

In March 1969, I went to Lake Geneva. I had to see it. I did not have a car, and it was indeed an arduous trip. I took a train from Champaign-Urbana to Chicago, where I stopped briefly to see some friends, and then rode a series of buses from there to the town of Lake Geneva, Wisconsin. I had little money, and fortunately for me, it was fairly warm. I walked to the Point from the town of Lake Geneva, along the shore path, which was a distance of about ten miles. I stayed at the Point for about an hour. I was exhausted and hungry, and had to start back almost immediately in order to get to Lake Geneva before dark, and get a bus back toward Chicago. It was one of the strangest trips I ever made to the lake. But standing at the Point, although tired and depleted, I looked beyond the birches, out over the expanse of waves, and felt the great power and consciousness within the water. I sensed the spirit that existed there and felt its being, out there, moving over the surface of the water, stirring a memory within me. It would never release me, nor I it, and I knew that I would find a way to come back. Somehow, I would manage it. With this resolve, I set out to return to the town of Lake Geneva. I took the highway this time, and was able to find a ride after I had walked about halfway back. I returned to school by way of Chicago, in the same manner by which I had come. I had been away for at least two days and had traveled about four hundred twenty miles, in addition to which I had walked at least another fifteen, in order to spend only an hour at the Point. But I had seen it, and that was enough to set my resolve to return.

I was very active musically that year, and I remember playing the Third Piano Concerto of Prokofiev in April 1969. This event, however, had an ominous overtone. My mother and father had come to the university to hear this performance, and although no one was aware at that time of any problems, I felt for certain that it was the last time my father would ever hear me play the piano. I was troubled about him, and had had several frightening dreams about his death. I had even cautiously asked my mother about his health, and she replied that, as far as she knew, he was fine. I had no choice to accept this, although I remained troubled.

Since I felt cut off from the light I had encountered in the practice of yoga, I was compelled to seek elsewhere. I was able to visit Bess from time to time, and actively resumed my theosophical studies, particularly in the area of controlling my own mind. In conjunction with this, I made a few attempts to practice yoga, but these sporadic efforts were short-lived. I became deeply interested in the I Ching through a very fine friend which I had at the university, and I became rather adept in its use. I respected it very much, and I found it to be a remarkably accurate and profoundly revealing means of divination, which I employed in considering several decisions which I had to make at that time. I was very much exposed to the extensive drug culture at the university, and was very curious about these drugs and their effects. At that time, however, I confined my experimenting to a very limited use of marihuana and, on two or three occasions, the use of methamphetamines, or speed. I found the results somewhat interesting, but of no real value.

During the summer of 1969, I worked again at the camp on the lake where I had worked the previous summer. It was a difficult time. I was involved in an unhappy personal relationship, and on June 28, my father died. Shortly after my troubled dreams about him, it was discovered that he had developed an aortic aneurysm, and he had subsequently gone to Chicago for an operation. I was completely unaware of the seriousness and potential danger of such a condition, and had said a very casual good-bye to him. Shortly thereafter, I received an urgent telephone call from Chicago and was driven up to join my mother at the hospital. I saw him twice in the intensive care unit before he died, and once he opened his eyes and looked at me. He was not able to speak, and I said nothing, but I will always remember the look of profound relief in his eyes when he realized that I was there at his side. After the funeral, I resumed my job at the lake near my home for the duration of the summer, before returning to my junior year at the university in September.

In the midst of the sadness of my father's death, I had an experience two or three days after he died that I will never forget and which greatly influenced my feelings about death. In my sadness, I had gone to meditate in order to replenish myself, and I had a vision of him. His soul expressed an enormous light and power he had never been able to manifest while he was in his physical body, and he was likewise surrounded by a world of energy and warmth and light. I returned from this experience with a tremendous joy and a feeling of gratitude, to be confronted by the grimness of funeral arrangements, and I realized then that, if anyone was enveloped in death, then it was us, the "living," for it was certainly not the soul of my father, which now lived in light. I later related this experience to my mother, although I am sure that she did not quite know what to think about it. But I know that she wanted to believe me. My father appeared to me very clearly once again several months after that, and then I had no more contact with him.

With all the gravity of the events of the summer, I did not think much about Lake Geneva. Soon it was September 1969, and I found myself back at school, negotiating my junior year. I worked enormously hard in developing that force which is often referred to as the "creative imagination." I began to regain and develop a great amount of what I might call personal, or psychic energy, and without realizing it, was laying a mental foundation and framework which would eventually lead me into occult experiences. But wherever my searches led me, I was really, in the final analysis, trying to regain the beautiful power which I had known at the lake, and to find the knowledge which would enable me to understand it and to exert control over my own life and being.

My spiritual teacher had warned me about the use of drugs, and I was wary of them. But I was also genuinely curious about them, particularly the hallucinogens. I took mescaline on several occasions, which I found to be a very intense experience and therefore aptly suited to my nature and personality. These experiences could be either disturbing, even frightening or deeply repugnant, or intensely beautiful, depending on my state of mind at that time and the nature of what I was perceiving. Although they could enormously enhance the quality and vividness of my perceptions and thoughts, I attributed no real or lasting spiritual value to them. I could not do so, because of the incomparable beauty and power and authenticity of the perceptions and experiences which I had encountered at Lake Geneva. The experiences could not even be compared. I wrote a great deal that year about various personal experiences. I had lived on a lake for the past two summers, and thus much of my writing dealt with images in nature, to which I was very much attuned, and also with sailing, since I had learned to sail my first summer there, and had sailed frequently when I returned for the second summer. I had always loved canoeing, and I had quickly developed a corresponding love for sailing. I had begun to think a great deal about Lake Geneva again, and woven in and out of my writings from that year were numerous references to it and to the mystical impact my experiences there had had upon me. My mind became filled with intense memories of what I had encountered there, and I felt a vacuum inside which I sensed could only be filled by the pure and sublime and mysterious consciousness which expressed itself there. But I did not know when or how I would go back.

I returned to my waterfront job during the summer of 1970, but various circumstances had made it a less desirable work environment, and I was certain that I would not return the following summer. I saw a lot of Bess, and I worked even more intensely in developing my "creative imagination." I am not sure why, but I became deeply interested again in yoga that summer, and I practiced the techniques and reread intently the books which I had on the subject. I really did not know where I was going spiritually, but I felt a deep need to be going somewhere. In July, I decided to return to Lake Geneva. I had not been there in almost a year and a half, since March 1969, at which time I had spent little more than a few hours there. I arranged for some time off from my job, and made a reservation at Conference Point Camp for a couple of days in August.

I can best describe the sensations which I felt then by offering below the words which I wrote at Conference Point, Lake Geneva, in August 1970:

I think that I felt drawn back here, to Lake Geneva, at least in the beginning, to reaffirm to myself the fact of God's special Presence here. I had only to enter upon the grounds of Conference Point, and that goal was fulfilled. That awesome, cowing, totally crushing and overwhelming Reality dwells here, not glaring or noisily proclaiming Itself, but gently, yet with magnificent power, by the eternal prayer which the waves whisper, washing away the troubles of the mind and the burdens of the heart. Conference Point shines with the most sublime Reality, the highest Truth—that wholly natural, Primordial Essence, the Divine Nature. The verification of this Truth washed away all the muck and sham in me, leaving me numb, empty, and alone. But then the emptiness was filled to overflowing with a most subtle and pure joy, the Bliss that is the Celebration of the Presence of the Eternal, Loving God, my Father, my Mother, my whole Being.

Perhaps the waves whisper the mystical Om. They soothe the distur-
bances of the mind and the heart like sand on a beach made flawlessly
smooth by the washing action of the waves. I pray that I might dwell forever
in the greatest Heights and the most profound Depths of that Sublimity. That
I might be drawn back again and again to my Home, the Source of my Life.
Though my heart by some misfortune might forget Lake Geneva for a time,
may my separation from It be only a temporary one. May the day come
when I am united forever with It, and that Spirit, that Shining, Loving,
Boundless Eternity which is God. May my heart be made to contain It.

I did not stay quite as long as I had planned. It was as if I could not endure
too long such purity of beauty. I could only sustain so much of it; I was filled by
it, and I had no more capacity. I had confirmed what I had come for. I knew
again that there was an incomparable power there for me.

During my stay there, I obtained two applications for jobs on the lake for
the following summer, both of which were for waterfront work. As well as
securing an application for Conference Point itself, I also picked up an application from the George Williams College Camp, a very beautiful conference center which was about a ten-minute walk down the shore path, west from
Conference Point. On a lovely plateau, above the hills upon which George
Williams College Camp was situated, was the site of the magnificent Yerkes
Observatory, which housed the largest refractor telescope in the world.

With intense hopes for the following summer, I left the lake and returned to
finish my summer waterfront job. It was soon September, and I returned to the
University of Illinois and my senior year, and to a very full and eventful life. The
early fall was marked by an incident whose impact will never leave me, for I
believe that I came close to losing my sanity as a result of taking LSD. I experimented with it for one reason: I had heard that it could induce intensely mystical
and religious experiences. I wanted to know if this was true, and I felt that there
was simply no way I could justifiably express an opinion about it until I had tried
it. Over a period of approximately two months, I took LSD about four times. All
of the resulting experiences, with the exception of the final one, were very similar.
Although I experienced very strong visual hallucinations, I always knew where I
was and was able to maintain control of myself. I had no excessively strong mental or emotional reactions, and never felt that anything was taking place which I
could not handle. During these first three experiments, I was not alone.

The final time I took the drug was on a warm fall afternoon. After ingesting
it I set off on foot, alone, out into the open country. As I sat in a field, in the hot
sun, the land gradually turned to liquid and began to undulate gracefully. There
were large power lines nearby, and the electrical buzzing from them was trans-

formed into a roar. I felt as if the sun were frying me. I caught sight of a grasshopper a few feet away, and when I looked at my own body again, it had become that of an insect, down to the last incredible detail. I became frightened and, getting to my feet, began to move quickly back toward the campus. I had to cross a large cemetery at one point, and as soon as I had entered it, the tombstones and grave markers began to run about wildly, sliding over the ground, as I negotiated my way through them. I remember looking up into the blue sky and seeing an enormous hawk, gliding motionlessly along the air currents. I approached the football stadium and the screams of thousands of people struck my ears. I became obsessed with making it back somehow to the safety of my apartment. I lost my sense of movement. I was a disembodied consciousness which saw its surroundings like a frozen negative on a photographic plate. Suddenly, I would register another perception, a few hundred yards beyond where the previous one had imprinted itself upon the screen of my consciousness, but I had no awareness of moving or of what took place in between. Somehow, I made it to my apartment. I got the door unlocked and, after entering, quickly shut it behind me to keep out the distortions. But I sank into the floor up to my knees, and the walls melted and I could see the sun. It emitted giant waves of colored light which struck my thoughts and pulverized them. I could not think. My terror became uncontrollable and my emotional state escalated to pure, unbounded panic. I tried to get back out the door of the apartment, but the light from the huge window in the hall blinded me and beat me back into the apartment. I tried several times to telephone for help, but the phone had melted into a blob of jelly and I could not find all of my arm. But I managed to call the numbers of several friends who did not answer, and after what seemed like an eternity, just before I called the police, I finally reached a friend who came to me as quickly as she could.

By the time she arrived, I was almost hysterical. I had her shut all the windows because I thought I was freezing to death, but as soon as she had done so, I began to burn and experienced an intense suffocation. I looked to my friend for help, but she had only one, enormous eye in the center of her face, and I could not look at her. I vaguely realized that I needed to urinate, and I had my friend guide me to the bathroom. I literally could not find my body. There were no sex organs, so I gave up in my attempt. After several hours, I gradually reclaimed my wonderful materiality, and experienced again an exquisite sense of weight and mass.

I had experienced the most helpless, debilitating fear I had ever known. It was degrading and humiliating. During that LSD experience, I had grasped moments of intense beauty, but they were beyond my control and overcome by wave after wave of paranoia and terror. I have never taken a drug since then, and I experienced vivid and frightening flashbacks for many months. I lived in constant dread of them, and spent several nights in clinics which were set up to deal with such experiences. I found that the smallest amount of marihuana could touch off intense flashbacks. Even a small drink of beer had the potential to throw me into terror, and thus for months afterwards I did not even drink beer. Although I have occasionally used marihuana since then, it has been rare, and I eventually abandoned all such practices as essentially valueless and unnecessary. I would stress again here the fact that none of the perceptions and experiences which I have described in this book, neither those which I have encountered at the lake nor others related to them, are related in any way whatsoever to any kind of drug. I found no true relationship between such drug experiences as I have described above and those matchless perceptions of unbounded reality and consciousness which I have embraced at Lake Geneva.

My writing that year dealt exclusively with images from the world of the lake; its beauty, its sparkling waters and blue skies, and the deep green hills which encircled it. I called forth images from my early experiences there. My visit to the lake that past August had reawakened a world of sensations and memories, and now the lake was often in my thoughts. I contemplated the possibility of returning there for an entire summer, and waited anxiously to hear some word about the jobs for which I had applied. I stayed more closely in touch with Bess Hibarger that year, and the techniques which I used in furthering the development and control of my own mind were still strongly associated with the knowledge and teaching that she had given me. These techniques were presented as having a Christian foundation, but I was not concerned about this aspect of them. I was simply looking for power to control my life. Many of the techniques had appropriated and adapted Eastern concepts, such as increasing one's spiritual power and consciousness through energizing and developing the various chakras, or psychic centers, within one's self, and thereby releasing their respective latent forces. I was very familiar with such principles through my saturation with yoga and other Eastern teachings. Therefore, I began to develop a tendency at that time which, although I did not realize it then, was perhaps not very wise. I began to devise my own systems of meditation and release of power by combining the techniques which I had become aware of through Bess Hibarger with the various yoga practices I had acquired through my study with Swami.

Although I did not seem to notice any harmful effects from this at the time, such tendencies were to cause me a great deal of trouble in the future. With respect to the techniques I had acquired through my contact with Bess, I found it appropriate to describe them and refer to them as "applied metaphysics," or, in other words, a system whereby one developed energy and power within the mechanism of their inner being and used it to transform both the nature of their own consciousness and the conditions in the outer world. I was developing a change of perspective about the manner in which I sought to control my life. A change had begun months before, during my junior year, when I began to work more with that force known as the creative imagination. Some of the results I had achieved in terms of influencing the nature and course of outer events in my life were truly astounding to me, and now, during my senior year of study, I was involved with developing these tendencies further. I sought to exert more control over the events in my outer world. I wanted more power over the exterior conditions of my life. To put it another way, I wanted to manipulate my circumstances so as to realize my personal ends and desires. I do not necessarily see myself as having become more selfish. Rather, I was seeking a control I had never had over my life. I had experienced years of loneliness and wandering and uncertainty, and I eventually came to seek more control. But the major shift of focus in my attitude during this period was that I concentrated more increasingly on molding the outer world to mirror my desires, rather than looking primarily within myself and searching my own being, which was what I had done for several years after my first experiences at Lake Geneva. At that time, there seemed also to be no apparent danger in this, just as there seemed to be no danger in my combining various techniques of inner development. But I learned differently.

In March 1971, I met Sarah. She was a lovely girl and a fine person, and she was a voice student in the music school. We developed a close relationship and fell in love. Just around the time I met her, I received job offers both from Conference Point Camp and from George Williams College Camp. The job at Conference Point offered a position as lifeguard, but, much to my surprise and delight, George Williams had offered me a contract to teach sailing. I was ecstatic. I had obtained the desire of my heart. My sense of well-being and security, and control over my life, was growing. I felt a new strength and solidity. I had developed a relationship with a beautiful young woman, and now I was looking forward to spending a summer on Lake Geneva as a sailing instructor. Sarah would be in Europe for most of the summer, touring with a choir. It was our hope to be together in the fall, when I returned to the university to enter graduate school. But there was a catch to this, which I became aware of during my senior year.

My piano professor was on sabbatical that year, touring and making some recordings, and so it was necessary for me to study with another teacher. However, we did not get along, and after three months, to our mutual satisfaction, we terminated the arrangement and I studied with someone else, which proved to be a more agreeable situation. I was able to finish up my undergraduate studies and I gave a recital in April. But due to this situation, in addition to some other personality differences and the fact of my own teacher's absence that year, it looked as if I would not get into the graduate department in music there. Although my abilities as a pianist were beyond reproach, certain personalities were determined to keep me out, which had serious consequences both for my training and for my relationship with Sarah. But the force of my mind was centered on returning, and even though I had no outer indications that this would be so, for indeed I had been told quite plainly that I could forget about returning in the fall, I turned down several attractive teaching assistantships from various schools. I went way out on a limb and put my entire future at stake. One day, after I had said good-bye to Sarah for the summer and returned to my home to await the date upon which I was to depart for Lake Geneva, I experienced an intense flash of intuitive knowledge. I knew beyond all doubt that I would return to the University of Illinois in the fall. It was like a burst of light inside my mind, and I felt an immovable conviction and certainty. Bringing the techniques I had developed fully to bear, I centered the force of my consciousness upon this end. Sarah was in Europe, and in a few days I would be living on Lake Geneva.

In June 1971, I went to the lake and spent the summer there, as I did again the following year. From after the time of my first visit to the lake, in August 1964, until the early 1980s, those times were the fullest and happiest periods of my life. After I had arrived at the lake in June 1971, it was, as I remember, only two or three weeks until one day when I received a letter from the University of Illinois. It announced my admission to graduate school. I experienced a sensation of supreme victory. That period of my life had become one of those extraordinarily rare times at which I felt that I possessed everything I wanted in order to be happy.

I had been in close touch with Bess that spring, and during my stay at the lake I wrote to her and telephoned her several times. The writing I did that summer expressed an intense preoccupation with the enormous power of the mind. The primary nature of my experience on the lake that summer was that I simply existed and savored the joy and exuberance of each moment. The first shining morning that I sailed upon those gently undulating waters is an image that will be with me forever. I virtually lived in sailboats, and the movements and sounds of the wind and waves filled my perceptions for many hours each day. The Point was only a ten-minute walk down the shore path, to the east, and I was free to go there whenever I was not sailing. I enjoyed the people with whom I worked and every other aspect of the summer.

I did not spend a great deal of time in solitude. Never was I more aware of the evanescence of time. It flowed inexorably through my fingers. Somewhere inside myself, I was a bit troubled that I was not focusing more of my energies seeking that ultimate state of perception I had encountered in 1964. For in spite of the fullness and adventure of living that characterized that summer, I knew deep inside that I was not placing myself in a decisive position of accessibility to the incredible forces that once touched me there. I was still not to realize for some time that those perceptions and experiences were ones of ultimate solitude, and, whether or not I was actually conscious of it, I was cutting off the possibility of such experiences by remaining surrounded, or shielded, by people, activities, and all those things that pulled my consciousness away from that mode of perception. Although my mind did not let me face it then, I see clearly now that the explanation was very simple. I was not ready to face the aloneness. Some part of my being knew that even then, but another part of me avoided confronting the truth. Nevertheless, I spent many hours walking upon the path along the shore and sitting among the rocks and birches at the Point, feeding my hunger for perception, breathing into my being the exquisite, living consciousness of the lake.

I looked forward to seeing Sarah again with great anticipation, and she returned from Europe while I was still at Lake Geneva. She came up there to visit me from her home near Chicago, and I recall driving to Chicago from the lake to pay her brief visits, for although I still did not own a car at that time, I was able to borrow one to make the trips.

The lake had refreshed and rejuvenated me, and I left it fully with the hope and intention of returning for the following summer season. In September 1971, I began my first year of graduate school. Lake Geneva was never far from my thoughts, and I eagerly anticipated receiving a contract from George Williams for the following summer. I wrote a great deal during that academic year, and the subject matter dealt almost exclusively with the lake, and my memories from the past summer there; its beauty and richness; the joy and exhilaration of sailing in that world of sparkling water and radiant blue skies, and the majesty of the Yerkes Observatory. I look back now and contemplate the words I wrote in November 1971, regarding my previous summer at the lake:

At times, the future seems dark and twisted, but the light of that one vision is always shining, guiding. I approach it in the realm of the soul where the subjective sun perpetually shines, and where time has no meaning. And I see Conference Point always in the future. Through this spiritual revelation, there will be a way for me, a road.

I worked very hard at the piano. My own professor had returned, and thus things went more smoothly again for me in the music school. I performed the First Piano Concerto of Liszt in April 1972, and I was awarded a teaching assistantship for the following year. The metaphysical knowledge I had acquired as a result of my relationship with Bess, and which had served me so well over the past months, was still very much a part of my way of life. I saw her occasionally during the fall of 1971, when I made trips home. But my life had begun to take a new direction that fall, and my contact with her greatly diminished over the winter. By spring, I was intensely preoccupied with certain new concepts and ideas, and, without really realizing it, I had lost touch with her. In the fall, I had come to discover a whole new world of ideas, although from then until the late spring I continued to explore the potentials of the techniques which I had been involved with over the past many months; that is, using the yoga techniques I knew, as well as the knowledge of the practices I had obtained from Bess's library, in conjunction with intense efforts of creative visualization, in order to exert yet more control over the circumstances and events that made up my outer world. But other possibilities had opened up to me as well.

When I became a graduate student, I gained a direct access to millions of books in the graduate shelves, a privilege denied to undergraduate students. The university library was awesome, and I discovered shelf after shelf of books dealing with every imaginable facet of the metaphysical and occult world. During my university career, I was always a member of the Dean's List, and a Graduate High Honors. And yet, when I consider the countless hours I devoted to these personal studies, not to mention the thousands of hours that I practiced the piano, it is a wonder that I ever did any academic work at all.

And it was thus that I first discovered the writings of that esoteric Russian philosopher-mathematician, P. D. Ouspensky. At that time, it was his work entitled *Tertium Organum* that made a particularly powerful impact upon my thinking. In his explorations into the nature of perception, both human and nonhuman, in his discussions of the nature of time and space, and particularly the properties of four-dimensional space and space of yet higher dimensions, I found great new vistas of thought awaiting my exploration. I endeavored to find possible connections between the concepts he set forth and the experiences I had had at the lake, and I was particularly struck by the connection between his ideas and concepts and those which comprised the principles of Hindu cosmology. What was most astounding were the implications in his work that the universe and everything it contained was, although perhaps in some way unapparent to us, living and conscious. Not only was this in accord with the concepts of yoga and Hinduism, but it reflected a truth I had perceived at Lake Geneva; namely, that within the natural world was a tremendous consciousness.

Later, in the spring of 1972, I recall finding a similarly astounding work entitled *The Theory of Celestial Influence,* by Rodney Collin. In it, I found an incredible extension of Ouspensky's ideas, particularly with respect to the nature of the manifested universe. It also correlated with certain aspects of

Eastern thought, and strongly reinforced one of the most overwhelming and beautiful perceptions I had attained at the lake, which was that the universe was the embodiment and expression of incorruptible law, rooted in an order and harmony that was sublime beyond comprehension.

I had never had any use for purely speculative philosophy, and I sought intently to find applied uses for the ideas I had discovered in the works of Ouspensky and Collin. Thus, to a significant extent, I enhanced my understanding and perceptions of time and space, and while I pursued this line of thought, I was simultaneously exploring another new discovery which had come to my attention about the same time I had come upon Ouspensky; that is, during the fall of 1971. This, of all things, was a system known as Huna, which was practiced in Polynesia, although much more so formerly than at the present time. Although one might refer to it as a form of magic, such a description is misleadingly esoteric. And although it had many interesting facets, there is not space to describe all of them in detail here, except to convey its primary attraction for me, which was that it embodied some very specific techniques related to creative visualization. I saw in it another tool by which I could control my outer world.

In my desire to have power over my life, I was devoting my energy more than ever to finding ways of influencing events around me, rather than looking within to examine and explore my true spiritual needs. And indeed, I had enjoyed a certain success, in that I had obtained a number of desires whose fulfillment had been important to me. Among them were that I had developed a beautiful relationship with Sarah, I had spent the summer at the lake and was intending to return to following summer, and I had returned to the University of Illinois to do my graduate studies in piano, with the assurance of a teaching assistantship for the following year. On one level, I was enjoying a kind of peak in my life.

But on another level of consciousness, I was not satisfied. I felt this deep inside, but I do not believe that I really acknowledged it. Or if I did acknowledge it, I did not seem to recognize what it was that made me feel that way. Perhaps I did not want to recognize it. For if the underlying source of this restlessness was the fact that, in truth, I had not yet reattained that ultimate oneness with the exquisite consciousness I had once encountered at the lake and which I was still seeking, then that was something I did not know how to face directly. It was too disturbing, and, above all, it made me feel lonely. I had felt alone for much of my life, and it was a prospect that had always frightened me.

The lake embodied a great mystery for me. I do not believe at this point in my life that this will ever change. But almost from the very outset, I sought to solve this mystery by seeking "knowledge," by exploring and accumulating facts and ideas and techniques, and by looking into every available avenue for explanations and for some relevant frame of reference for my perceptions and experiences. Although I had done so unwittingly, I had progressively lost myself in a labyrinth of facts. I had become almost inextricably entangled and mired down in a mountain of information and techniques. On one level, they had given me a great deal of security and had enabled me to realize certain desires in my life. But they had not really brought me any closer to the fulfillment of my deepest and most unrelenting longing—to become one with the consciousness and mystery which had confronted me at Lake Geneva.

I do not regret those years of searching, from 1964 until the early 1980s, because in many ways I evolved through those circumstances. I acquired extensive insight, perspective, and understanding in terms of the many paths of knowledge that one can follow, and would it not have been for all those experiences, I would be someone else today other than who I am. Those experiences deeply enriched my consciousness and my life, but during that process, I also struggled and wandered for many years. The purpose of this chapter is to present a truthful and balanced picture of those searches; to show ultimately not only the light and beauty which I found, but also the confusion and wandering that characterized my seeking.

I was limited in terms of the time and energy I could commit to exploring directly the mysteries of the lake. It was not nearby, and I still did not even have my own transportation. And deep inside of me was the suppressed fear that if I did perhaps indeed make the step of reaching out and confronting the world of the lake, I might not find what I had sensed was there. Perhaps I would even discover that everything had been only within my mind, that, in other words, it was not real.

I would be returning to Lake Geneva during the summer of 1972. I had received a contract from George Williams, this time for the position of director of the sailing department. Sarah, who was planning on attending summer school at the university, would be able to come to the lake and visit me occasionally during the summer. She and I had developed a close relationship during the year, but in spite of this, I had begun to experience a sense of restlessness. Not too many months previously, I had felt as if I had everything I wanted. But gradually, my feeling of satisfaction had begun to deteriorate. Whether or not this was due to some flaw within the relationship, or the manifestation within my own being of some unfulfilled spiritual longing that I thought Sarah should be able to fill, or simply the inevitable expression of some aspect of that insidious perversity that seems to be innate to the human condition, I am not totally certain. But whatever the reason, my attention began to wander. During spring 1972, I had an intensely disturbing dream in which my relationship with Sarah had ended as a result of some tragedy. We seemed to be separated by a great physical distance, and I saw her flying to California. I feared her death. But I kept silent until, shortly after that, she announced to me that she and her girl-friend were planning to fly to California that summer. In light of this, I related my dream to her and asked her at least to reconsider her plans. The matter was left there for the time being, but I could not shake my fear, and I sensed that the end of our relationship was inevitable. I had had that feeling of inevitability before. It had haunted me during the months before my father's death.

Sometime around March 1972, I began to develop an interest in the true occult. I was amazed at some of the texts I discovered within the shelves of the graduate library, and I began to study the mechanisms of magic. This could have proven unhealthy enough, but I was at the same time also involved with the practices relating to yoga and to Huna. I was unaware of the dangers of combining various esoteric techniques in such a fashion, and it would be several months before I would feel the repercussions of this practice. It became clear to me later that, by the time I had gone to Lake Geneva in June 1972, I had opened the door to the occult realm far enough that I had become accessible to some very dangerous forces, but I did not become aware of this until several months after that summer at the lake. But by the end of May, I had experienced enough to satisfy myself that there was real power there.

In June, after making a trip to Florida with my mother, I went to Lake Geneva. Sarah's plans to go to California had fallen through, and although I was relieved about this, my apprehension remained. I had taken a collection of notes pertaining to magic with me to the lake and, although I have never been able to ascertain when or where or how, they disappeared. But my attention to such things was suspended for the summer anyway. My feelings toward the lake and the power there were the same as the summer before. I felt exuberant and happy, and all of my senses drank in the warmth and light and opulent beauty of that living world. But I did not seek intently those isolated conditions and reflective states that might have challenged me to confront the deeper and more mysterious aspects of that environment. There were many occasions that summer during which I experienced times of fulfilling solitude and reflection. I loved to walk along the shore path to the Point, where I sat upon the rocks and listened to the waves and looked into the depthless skies, and I often followed the trail that led up through the hills to the plateau upon which was located the magnificent observatory. I enjoyed the quiet and elevation there, and the nearness to the open expanse of sky.

Sarah came up to the lake and visited me from time to time, and during what was to be her final visit for the summer, she informed me about the development of some unexpected circumstances under which she would be doing some traveling in the western part of the United States and ending up in California. Remembering my dream and my persistent feelings of apprehension, I again expressed my concern about such a trip. But Sarah was certain that everything would be all right, and I could not dissuade her. I resigned myself to her decision, but inwardly I felt a sensation of inevitability and dread. Our relationship was finished.

I had not actively sought new relationships, but I was emotionally open to the possibility of one. However, I experienced a conflict of feelings, because I was not willing to let go of Sarah. Not too many days had passed after Sarah's final visit when I met someone by whom I was totally subdued the first time I saw her. She was visiting the camp with her family, and was a relative of the president of George Williams College and his family. The college was located in Downers Grove, just outside of Chicago, and the camp on the lake served as a summer campus. The president and his family had a summer house there, and I was friends with them. Nancy's youth and sparkling beauty, in conjunction with the exquisite magic of the lake, was instantly fatal. We did everything together. We walked the shores of the lake, and in fact walked around its entire perimeter one day, which was about thirty miles. Among all the days of my life, that one will always be one of the most unforgettable. We swam together and sailed together. It is impossible to describe, to one who has never done it, the ultimate beauty and mystery of sailing at night.

I allowed myself to become happier in a personal relationship than I had ever been in my life, and my feelings toward her were pure and unrestrained passion. I forgot everything else, and I could not be separate from her for even a moment. Whether or not it was true, I told myself that if I could just have stayed in touch with Sarah, it might not have happened. But she was inaccessible. I did not even know where she was, except that it was somewhere in the West. But regardless of what the future held, I was compelled to live this experience to the fullest. I never knew such happiness, or such desire.

Nancy's family returned to Colorado, but she was able to remain there with me for several more days, before returning to Colorado herself to begin college. It was getting late in August, and many people had left the lake. I could not think of the end, but I felt it stalking us, and that impending day when she would leave me.

The day that Nancy left was gray and heavy and foreboding. After we said good-bye, she turned from me and, without looking back, walked to the car and was driven away. I had agreed to stay at the lake for another week to help finish up the season and prepare things for the September sailing school. But I could not bear to remain there for even another day, let alone a night. Some friends who had also worked at the camp that summer were leaving that day, and I was able to arrange a ride with them to my home, since they were going in that direction. I felt so numb that I could hardly move, and I dared not think. I went to my living quarters and mechanically packed my belongings. My surroundings were becoming unendurable. Just before I left, I walked down the hill to the edge of the lake. The water was quiet and sullen and opaque. The waves were leaden and grey. There was no sun, and it was almost cold. The atmosphere was grey, like the lake, and a mist was settling over the hills. In the distance, enveloped in the grey mist, I could see the Point, jutting out into the water. For a moment I stood and looked at it, without feeling or thinking, and then I turned, and quickly left the world of the lake.

In September 1972, I began my second and final year of graduate school. I felt compelled to be honest with Sarah about what had happened at the lake. She was devastated, and our relationship collapsed. My dream and my fears had become reality, for although I had not foreseen all the details of the circumstances, the end result was the same. I lost Sarah. There were some intermittent and extremely painful attempts at reconciliation between us, but ultimately they failed. I saw her almost daily at the music school, which was almost unbearable, and I remember that she came to my graduate recital the following March. She even went to dinner with me and some other friends later that evening. I think that she tried to reach out to me again, but she had been hurt too much, and simply could not do so.

My correspondence with Nancy began to dwindle. The summer had not had the impact upon her that it had had on me. She was younger, and it was her first year of college. She was very beautiful, and new experiences were waiting for her. By winter, she had almost completely stopped writing. My emotional and personal life collapsed. I felt as if I had lost everything. With the exception of one or two brief and unsuccessful attempts, I had no relationships whatsoever with women for over a year after the summer of 1972. The time that Nancy and I had shared at the lake had seemed like paradise, and now I had fallen into a pit. I began to think that somewhere I had made a horrible and irreparable mistake. On the one hand, with respect to Nancy, I feared that perhaps the one great love of my life had slipped away from me, never to be regained, and yet I wondered if it had not all been some kind of overwhelming illusion through which a truly meaningful relationship with Sarah had been destroyed. I was completely confused and torn. I had no rationality left. In my mind, it was as if, through some irreversible cosmic mistake which I had made, I had fallen from an ecstatic state of fulfillment and grace. I almost felt as if some great, cruel joke had been played on me, and yet it was I who was ultimately responsible for the consequences. I had erred gravely in thinking that Nancy could give me something spiritually that Sarah could not. No relationship could give to me what I longed for. The fulfillment of this relentless drive lay elsewhere, and I had begun to realize it. I had tried to combine this idealized relationship with the power of the lake, to fuse them into one transcendental experience. This had shattered my judgement, and had alienated me even further from the possibility of a real answer. I felt enormously responsible, and I saw myself as doomed through my own irresponsible actions and hunger for power.

I thought very little about the lake. The associations were too painful. I did not write much, although I wrote about my summer experiences with Nancy in September, while we were still sharing some degree of communication. In February 1973, I began a poem that conveyed my profound restlessness for the power I had once known at the lake, but I abandoned it for several months. In October 1972, a letter which I received from my mother was accompanied by a newspaper clipping. Bess Hibarger had died. I had been out of communication with her for several months, and had been completely unaware of her circumstances. I was truly grieved, and I felt with great impact the realization that I would never see this wonderful being again. The emptiness that now characterized my life could hardly have seemed more total. All of those people who had been a source of light were now gone. I felt that all the guiding forces which had once been a part of my life were now taken away. I was alone.

If it had not been for the piano, there would have been nothing in my life to hold me together. For the majority of my life, any emotional turmoil I experienced often had the effect of somewhat disrupting my attention to the piano, but that year I turned to it with fierce attention. Each day I practiced between eight and eleven hours. My hands became like machines, and seemed to acquire a life of their own. I did not want to drown in the turmoil of my personal life, and so I riveted my consciousness on my practicing. Thus, in the midst of this very dark period, my musicianship and technique evolved dramatically, which was fortunate, because I was preparing for my graduate recital. Because of my ceaseless practicing and the teaching load I had assumed from my graduate assistantship, not to mention my academic work, I was able to remain heavily occupied. Even so, the condition of my life preyed constantly upon my attention, and I did not allow myself to remain motionless for even a moment. I continued this relentless pace until the time of my graduate recital, which I presented on the fifteenth of March, the Ides of March 1973.

After Christmas, in December 1972, I went to Lake Geneva for three days for a staff reunion from that previous summer. I took a train to Chicago, where I stayed with the president of George Williams College and his family, and we all went up to Lake Geneva together. I had never seen the lake in winter, and it was extraordinarily beautiful. This fact made it perhaps even more difficult to be there, for although I had hoped that Nancy might come for this occasion, she did not, and I thought of her constantly. The experience was grim. After I had left the lake and returned to Chicago with my friends for another day or two of visiting, someone suggested that we telephone Nancy and her family in Colorado, and although I remember expressing my apprehensions about this idea, I cannot recall whether or not we ever placed the call.

My spiritual state of being reached a very dangerous point that year. When I returned to school in September 1972, I became increasingly involved with the study of magic. From then until late February 1973, I became ever more occupied with the techniques I had developed that were the result of my knowledge of three primary esoteric systems; namely, yoga, the Huna, and kabalistic magic. As I have said, it would have been dangerous enough just to be involved with magic, but the fact that I integrated it with other systems, which in themselves were highly potent, created within me a precarious emotional and mental state of being. The fact that I was also very depressed only made matters worse. I was to learn that, to begin with, such things should not be undertaken at all unless one is well centered and inwardly strong. But I was not. I was very weak, and I could hardly have been more vulnerable. If a person is experiencing any kind of inner turmoil, such practices only tend to increase any existing imbalances. I was to learn from this experience a very fundamental principle: an uncontrolled influx of energy into one's mind will seek the channels of least resistance and tend to deepen them. My channels of least resistance were my emotional weakness and vulnerabilities. Thus, rather than beginning to feel better about my life and developing a healthier and less obsessive attitude, I became still more possessed by the desire to regain my losses.

I was trying not to lose a personal relationship, and I was not sure which one I wanted to keep. To be even more unmercifully clear about it, it depended on which relationship I had the most chance of saving. The area of personal relationships in my life was by no means my sole reason for exploring the occult sciences. My life was in utter spiritual confusion, and my immersion in the occult, although it was very unwise, was a kind of last stand to try to rectify this by exerting some kind of control. But my personal relationships had also become caught up in my occult involvements, and I believe that, during the months following the end of the summer, my primary efforts were directed toward holding Nancy. But as time went on and this situation became less hopeful, my mind began to convince me that the true loss had been Sarah, and that I should try with all my strength to regain her. But the truth was that, for several years after that, even the very sight of Nancy would have melted me.

I experienced two primary repercussions from this situation and from my involvement in magic and the occult. Anyone who has never been involved in such things can hardly imagine the stresses the mind can experience under such conditions, or the nature of the perceptions which can result. I grew more aware that what I had formerly distinguished and separated as clearly inner or outer reality began to lose its distinctness. I had once read or heard that the crux of magic was a state of perception in which the subjective and objective lost their definition and became one. There came a point at which it was not only irrelevant to make such distinctions, but impossible. Such boundaries were no longer operative. And I would point out that I am not talking about the distinction between something real as opposed to that which is not real. The power of magic is indeed real, and through it one is capable of transcending the traditional modes and boundaries of perception. I began to experience such states of mind, and as I looked at the universe around me, it became a living expression of the occult laws and principles that had become a part of my consciousness. I felt gripped by these perceptions, possessed by them. I felt that I could not control them, that I could not just walk away from them if I chose to do so, and my perceptions of the reality of the outer world were undergoing some kind of transformation. I found this to be profoundly unnerving. Although what I saw was intensely real, it frightened me because those experiences threw me back to a panicky feeling I had known in connection with the use of LSD; namely, that I was losing control of what was happening to me.

I was creating psychic, or emotional bonds with both Nancy and Sarah that were incredibly strong. This could have worked to my benefit or to my detriment, depending upon the circumstances. In my case, the consequences were painful and difficult to deal with. Through the use of specific occult techniques, I had deliberately and systematically established inner links with them that were even stronger, more persistent and tenacious than the ties that develop through ordinary romantic love. The natural romantic ties that already existed between me and those two young women were thus powerfully magnified, and when they were no longer an integral part of my life, and even though I sought to release them in my memory and emotional being, I was unable to do so. Through some inner knowing, I remained painfully in contact with them. At times, it was as if I was almost inside of them, feeling their very thoughts and beings. As a result, the thought of one or the other or both of them was perpetually in my mind. It was a constant state of awareness that plagued me, and it was truly terrible.

My involvement in the occult had a peculiar effect even upon my feelings for the lake. I began to long for it again, and for the mysterious power that existed there, but the longing was somehow different from what it had been in the past. It was more restless and consuming, and at times it became like a fever. This added to the feeling of crisis, and the situation became even more acute when I learned I would not be able to return to George Williams during the summer of 1973. The camp had extensively reorganized its employment procedures, and was now trying to hire only local people to cut down on expenses. The news that I would not be returning to the lake for the following summer was like confronting death. I was truly beginning to sink.

By early spring, despite a certain fluctuation of feeling I had detected in her in the past months, I knew that I had lost Sarah forever. In fact, she was already involved with someone else whom she eventually married. And after not hearing from Nancy for several months, although I had written to her from time to time, I finally received a letter from her sometime in the spring that convinced me we would never be together again. But what was even more galling to me than this was the fact that she said that her romantic love for me had changed into a friendly love that would now enable us to continue our relationship on the level of a warm, loving friendship. She had somehow gotten the impression from my letters that my feelings had grown to be much like hers. Nothing could have been further from the truth, and deep inside, I resented her for projecting her own feelings upon me. I could never have been merely her friend.

It was fortunate that I was able to present my graduate recital in March 1973. My responsibilities in earning my Master of Music degree were largely fulfilled, and my time was considerably freed up for the remainder of the semester. My attention became fully occupied with the state of my personal life. There was no one to guide me. I had lost my opportunity to spend the summer at the lake, and unquestionably, neither Nancy nor Sarah were any longer part of my life. All these things would have been hard enough to deal with, but in addition, my occult activities had activated forces that were exerting tremendous pressure upon my being, and I knew that I was becoming lost. I began to feel desperate. I was heading for a serious crisis, and I knew it. It was one of those few times in my life during which I realized that I needed help. I could not make it on my own. I was going under.

I needed spiritual help, and there was perhaps someone to whom I could turn. Irv Martin was the minister of music of my old church at home. I had come to know him around August 1966, about the same time that I had met Jerry Alber during my third trip to Lake Geneva. He had taken the position that Margaret Patton had vacated. He was a fine person, and he had been a good friend to me many times in the past. He had left the church and my home town around August 1969, to take another position. During the three years that I had known him, we had shared a fairly close relationship, even though we had some spiritual differences. Our musical interests had linked us together, and of course he also had known Jerry Alber well. And although our contact with each other diminished when I went away to college, we remained friends, and I often made it a point to see him when I went home. He and his wife had also met Swami

Nirmalananda Giri, and although they had resisted becoming involved with him or his teachings, Irv had been aware of my experiences with Swami and the resulting struggles I had experienced. When Irv left the church in August 1969, my father had just died two months earlier, in June, and it had been a year ago, in August 1968, that Swami, Jerry, and the rest of their group left for India.

Later, in 1971, Irv returned to my home town and to his former position in my church, but until my crisis in early 1973 we had only sporadic contact. Around February 1973, I went home to see Irv. The main problem we had had communicating in the past was that his viewpoint was thoroughly Christian, but because of my upbringing in the church, this was not a new problem for me. Irv was, however, a receptive and open-minded person, and I knew that, no matter what our differences were, he would accept me and listen to my problems. I related to him the circumstances of my life and the events that had created them. I could sense that he was deeply and truly concerned about my welfare and that he realized that I was in real trouble. He convinced me to do something I conceded to do only because I was in such a state of desperation. I needed help, and as long as I got it, I would accept it from anyone. I agreed to begin attending a Christian prayer group of which he was a part. I still did not own a car, and would not until later that spring, so I rode the bus to my home sixty miles away in order to attend the meetings. They were held once a week, and I tried to make all of them, although this was not always possible.

The couple in charge of the group were thoroughly steeped in a fundamentalist tradition, and they were full-blown charismatics. They spoke in tongues and laid on hands in order to effect physical and mental healing and to cast out demonic entities. Their beliefs were based totally and exclusively upon a literal interpretation of the Bible. I was immediately surprised by the influence they had developed over Irv, and I believe that he himself was surprised by it. This couple and the group in general expressed an energy and enthusiasm that was difficult to resist, and although I was really not sure what was happening there or what I thought of it, they seemed to manifest a kind of light to which I felt a certain attraction. When I looked at the incredibly complex knot that my own life had become, their lives and viewpoints seemed simple and pure by comparison, and I began to wish that I, too, could experience that. But from the very beginning, I began to feel an inner conflict because of my contact with them. They were suspicious and condemnatory of anything outside their own tradition. What this meant, in essence, was that everything I had experienced and which was important to me in my life was excluded from what they considered to be spiritually acceptable. Chief among these was magic, and I was willing to agree with them about the dangers involved in such practices, but also included among the things which they deemed as unacceptable were all aspects of the occult, astrology, yoga, Hinduism,

Buddhism, theosophy, metaphysics, and every other realm of experience one could think of that was foreign to them. Many of these paths had been meaningful facets of my quest, and had been instrumental in my own personal growth. It was, after all, an enormous world, and there were many roads to knowledge. And I had respect for them all, even for magic. All of this provided conflict enough, but in addition, my experiences at the lake were also discounted because they, too, lay outside the realm of the acceptable. This struck at the very core of my being. Those people shared so openly with me. Why could I not do the same with them? Did everything have to be exclusively on their terms? In time, I learned beyond all doubt that the answer to this question was an unqualified "yes."

The summer came and I was still meeting with them and seeing Irv Martin. I had acquired a car, so my transportation problems became simpler. My absence from Lake Geneva was intensely disturbing, and I longed for it. I had found a job for the summer as a lifeguard at a public swimming pool in Champaign, and the contrast between hot concrete and a few thousand gallons of chlorinated water, and the deep green expanse of the lake with its cool breezes was devastating. It seemed like hell. I went each week to the meetings at home. They were small, consisting usually of about ten or twelve people, and were always held in private homes. I tried to become one with those people. I tried to let go of all the things that had been a part of my life. They encouraged me and laid their hands on me and prayed for me, and they helped to alleviate the enormous spiritual weight around my neck. I accepted the conflict I experienced with them because, at least, I had kept my sanity, and had not gone under. I had to give them credit for that.

But I had become entangled in the occult world, and I had touched forces from which it was difficult to disentangle myself. I had forged bonds not easily broken. The people with whom I was meeting were experiencing difficulty in helping me get free, and they knew it. In June, some very bizarre things began happening. Three rings that I possessed and that I regarded as talismans, or objects of some degree of power, simply vanished without explanation, and I never found a trace of them again. They had been in a jewelry box that contained, among other things of personal or financial value, various pieces of jewelry and some religious objects. The three rings, which were the only objects in the box that were connected with occult uses, were the only items missing. No one knew anything about either their existence or their function. I have no idea whether they were stolen or whether they simply vanished into thin air. At one time, I had given one of the rings to Nancy to wear, and Sarah had had one of the others. But at a certain point in time I had requested their return, and had not let them out of my possession again. When they disappeared, I decided that it was desirable for me to move out of the house in which I had been living for the past nine months, and by early July I had taken a room in the home of one of the university music professors with whom I had studied music theory several years earlier.

Meanwhile, the members of the prayer group had begun to tell me about a man whom they were sure could help me get free from my occult ties. He was a black man from Jamaica named Cecil DuCille. He had been a minister there, but had come to the United States to engage in a speaking tour. I had driven to my home town one evening in June to meet him. I was to meet Irv Martin at his house and drive with him to the meeting place for that evening, which was in a little community several miles from the town in which my home was located. Irv never came home, and so I drove out into the country alone to try to find the meeting place, the location of which I had a general notion. But I never found it, and in fact, I became very much lost in the country. It was very dark that night and I began to grow apprehensive, for I felt that something very powerful and very evil was bearing down upon me. It was almost as if I could feel it breathing on me. The hair on my neck began to stand on end, and although I was lost, I refused to stop and get out of the car. My speed accelerated, and I drove simply to keep moving. My fear was escalating to terror. I stepped on the gas pedal and just kept driving until I found the little town again. From there I drove home, but I still could find no trace of Irv after stopping at his house a second time, although when I went to knock on his door I found the porch light on. I assumed that he had come home and left again in my absence. There was nothing else to do, so I returned to Champaign.

The following week I came home again, and my mother informed me that, shortly after my previous trip home, two detectives had come by the house looking for me. I had no idea what they were after, but as as precaution, I called my lawyer and informed him that I was going down to the police station to find out what they wanted from me. After entering the police station and introducing myself, I was shut up in a room alone. After some time had passed, two detectives entered the room and began asking me all kinds of questions. They were very vague and evasive about whatever it was that they were after. I felt confused and intimidated, and shortly thereafter, I was charged and booked for disorderly conduct and window peeping. It was necessary for me to telephone my lawyer and have him send over some money as bail, so that I could be released from jail. The case never came to court, but I suffered some embarrassment from it and a considerable amount of inconvenience. There had been some trouble in Irv's neighborhood the night I had gone to meet him, before I had come back to his house the second time. He had not made it home to meet me because of a commitment elsewhere, but had returned after I had driven to the county to try to find the meeting, which he himself had subsequently attended. But while I was parked in front of his house, after returning from the country to check on him a second time, someone had reported my license number to the police. After this incident, I wondered what might happen next.

I became more determined than ever to meet Cecil DuCille, and shortly after that I was able to do so, during one of my trips home. Cecil was a man who possessed a great abundance of personal power. His viewpoint was totally Christian, but he had an openness and warmth that I found very magnetic, and he exhibited extremely high intelligence. I liked him from the moment I met him, and although I have lost all contact with him long ago, I remember him very warmly. From the very beginning, he was kind and gentle to me, and I know that he liked me very much. In the path that he was following, he was completely dedicated and selfless. I could tell him anything, without fear of any automatic or potentially unjustified criticism. And I could not mistake the fact that he expressed a tremendous spiritual energy. During the time that I knew him, I always felt that he was really my friend. I trusted him completely.

I conveyed to him my spiritual predicament and the events and circumstances that had engendered it. He prayed for me the first time I met him, during one of the meetings, and when he stood behind me and placed his hands on my shoulders, as I sat in a chair in front of him, a tremendous rush of warmth and light and energy filled my body. It was like a flash of yellow heat which entered my head and shot through my body. My eyes were shut, and I saw it flood the inside of me. The power was so intense that my whole body shook. I could feel the emotional and psychic weight inside of me being broken up and released. It was like being cleansed. Much of the darkness that had become attached to me was falling away. The bonds that had weighted me were being shattered and dispersed. I could hear Cecil's voice, and it was full of authority and power.

Cecil's work was not complete. I saw him often through the months of June, July, and August. I met regularly with my prayer group, and we often went to the gatherings at which Cecil was speaking. He prayed for me several times as he had done the first time. I had difficulty in trying to embrace the spiritual viewpoint from which he operated, and with respect to the others in my prayer group and those who often surrounded Cecil, my difficulty was far greater. But Cecil understood all of this. He saw me very clearly, accepting me just for what I was, and his understanding was always there. He would often take me aside from all the others and talk with me. He enjoyed me, for he loved music, and had once been a musician himself.

Although I could not accept his teachings, I understood that he was helping me to become free of the occult forces. That was the most important thing to me. I was willing to use any means available to get free. I felt that my very life was at stake. It truly seemed as if there was a battle for my soul going on around me, and although I could not see it, I often sensed it, and things were happening to me that let me know that I was not entirely out of the woods yet. I know that people can become carried away with the idea of demons and the demonic world, and can use this idea as something upon which they can blame literally every negative aspect of their lives. I think that this reflects a gross perceptual imbalance. On the other hand, there are a few people whom I trust very much who have had real contacts with this aspect of the world. There have been a few occasions during my own life in which I, too, have seen this side of the universe. I believe that it exists, objectively, quite separately and independently of our own consciousness. This is something which, in fact, I know very well. There is a dark side to things, and it has great power. It is evil, and consciously and deliberately malevolent.

I recall an experience I had during that period of my life that I will never forget. It was daytime, but I had been sleeping, and I began to dream. I was walking by the ocean, and I saw a being come out of the water and approach me. It was like a man, but very hideous and frightening. As had happened a few other times in my life, I began to become conscious in the dream, and I reached a point of awareness in which I realized that I was no longer dreaming, and that something was really happening to me. It was as if my sleep had become disturbed by something and my mind began to represent this disturbance in dream symbols. But as I became more fully awake, I shook off the dream, and after a few moments I found myself utterly and completely awake and conscious. I was being physically attacked by this being. It was as if it was at the same time both upon me and inside of me. I lay on my bed, paralyzed. Although I struggled violently, I was completely unable to move for several seconds. My arms were at my sides, but I could not move them no matter how hard I strained to do so. I tried to scream, but I could not open my mouth. As much as I wanted to yell, it was as if my jaws were clamped shut by a powerful vise. I felt as if I was in a kind of straightjacket, the substance of which was some kind of vibrating power. Finally, after violently exerting myself for several seconds, I was able to get free and, with a kind of gasp, I jumped from the bed and the experience ended abruptly. Although it was not painful, it was as if my body had received an intense electrical charge of some kind. I was truly stunned, and although I remained apprehensive for several days, I did not have such an experience again.

During that same period of time, at the urging of Cecil and other various members of my personal group, I destroyed all of the notes I had accumulated pertaining to magic and the occult and various practices related to it. On one level, it was a difficult thing to do, because I had spent many months collecting and compiling them. Much of the material, besides being specific and detailed, was virtually irreplaceable. But I realized it had to be destroyed. To stash it away someplace was not enough. I needed to make the gesture of cutting it completely out of my life. I built a fire specifically for the occasion, and burned all of it.

After talking with Irv Martin about it, I offered my services as a counselor for the group from my church, which would be going to Lake Geneva in August. It was the same program under which I had gone to the lake in August 1964, and the three following Augusts. The church was pleased to have me go along with them, and it was thus that I was able to look ahead to the prospect of being at the lake for a week. But I must admit that my motives for going with the church, as was true also of my early years at the lake with them, were not entirely pure, so to speak. That is, although I believed that I had something to offer, I was going primarily because it was a means to see the lake again, and any other reason I could come up with was simply a rationalization. I was in a strange situation, philosophically. On the one hand, I had completely renounced my ties with magic. On the other hand, many of the paths I had followed during my life had great meaning for me. This was certainly true of yoga, and of supreme significance and impact were the experiences I had encountered at the lake.

And yet, after many years of separation, I had again found myself within a Christian circle. It was not an environment in which I could seek the full expression of my personal ideas, for they were foreign there, and they did not fit. They were neither understood nor accepted. Ironically, I was, at age twenty-four, in a situation not entirely dissimilar to the one in which I had found myself at the age of fifteen, after my initial visions at the lake. I was also experiencing my old feelings of wanting to belong, and to be accepted. But as it had always been, my acceptance seemed to be conditional upon my demonstrating a certain conformity, in terms of my spiritual ideas, with those around me.

It was with this general feeling and awareness that I went to Lake Geneva in August 1973. I became very much involved with the activities that week. I was popular and accepted. I became very close to many of the young people there, and I spent most of my time and energy in interaction with them. I had come to a point at which I told myself that I really wanted to live my life as they did. I wanted to become a part of their Christian fellowship. I really became convinced that I had done this, and that through this, and because of the light which was now in my life, I had given up all the old ways. The wandering, the searching, the confusion, would now all be a part of the past. And somewhere in all of the ties that I would leave behind in favor of this new kind of life was the lake and the mystery which it had held for me. I would regard it now as something which had once happened to me that was very beautiful, but which had also had a dark and elusive aspect to it that I had never been able to understand, and from which I had now evolved into a different way of living, characterized by the light of this Christian environment, and the clarity which it seemed to bring to my thoughts. I even did some writing that week at the lake which strongly expressed my new sense of direction.

And yet, the lake called to me. In the whispering waves, in the voices of the night, in all things, it touched my soul. But I had decided that this was now something for me to overcome, something I should leave behind, and go on. Being there that week was very strange from the standpoint that it called to mind overwhelming memories from the previous summer. In my mind, I saw Nancy everywhere, and I remembered all the places we had been together and the things we had done. The ghosts from the past were almost devastatingly powerful. I walked to George Williams several times, and took some of our group sailing. I had not been in sailboat for a year, and it was a wonderful feeling. I kept hoping that perhaps Nancy would have come back to the lake to visit, and that I would encounter her there, but it did not happen. However, I talked with her cousin, who, as usual, was there for the entire summer, and learned much to my surprise that Nancy had moved to Chicago. It was thus that the lake flooded me with the most powerful memories and sensations which touched almost every area of my life. But I struggled to resist them, to turn away, and to set forth in a new direction.

After that week at the lake, I returned to Champaign to finish up my summer lifeguarding job. In September, I took a position with a very fine, new, high school level performing arts academy that had just opened there the previous year. Although I taught piano, my primary responsibilities involved working with ballet, which, although it was quite traumatic at times, was also very exciting, and a completely new experience for me. Although I liked very much where I had been living, it had become necessary for me to find other living accommodations, since a member of the professor's family in whose house I was living was moving back home for a time, and they required the extra space. I moved into the home of another university music professor. He was divorced, but his son, who was about my age, and an enormously talented artist, also lived in the house. I became well acquainted with this young artist and with many individuals within his circle of friends. They were not a healthy group of people to associate with, and the character of their lives was certainly very far removed from my own, both in terms of social behavior and spiritual ideas. The same could be said of many of the individuals with whom I was then working in artistic contexts. But this was where I found myself, and these were the conditions under which I could then make a living as a pianist. I felt that I should be strong enough to flow with any situation, to embrace it without criticism, and to be comfortable in it.

There was an enormously contradictory contrast between this everyday world in which I lived and functioned, and the one which I encountered when I went to my home town to associate with my Christian friends there. Furthermore, I was experiencing more and more dissatisfaction over the fact that I simply could not share with these people those things in my life and thoughts which were really meaningful to me. They could not understand them, and they did not want to. They would not accept me on my terms, and this began to frustrate me very much. Although I never returned to the occult, I recall that, sometime around September 1973, I began to study the ideas of Ouspensky again. I needed something substantial and challenging. I could not live on the almost exclusively emotional level that characterized the frame of being of most of my Christian associates. Besides, after my August visit to Lake Geneva, Cecil DuCille had left my area to do some speaking elsewhere. Thus, I was no longer seeing him, and shortly thereafter, he returned to his home in Jamaica. In truth, it was really only my interest in Cecil and my affection for him that had kept me coming home, and now that he was gone, there was little there that interested me. Thus, by around October 1973, I had stopped going home to the meetings. I was no longer involved in the prayer group, and I pretty much lost contact with Irv Martin. I had really wanted to belong, but I could not tear my inner being apart in order to do it, so I became, instead, a member of the set of people with whom I associated in Champaign.

For several months, I turned my back on almost everything that had been a part of my life, except music, and the emotional environment of the academy where I functioned as a pianist was a very difficult one in which to be happy. It was filled with aspiring professional dancers whose lives were, for the most part, in constant emotional turmoil. Those who ran the academy and taught there were anything but stabilizing. And yet, I opted for that world in favor of the one I had known with my Christian colleagues. Their narrow view of life and of others was unacceptable and repulsive to me, and so I became one of those whom they would not have approved of. But the situation of the house in which I was living became more and more undesirable. The influences there were profoundly unhealthy, and in my directionless situation, the effects upon me were very negative.

Two interesting things happened in December. I telephoned Nancy and talked with her, but I have no recollection whatsoever concerning what we said. I only know that, for me, it was a strange and disturbing and inconclusive experience. It was only an impulse that had made me call her, and I do not even remember if I called her in Chicago, or at her parents' home in Colorado, since it was around Christmas. The day after Christmas I left for Jamaica, with two of my friends from Champaign. I had written to Cecil, and he had warmly invited me to come and visit, and to bring others if I wished. It was wonderful to see him again, for no matter what, I knew that he was my friend, and he expressed to me a feeling of unconditional love. But the trip was not very spiritually helpful to me. I talked with him at length about the state of my life, but I could not embrace his way of life. In my own way, I was unaccepting, too. I could not deal with the kind of people who surrounded him. While my friends and I stayed with him, his house was filled with other guests who were much like those I had known the previous summer and fall, in the meetings which I had attended. Although Cecil overlooked it, the two friends who had accompanied me to Jamaica were creating a tension in the house. But I had come with them because none of us could have afforded to make the trip individually.

With a very inconclusive frame of mind, I returned from the trip to Jamaica in the middle of January 1974, to receive some very interesting news. Jerry Alber had returned. He had left the ashram in Oklahoma City where he had been living with Swami Nirmalananda Giri since their return from India. Several of the others who had accompanied them to India were now living in this ashram also. Jerry was also experiencing a state of spiritual indecision, and had left the ashram to consider the direction of his life. During the three months that he stayed in my home town, I was able to go and visit him several times. It was strange to see him so unexpectedly again after all that time. I had been completely out of touch with him since August 1968, five and a half years. Both of our lives were in turmoil, and somehow, I did not feel up to recounting to him all of the changes and experiences in my life that had brought me to that point. I was truly glad to see him again, but I think that we both were heavily caught up in our own problems. I remember that one day I asked him what he saw when he looked at me now, to which he simply replied, "The light in you has gone out." I was very curious about Swami, and Jerry told me a great deal about him, and about what life was like in the ashram. I was also deeply interested in the stories which he had to tell about their trip to India, and Jerry related to me the circumstances of Swami's automobile accident and his resulting change in personality.

In March, I moved out of the house in which I was living in order to save myself. The effects of that environment were too detrimental, and I could not deal with them. Again, I was tired of floundering. Much to my delight, I was able to move back into the music professor's house which I had left in the previous September. They had rearranged their space, and I was able to reclaim my old room there. The change of environment was very beneficial for me, and besides, I had become like one of their family. Through the present time, they have remained my very best friends. At the beginning of March, I called Nancy again, in Chicago, and although again I do not remember our conversation, I recall that she was not very friendly toward me. I am sure that she felt threatened. I decided that I would not try to reach her again.

It was also in March that I renewed my contact with Irv Martin and the associates of my former prayer group. I began attending their meetings again.

My feelings at that time can best be explained by the words I wrote on March 10, 1974. The first thought makes reference to my trip to Lake Geneva during the past August 1973, as a counselor for the church camp.

Within a short time after my August experience of Lake Geneva, my life began to fill with darkness: dark people, dark experiences, dark thoughts. I looked at it as a kind of growing experience, but it was negative in a very powerful and malevolent way. I felt as if I should be capable of absorbing and embracing all things, all life styles. This was a grievous mistake in judgement. My loneliness, frustration, and jarring conflicts of ideals and interests (initiated in part by the apparent irreconcilability of my various worlds: Christian, occult, artistic, etc.) gradually led me from desperation to desperation, to a severe splintering and fragmentation of personality, and finally to an agonizing apathy and loss of faith and direction—to loss of dream, ideal, balance and harmony, hope, and method.

Among the losses referred to in the above passage was the lake. Even that was not in my thoughts much anymore. Everything had seemed lost, part of the past. After references to my talking with Nancy and my visit with Cecil DuCille in Jamaica, the passage then continues.

But the road continued downward, into more darkness: to more frustration and bitterness, tremendous resentment, cynicism, and dangerous hostility. But my musical growth has continued in spite of everything, strangely. It has kept me together as a functioning, creative, sane being. But music, although indescribably most wonderful in itself, was far, far short of being enough. And I could not, I dared not turn back to the occult in any form, and certainly yoga and even metaphysics seemed only to lead to a more confusing and self-entrapping jungle. But I cannot accept that which I do not believe; I cannot abide in my soul nature doctrines which I either do not understand fully or which I suspect as artificial or superficial. And yet the realization has come upon me that my very life and salvation depend upon finding a road out and upward—I need a Savior. I need a Christ. I need Grace.

It was a very confusing time in my life. I had again reached a point of having to start all over, just as I had done when I first sought help from Irv. My spiritual quest had become erratic, leaning first in one direction and then in another, and in frustration, I had turned my back on all of it for a time. But this led only deeper into the pit in which I found myself, and since my Christian friends had succeeded, at least in part, in undermining my faith in everything that I had ever explored in the past, I felt that there was nothing to be done except to reconcile myself with them. I convinced myself again that this was the true path for me, and I tried very hard to accept the viewpoints of my Christian friends. Perhaps I would not have felt such a need to become one with them if I had only lived my life in some kind of sensible and consistent manner. But I experienced a relentless dissatisfaction with the condition of my life, and it drove me to seek meaning and stability in everything around me, although I did so in a fashion which was indiscriminate and almost reckless. But what was it exactly that I was searching for? At that point in my life, I failed to recognize clearly what it was. I had once known, though, and I had then lost sight of it, and I know now, in retrospect, what drove me: it was the visions and experiences of the lake. At that point in my life, my perspective had become greatly clouded, and my path twisted and confused. But underneath it all, the lake had never released its hold on me.

In March 1974, when I rejoined the prayer group, I had again abandoned my other metaphysical pursuits. For although I had resumed studying the works of Ouspensky during the previous September, I now set them aside. I sought to devote the totality of my spiritual energies to my Christian associations. But as the case had always been, my mind naturally sought other avenues of exploration and expression. I had begun to recognize my longing for the lake again, and I was compelled to embrace it as part of my life. I just could not give it up. After making some inquiries, I was able to secure the position as waterfront director for Conference Point for the summer of 1974. I cannot express how much I looked forward to going. After the previous summer, which I had spent in miserable separation from it, the prospect of returning now seemed like a return to paradise. I offer below some of the thoughts which I recorded in May. It is very apparent from them that my life simply could not be complete without the lake. I had tried to turn away from it and to live according to the expectations of others, but I could not do so. I was willing to try to live within a Christian framework, but not without the lake. Thus, detected or not, there remained an element of conflict in my being. But why would I not just accept the lake on its own ground, and abandon the rest? The answer was still not apparent to me then, but it had always been a part of me. I still wanted to belong, and to be accepted. I was afraid of standing alone, and the idea of solitude was overwhelming. The words below are dated May 17, 1974, and are excerpted from a longer passage. The thoughts are in reference to Lake Geneva.

> She has been many things to me: a place of great beauty and unimaginable joy, with whom I have also shared fear and tragedy; a companion and counselor; a lover; a source of power and mystery, and strength. She has perhaps even been God to me.

The final statement said it. The lake had been God to me, and it still was. I still did not understand the lake. It had remained a mystery to me. I would be drawn back to it time after time until I became one with it again, and breathed its light. And yet, my fear of solitude drove me to persist in not acting upon this instinct, and thus I knew conflict. My Christian friends could not understand the supreme power which the lake held for me, and I could not openly tell them of my devotion to it. It would be like admitting to idolatry.

In April, Jerry Alber had returned to live with Swami. He had gone as suddenly as he had come. He had disappeared from my life again, and this time I was not to hear from him until August 1978.

Something else had developed in April which was to have considerable significance for me. I encountered for the first time the writings of Carlos Castaneda, which dealt with his relationship with a Yaqui Indian sorcerer named Don Juan. They were significant because I found in them, for the first time in my life, accounts of perceptions and experiences which were akin to many of the things which I had encountered at Lake Geneva. Between April and November 1974, I had read all four of Castaneda's books that were in print at that time. Within these works I found another voice which called attention to what I had seen at the lake; namely, that the world was a place of limitless mystery and incredible power, and that there were awesome and beautiful perceptions awaiting those who were able to embrace them. I had known such perceptions, but I had had great difficulty in sharing them and finding acceptance for them. Furthermore, I had never really understood them myself, and when I discovered Castaneda's works, I found extensive substantiation for the nature of many of my own experiences.

My inner life became dominated by two things which, before very long, would again dictate that I make a choice of allegiance, although I tried to integrate them; namely, the ideas of my Christian friends, and my personal ideas as they had been formed by my experiences at the lake and influenced by the writings of Castaneda. Meanwhile, in the bewildering process of trying to make my way through life, I made a choice which for me was very strange and that I eventually regretted very much. By the end of May, after anticipating going to the lake so much, I elected not to spend the summer there. Not only does such a decision seem actually crazy to me now, in retrospect, but it was not long after I made it then that I pondered over the credibility of my actions. Very simply, I was still bouncing back and forth between conflicting tendencies. In this case, circumstances led me to feel that the right thing to do was to remain in Champaign for the summer, so that I could continue the activities which centered on my Christian affiliations. I really believed that this was the right path, and those within the Christian circle certainly encouraged such a decision. I had again decided that the lake would always be special, but that the center of my life should be elsewhere, in a Christian context. It was an easy way out. I would have fellowship and acceptance, and I would not have to face the solitude and independence required for me to explore the mysteries of the power embodied in the lake. Thus, I remained in Champaign for the summer, and while I worked as a lifeguard at an air force base in a nearby town, I went to summer school at the University of Illinois in order to study piano, and made frequent trips home to pursue my activities with my Christian associates there.

I had also arranged to go to Lake Geneva again that August, as a counselor for the group from my church which went to the Point every year. But during that entire summer, in which I went home regularly to meet with my Christian friends there, I was becoming more and more absorbed in the works of Castaneda. They were irresistible to me because within them I perceived a framework that embraced the nature of many of my perceptions and experiences at the lake. Castaneda's works were, insofar as I saw, nonreligious in nature. This did not bother me, even though I viewed at least my early experiences at the lake in a spiritual context.

The perceptual framework within Castaneda's writings embraced many of my own ideas. Among these was that the world was a marvelous, insoluble mystery. It was incredibly and infinitely alive. Science, and the human ego, had deluded us into thinking that we were really solving the mysteries of life. But science had only done what I had done in my own life; namely, amass mountains of facts and techniques that, in truth, got no closer to confronting the profound and inscrutable mystery of the world. The only real way to "know" the world was through direct experience, through embracing the infinite and wonderful identity and consciousness within the being of the world. The universe was not an inanimate lump for us to poke and prod. It was an essence, an identity, and living consciousness. This is what the lake had taught me, and I could not forget it or ignore it. Through the eyes of my Christian friends I saw a living God ruling over a dead world, comprised of objects he had created. This view of things was flat and lifeless to me, and I knew it was incorrect.

The world required one to live a strong and responsible life; to be ultimately responsible for himself and for his actions. This was the way that I had always wanted to live, although I had not been so successful at it. But why had I not been? It was because I had not taken responsibility for myself. I had not properly handled my independence. In truth, I did not want a savior. I did not want to be crying to a higher authority for help all the time. I wanted to live a strong, clean life, and I had been looking many years for the power to do this. But I had made many errors, and I had not faced the responsibility of embracing the independence and solitude necessary for me to truly confront the wonderful power and mystery of the lake.

I realized again that, as it had always been during all my attempts to embrace Christian fellowships, all the emphasis had been on the differences that separated me from them. Why could they not acknowledge the integrity and worth of paths other than their own? Why were they so persistently intolerant of other views, and so determined to discredit them? Because of my past exposure to yoga and Hinduism, I was quite open to the idea that the consciousness of God could incarnate itself in human form, and even Hindus were accepting of Christ as such an incarnation. But they regarded him as one of many, whereas the Christians interpreted him as utterly unique in this way, and therefore they regarded any way of life which was not centered around this idea as incomplete and unfulfilled. I regarded this attitude as simply another form of immaturity and egotism, and it ate at me.

Castaneda introduced me to the idea that there were places of unique and special power in the world, where marvelous and incomprehensible things could happen. This indeed described my beloved lake. It was truly a place of power for me. From that time forth, this idea was to play an important role in my thoughts. Castaneda's work also presented me with something else that took me years to understand and embrace, and I only began to do so when I overcame my fear of aloneness. This was the idea that a passionate love for the splendorous being of the earth could save us from our sadness and loneliness. I had known this passionate love in my relationship with the lake, but I would have to grow a great deal before I could truly understand the full meaning and implications of it.

My life needed strength and control and impeccability. Thus, although I continued with my Christian associations through the summer of 1974, my thoughts took on more and more of the character and direction which I have just described.

At some point during that summer, I had a very peculiar dream that evolved into a vision and another direct confrontation with some kind of spiritual entity. Although the experience was somewhat disturbing, I did not sense in it the malevolence that had confronted me in the experience of the previous summer. I was suspicious of it because I did not understand what was happening, but it did not frighten me. Whatever the entity was that approached me, it took on the form of a man, and was rather beautiful, rather than ugly. It had come into contact with my hands and forehead, and I had looked into its mind and seen a radiant and powerful consciousness there. After the experience had ended, the palms of my hands and my forehead "buzzed" for about half an hour with a kind of electrical energy. I simply accepted the experience and went on with my affairs. Such an experience has never repeated itself since then.

In August 1974, I returned to Lake Geneva with the church group. Irv Martin also made the trip. One day while I was there, I walked down the shore path to George Williams, where I encountered the daughter of the president of the college, whom I had not seen since the previous year. She told me that Nancy was there. Shortly thereafter I saw her, and we talked. I was overwhelmed. It had been almost exactly two years since I had seen her, and we had said good-bye in that very place. My mind was flooded with the memories and sensations of the past, and I could not deny the fact that my intense love for her had never changed. I wanted more than anything else to take her in my arms and tell her so, but I could not. That experience was gone forever. I saw her two or three times that week before she left. Although she was very cordial to me, I perceived that I was not very welcome among her relatives who lived there for the summer, and who had once been very friendly to me. I felt very estranged, and perceived quickly that I should make no attempt to renew acquaintances with them. Even Nancy herself advised me about this, but to this day I do not understand why. Perhaps they felt that I was threatening to her. I do not really know. But it was obvious that they did not want me in their lives, and so I turned my back on them and made no attempt ever again to approach them. That was the last time I ever saw Nancy, although she remained in my thoughts for many years, and I never completely got her out of my heart.

That was the last time I tried to integrate my life with that of the Christian community, both in terms of that church and the prayer group with which I had been involved. I wanted the warmth of fellowship and understanding, but the lake would not release its hold on me. Or perhaps I should say that I could not release my hold on it. I had still not become independent enough to resist my tendency to integrate worlds that were not meant to fit together. In truth, these were attempts to make myself feel more secure, and they were always ultimately a failure. Nevertheless, I had convinced myself once again that I could take what was presented to me as the Christian life and embrace within it the world of the lake and its mystery, and along with it, the exciting new thoughts which I had encountered in the writings of Castaneda. But even if I myself could have reconciled such a proposition, my close Christian friends would not let it lay. They regarded my experiences of the lake as threatening to what they perceived as a true Christian way of life. The mystery and inexplicability of my perceptions frightened them. They regarded them as dark.

I recall a late afternoon that week when I was sitting with Irv Martin at the Point, on the rocks near the edge of the water. As we talked, and as I endeavored to share with him the nature of my deep feelings for that place and what I saw as my relationship with it, I could strongly sense his concern. He expressed to me his feeling that I seemed deeply attracted and pulled by something there which he himself did not understand. He was frightened by this, and his only answer was for me to resist it and follow in his path. This brief conversation I had with him epitomized the recurring and consistent conflict I had always experienced with my Christian friends. At various times that week, I was very uncomfortable within this circle of people, and I could not seem to avoid little conflicts that kept surfacing in different ways, and which led me to feel more strongly that I did not really belong there. I felt hypocritical because I had gone there as a counselor for a Christian group when, inside of me, I felt such conflict. There were individuals there who, because of their awareness of the various paths I had traveled in my life, expressed an open criticism of me that bordered on hostility. And I began to feel more acutely something that had always troubled me. These people could not answer the philosophical questions which had posed themselves to me all my life. They could not help me on my individual path. Indeed, they claimed to have all the answers, but they did not fit my questions.

After that week at the lake, I returned to Champaign and to my position with the arts academy. It was an extremely difficult environment to work in, emotionally speaking, and I began to wonder how much more of it I could reasonably endure. But I was at least able to function as a pianist, and therefore I held onto the work. I did not have a great deal of contact with Irv Martin, and I never returned again to the prayer group. My contact with the church also quickly diminished, and within a few weeks, I was out of touch. I remember a conversation which I had with its minister early that fall. I was still searching for answers to spiritual questions, and I had shared my feelings with him about this. I had thought that perhaps he could offer some guidance, but I perceived that he was actually very bewildered by my comments. With regret, I expressed to him my disillusionment with my attempts to follow what had been presented to me as the Christian path. I was again experiencing great doubt and uncertainty. I saw that what I was saying had actually embarrassed him. He felt uncomfortable because he simply did not know what to say. I could not blame him. He wanted to help, but he felt inadequate in trying to reach me, and since I saw no point in prolonging this uncomfortable situation, I ended our conversation shortly thereafter.

Jerry Alber said many years later that my perceptions were "beyond religion," and that indeed is how I see them at the present time. My study of Castaneda's works was a major step in embracing that attitude. I related to the lake more and more in terms of its consciousness and power, and sought to make that power part of my life, as I had always done. But in my everyday life, this was a power which, as well as being divorced from any specific and therefore limiting religious connotations, had none of the former characteristics of my efforts to exert control over all my surroundings. It was an immaculate power beyond the clutching demands of ego, and it was characterized by balanced and harmonious actions, directed by a strong and impeccable will. It was true control, but of my own self, in the face of the infinite and mysterious world by which I was surrounded.

I went to Florida for almost three weeks after Christmas. I went alone in order to face my solitude, and I found it to be a deeply rewarding experience. I scrutinized my past life and wrote down my observations in the form of extremely detailed letters, which I mailed to Irv Martin with instructions for him to keep them for me. I explored all of the events which had brought me to that point in my life, a process sometimes very painful, but also very revealing and therapeutic. I came to a certain understanding with myself, and was able to forgive myself for putting myself through all of the conflict that I had experienced over the past years. I thought a great deal about Sarah and Nancy, and I faced the fact that those were experiences which I would simply have to live with, and go on with my life. I thought about Lake Geneva and the influence it had had over my life for so many years. I sought intently to relate what I had found in Castaneda's works to my own life and the manner in which I wanted to live it. I realized and accepted that I could not embrace the kind of life that my Christian friends had, and that I would have to take full responsibility for myself and for my life.

When I returned from my trip in January 1975, I visited briefly with Irv when I went home to collect my letters from him. I remember seeing him very little after that, and I am certain that, shortly thereafter, I completely lost touch with him. He had been my last contact with the spiritual environment of which he was a part. Although I do not remember exactly when it was, sometime during that winter of 1974-75 I saw Cecil DuCille one last time. I think that it was after my return from Florida. He had returned to the United States to do another extensive speaking tour. I went to a meeting at which he was speaking, and I was so utterly repulsed by the behavior I saw there that I almost left before speaking with him. After the meeting was finished, he ushered me away to an empty room where we were able to talk privately. As always, he was open and loving to me. He listened to me with understanding and patience. We did not talk long. I told him that I would always love him and respect him, but that I could not live in the manner of the people around him. That was the last time I ever saw him. My life was turning in a new direction.

Between March and August 1975, I made four trips to Lake Geneva. The first trip I made alone, on March 30, Easter. I had driven up there after going home to visit my mother. It was extremely cold, and the hills surrounding the lake were covered with snow. It was the only time that I ever saw the lake when it was covered with ice. The sun shone brightly and its light reflected off the frozen surface of the lake. Everything was extraordinarily quiet. Occasionally, I heard the eerie, unearthly sound of ice cracking on the surface of the lake, and the vibration shot through the ice to strike the banks along the shore near where I stood. I walked along the shore path between George Williams and the Point, surveying the lake and hills. I stood at the point for a long time, until I became very cold, envisioning the summer waves singing at my feet. I walked through the hills of George Williams and surveyed the ghosts of the many memories that still lingered there. Standing motionless in the quiet of the snow, I contemplated my life, and then, as I had done so many times in the past, I said farewell to the lake.

It was my hope that I might perhaps have returned to the lake for the summer of 1975, but I was unable to find any waterfront work there. However, I made a one-day excursion to the lake with a friend from the arts academy where I worked in Champaign, on May 17. I did so again with another friend from the academy on June 15, and we went sailing. These trips were really nothing more than outings. I did no great inner work at the lake. I just wanted to see it. I had come through so much in the last few years that I was, I suppose, taking a kind of spiritual sabbatical. There had been many stormy and difficult periods in my life over the last eleven years, and I was resting now. My life had become more calm and stable, and I was weary of the violent fluctuations in experience that had characterized the last few years. Now, I sought a more consistent and steady way of life.

In June 1975, I spent the summer at the Interlochen Arts Academy in Michigan, as pianist for the ballet department. It was very beautiful there, and in my spare time, I did a great deal of swimming and canoeing. Over the past few years, my romantic life had also known a great deal of turmoil, and that, too, had now acquired a more even keel. During that summer, I met the young woman who was to become my first wife. She was a professional ballet dancer, and was teaching there for the summer. Merritt and I decided that we wanted to marry, and planned on a wedding that fall. After the summer season at Interlochen had finished, we drove to Lake Geneva to spend a day there. The church camp from my home was there that week, for their yearly August visit. Some of the young people who knew me were very warm to me. Irv was there, but he did not seem to have a great deal to say to me, and the young minister with whom I had talked the previous fall looked at me as if he had seen a ghost. Merritt and I were generally uncomfortable and did not feel welcome, but we stayed the night and left promptly the following day.

After visiting my mother, and then traveling to Louisville, Kentucky, where Merritt's parents lived, we returned to Champaign. We stayed with my adopted family for a few days until we could locate an apartment. I hated to leave them, for I had lived with them for the last year and a half, in addition to the first time I had occupied their household. But I saw them often, and through all the changes and moves which have occurred in my life since then, I have never lost touch with them. I returned to my position at the academy, and since Merritt was a professional ballet dancer, she was able to secure a position there as an instructor. We were married on November 26, 1975.

I had retained my interest in the works of Castaneda, but after June 1976, my thoughts became occupied with other things. Periodically in my life, I seemed to develop an interest in yoga. The techniques had never lost their power. Around March, I began to explore them again, but with little depth or continuity. I remember, however, that in May, I made an appointment with a Sanskrit professor at the University of Illinois and talked with him about various aspects of yoga. I had been particularly interested in acquiring certain specific information about the nature of my own personal mantra, which had been given to me many years ago by Swami Nirmalananda Giri. With respect to this, the results of my inquiries were extremely enlightening, and I was able to have many of my questions answered. I approached yoga sporadically for the next four years, but often in a tentative manner. Through the spring and summer of 1976, I used the I Ching again after many years, I think primarily as an aid to determining the course of my career. By late spring, both my wife and I had decided that we would not return to the academy in the fall, since neither of us were happy there. However, we were not certain as to what we would do as an alternative.

In early June, I went to Lake Geneva alone for two days, but I was very unreceptive to its environment. I left with very mixed and inconclusive feelings, and I did not know then that I would not return for three years. Without being aware of it, I was entering a period of my life in which my relationship with the lake took on a kind of dormancy. It would be the longest period of separation from it that I had ever experienced, from the time of my first experience there in August 1964, until the present. After my visit to the lake in June, Merritt and I returned to Interlochen for the 1976 summer season. The summer was quickly over, and we had no job prospects for the fall. After making a trip to Texas in September and deciding that it was not where we wanted to pioneer new lives, we moved into my home with my mother until the end of December. I arranged to do some postgraduate study in music at Indiana University in Bloomington, in January 1977, and was able to line up a position there as accompanist for the ballet department. In the interim, I studied piano with the fine teacher with whom I had worked for several years before going away to college, and I completed the major work on a book, written for pianists and teaching them how to survive and function successfully in the professional ballet world. This work, entitled *A Handbook for the Ballet Accompanist,* was subsequently published by Indiana University Press in 1978.

We moved to Bloomington, Indiana, at the beginning of January 1977. I was not happy at the university, however, and I stayed for only one semester. I had to accompany so much just to maintain an existence, and my academic work was so heavy, that I had little time to devote to my personal piano studies. It seemed like a hopeless situation, and we had little money. Besides, I did not like being a student again. During my semester there, I again devoted some time to Castaneda's works, and in the late spring and early summer I worked with the I Ching in conjunction with trying to determine our futures.

We returned to Interlochen for the summer of 1977, and in August I was able to secure the position of music director for the dance department of Wayne State University in Detroit. We moved there in September, and while I pursued my work at the university, my wife was able to find a job performing with a modern dance company which was based in Detroit. Much to my interest, I heard in November from my mother that Jerry Alber had contacted her in order to determine my whereabouts, but I heard nothing from him. The winter that we spent in Detroit, in 1977-78, was perhaps the deepest point in the spiritual sleep I was undergoing during that period of my life. Merritt was very different from me in many ways, and I was able to share with her very little of those aspects of my life and being which are set forth in this book. I had done no writing whatsoever about my personal life or my spiritual searches since I had written to Irv Martin from Florida, after Christmas in 1974. In fact, I had made only one effort at writing since then, which was a very short poem that I wrote at Interlochen in August 1976, during my second summer there, and which, in the briefest way possible, dealt with certain images of nature after the fashion of Japanese haiku. This suspension in my writing endeavors was a sign of my spiritual dryness.

I experienced a growing void in my life and within myself. I do not know where Lake Geneva was in my thoughts then, but it, and so much of my past life, now seemed like a distant, obscured memory. The emptiness I was experiencing during that period was a culmination of the process that had begun around the end of 1974. I had severed my Christian ties that fall, and after returning from Florida in January 1975, I lost contact with Irv. I had studied Castaneda's works a great deal, but after my marriage I had not applied myself to them with the consistency that I previously had. Not only had I devoted very little time to them since the spring of 1977, but I had engaged in no other related pursuits or searches. I had become more and more preoccupied with trying to build my career as a pianist, and had overlooked those inner needs that were so basic to my character. Furthermore, since I had gone to the lake for a week in August 1974, for the second time as counselor for my church group, I had been back there on five occasions, but all of these visits had been very short and extremely inconclusive, and now I had not even seen the lake since June 1976.

In December 1977, when I went home for Christmas, I was able to obtain some information about Swami Nirmalananda Giri, and I wrote him a long letter in January 1978. Perhaps this was prompted by the fact that my mother had heard from Jerry Alber the previous November, or perhaps I just wanted to reach out to someone who represented some kind of spiritual authority. I felt that I wanted to put things to rest between my spiritual teacher and myself, even after all those years of separation. There had been a couple of times over the past years that I had tried to reach Swami by telephone, but I was never able to do so. The phone was either not answered, or when it was, I was told that everyone was away, travelling in India. Swami remained true to his vow of separation from me, for my letter never received an answer. It was also in December 1977 that I obtained Castaneda's fifth and most recently published book, which I read with interest, and as a result, I studied his previous works again rather thoroughly for several months afterwards.

I did not want to face it, but there was a gap between Merritt and me that had existed for some time and which I felt was widening. I did not feel comfortable about sharing many of my feelings with her, and yet I felt a strong need to talk with someone. In May 1978, I made the acquaintance of a Catholic priest named Father David. He was Oriental, and a kind and loving and thoroughly charming man. He never quite got over his amazement that, of all the priests in Detroit, I picked his name out of the telephone book. I had really not known where to seek counsel, but I had always felt an instinctive liking for priests, and Father David's office was the first one that I called. I was surprised, somehow, when I met him and discovered that he was Oriental. He had not only a Christian background, but an extensive background in both Buddhist and Hindu traditions as well, and after I talked with him in some detail about my life, he remarked that he was probably the only priest in Detroit who could have really grasped and understood the nature of the quest that had characterized my life. For that reason, he was convinced that I had been led to him. I talked with him only once, but I will never forget him, or something that he said to me. When I had told him about my life, and the lake, and the circumstances which had led me to that moment in time, he said that I was very blessed and fortunate to have been given such experiences. There was something in this, or in the way that he said it, that brought tears to my eyes. After so many years of wandering and confusion, and seeking for real understanding from even one person, here was a man who was telling me that, in essence, he understood, and that he saw me as fortunate, instead of as an oddity or a threat. These few words gave me a beautiful peace and strength, and I felt an indescribable and unparalleled sensation of relief. Indeed, I have since noticed, over the course of my life, the great power that even a few words can have, when spoken by the right individual. To hear such words even only once every few years was sufficient to renew me and to give me new courage and drive. It had been so difficult to maintain my identity and my belief in what was real without ever hearing such words, and I valued them deeply. And for those people who have offered them to me now and again during my life, I have warm memories and lasting gratitude.

June came, and my work at the university was finished for the summer. Neither Merritt nor I were happy with Detroit, for various reasons, including professional ones, and we decided to move elsewhere in the fall. She returned to Interlochen for the 1978 summer season. Professionally, it was a busy and rewarding summer for me. In June and July, I was a pianist for the American Dance Festival at Duke University, in Durham, North Carolina. After my work there was finished, I went to New York City to make five solo LP records for a record company that specialized in music for ballet. It was then early August, and I drove from New York City to Detroit in order to do some personal business before driving up to Interlochen for the rest of Merritt's season there. When I arrived in Detroit on August 7, I was much surprised and interested to find a letter from Jerry Alber waiting for me. I had not heard from him since he had returned to live with Swami in April 1974, almost four and a half years before that. Jerry had left the ashram in Oklahoma City where he had been living with Swami, permanently this time, and had moved for a time to South Bend, Indiana. I wrote to him and told him that we were moving to Louisville at the end of the summer, and that I would like to have him come to see me when we were settled there.

I left for Interlochen, to join Merritt and to appear as guest pianist on the final ballet concert of the season. We returned from there to Detroit, and moved to Louisville, Kentucky, Merritt's home town, in late August. After we were settled there, I began to do yoga again on a steady basis. It was something I had been meaning to do for a long time, but I had not undertaken it until we moved to Louisville, where I had a room to myself to practice. Merritt secured a position as ballet instructor at a performing arts high school there, and I began a rather low-paying job, playing for the Louisville Ballet Company. Merritt and I were not getting along very well, and there was a great deal of tension between us. It was at this point that Jerry Alber came to stay with us for two weeks. He arrived in the last week of September. Out of the last ten years, since he had left for India in August 1968, I had seen him for only a few weeks during the early part of 1974, when he left the ashram for a time in order to assess his life.

We talked in depth. He had reached a point in his life where he knew that he must seek a new direction, and he longed to return to Germany. I questioned him about Swami and about life in the ashram. I talked about the last ten years of my life, and expressed to him my restlessness in my relationship with Merritt. But I did not know what to do about it. Jerry decided that he would remain in Louisville for the time, and secured a job at a local organ builder's firm. On October 7, he moved to a hotel until he could find more permanent quarters. He was welcome to stay with Merritt and me as long as he wished, but I sensed a lot of tension from Merritt.

On October 10, only three days after Jerry had moved out, Merritt left me. We had never discussed it, and there had been no warning whatsoever. I was so stunned that I could hardly function. It was to be the beginning of a long and hellish period in my life. Although I am sure that Jerry wanted to help, there was little that he could do for me. Ten days later, he left Louisville and returned to South Bend. Although we corresponded between then and January 1979, we did not see each other, and after that I lost touch with him again. My personal life became so unendurable that I hardly wanted to live. I was alone in a strange city, with no friends, earning sixty dollars a week, looking for more work and another place to live. Merritt was bitter and hostile toward me, and she would never speak again about our personal lives. I never learned what it was that had made her act so impulsively, or if indeed it was even an impulsive act. I wondered if Jerry's presence had frightened her in some way. Could she perhaps have thought that I was going to run away to a monastery?

In early November, I found an apartment and some part-time work as an accompanist at the school where Merritt worked. I found myself in the insane situation of accompanying the classes she taught, and I saw her at the Louisville Ballet classes, which she also attended and for which I accompanied. But we never spoke except when absolutely necessary. I was still not making enough money to get by, and so in late November, I started working as a waiter in a French restaurant. The only metaphysical activity I pursued was yoga, and I believe it helped me keep my sanity. In my loneliness and fright, I began running through one unhappy romantic relationship to another, but they were doomed to failure. By the end of December 1978, my marriage had been legally dissolved.

In January 1979, I wrote once again to Swami. Since I was again doing the yoga techniques, I wanted to ask him about certain facets related to their correct practice. I hoped that he might respond this time on the basis of the questions I asked him, but I never received an answer.

In the middle of June, I went to Lake Geneva for three days, and then to Chicago to visit friends. I went because I simply had to get away from my life, if only for a few days. I was in no condition to be receptive to anything at the lake, and although I had planned to stay there for five or six days, I left on the third day. In spite of its beauty, and the gentle warmth of the summer sun, I was not ready to face my aloneness there. I drove down to Chicago, and while I was there with my friends, it seemed so wonderful to be away from the hellish memories in Louisville that I decided I would go back there only long enough to pack and then move to Chicago and look for a new job.

I gave notice to all three of my employers, and told my landlord that I was moving. On June 21, I received my first copy of the book that I had published through Indiana University Press. After all of the work that I had put into it, and the waiting, I had expected a real feeling of triumph in seeing that first copy. Indeed, it gave me a quiet pride, but I felt very weary also, for the last nine months had pretty well taken from me any feelings of triumph that I might have had. I began to be very troubled about my impulsive decision to move to Chicago. I felt that I was really only running away, and I was not even sure what I was running to. Finally, almost in a panic, I realized that I had perhaps made a hasty and unwise decision, and I changed my mind. I was in some respects very lucky, however, for I did not lose my apartment, and I was immediately reinstated to all of my jobs. As I began reorganizing my apartment, I felt a profound relief.

In July, I received my first copies of the five records I had made in New York City the previous August. The fall soon followed, and I left the Louisville Ballet to accept a full-time position at the performing arts high school. During that year, I worked with Merritt again, almost every day. It was still very difficult, but not quite so bad as it had been, and, after all, it was my job. I still needed more money, and I continued to work nights in the restaurant. In August, I resumed my use of the I Ching again, and consulted it occasionally over the next year. But those next twelve months were really dominated by my intense involvement with the writings of G. I. Gurdjieff. I had begun to read Ouspensky's works again, and in his book entitled *In Search of the Miraculous,* he dealt extensively with the teachings of Gurdjieff and with his own personal relationship with him. I obtained all of Gurdjieff's works and printed lectures. I came to accept that life could be very, very hard, and that evolution was a conscious process that required intense seriousness and incredible commitment and effort. I became very sober about my life, and I looked at myself more seriously and honestly than I had ever done. Instead of running from pain and struggle, I faced it and endeavored to use it as a tool for my evolution. It was a year of intense inner work, and although I struggled and could not yet clearly see the light ahead, I grew much stronger and more solid.

In April 1980, I heard once again from Jerry Alber, but it seemed as if our paths were not yet ready to realign themselves again with one another, and it was not until a year later, in April 1981, that he called me again. Only then did our relationship truly begin to grow again, and three months afterward, in July 1981, he came to visit me. We have been very close since then and, somehow, it was as if, from the first time that I met him in August 1966, at Lake Geneva, we had never been apart. Our relationship had stood the test of time and all manner of circumstances, and I feel that he has always been my spiritual brother.

But during the summer of 1980, I began to experience a powerful inner reawakening, and I became filled with a deep and passionate desire to see Lake Geneva again.

In August 1980, I went to Lake Geneva for five days, and although I took a female companion with me, I was able to spend a considerable amount of time there in solitude. Something happened to me at the lake for which I had waited sixteen years. The unparalleled power and consciousness that was there, that I had felt to varying degrees and that I had always been drawn back to again and again, was suddenly and overwhelmingly available to me once more. I had asked myself many times in the past if the power at the lake was indeed as real as I remembered it to be, or if perhaps after all it was some illusion to which I had fallen prey. But during that visit to Lake Geneva, all such doubts were put to rest. This was home. And it was during that visit, while standing along the shores of the point, that I first felt that I should write a book about my relationship with this unique and exquisite place. I returned to Louisville to begin some preliminary writing.

During fall 1980, certain aspects of my life underwent a significant change. The position I had held at the performing arts school had been funded by a government grant, but the school had been unable to renew the funding again. I had lost my job. I had known that this was going to happen for several months, and after exploring various possibilities during the summer, I had concluded that it would not be possible for me to make a decent living in Louisville as a pianist that fall. I did not wish to move again, so I accepted a position with a commercial interior design firm owned by a friend of mine. It was a difficult personal adjustment for me not to be functioning as a professional musician, but it was a reality which had to be dealt with.

My visit to Lake Geneva had made a deep and lasting impression, but there remained with me a conflict I had always known. It had become immediately apparent to me after my first trip to the lake in 1964, sixteen years earlier. How could I reconcile the beauty and knowledge and joy which I had embraced at the lake with the rest of my life? I had never been able to do so successfully, and because of this contradiction, I began to feel a sense of hypocrisy about writing with reference to things which, although they possessed great truth for me, I had not fully embraced and expressed in my own life. I grew discouraged, and by December 1980, my writing dwindled to a halt. And again, my life felt empty. I did not know what to do about it, but although I was unaware of it at that time, I was on the verge of being confronted by an incredible revelation concerning my experiences at the lake. I would gain enormous insight into the things that had happened to me there. Not only would it have great impact upon my life in general, but it would deeply influence the character of the book I was writing, and it would reveal an unforeseen and dramatic new direction in my relationship with the lake.

Negoya

Negoya, Whose Spirit did wander
    over the grass,
Whose Soul, over the rejoicing waters
    did pass,
Smiled, and the warm sunlight
    danced in the trees,
Sighed—And a summer wind
    stirred their leaves.

Rays of the summer sun danced
    on the sparkling waves,
A flourishing breeze drifted
    through rustling birches.
Negoya lingered near
    their whispering branches,
    And birds came,
    And sang there...

October, 1966

I would say that I began consciously to use the word "Negoya" during the few weeks prior to the writing of this poem. Until that period surrounding October 1966, I had no name for the essence I had discovered during those initial experiences at the lake. In my first poem, eight months earlier, I made no attempt to name anything associated with the experiences. Rather, I referred chiefly to my emotional state and my feelings of longing. But in the second poem, I confronted and resolved the problem of naming the force that I felt the need to identify. I do not have a clue as to how I arrived at the name, "Negoya." I do not consciously relate the term to any other word. There was nothing like it in the occult or metaphysical terminology with which I was familiar, and during subsequent years of various occult and metaphysical studies, I never came across any word that resembled it.

It was a term that simply came into my mind after brief reflection and that I used afterward to denote the force that was central to my experiences at the lake. No words I knew at that time seemed appropriate to embody the experiences of beauty and mystery which I had known there. I could not use "God." The religious training which I had received during my upbringing in the Presbyterian church had established for me an image of God which, to say the very least, was simply inappropriate, if not even antagonistic, to symbolize my own experiences. During all the years of my upbringing within the traditional church, with a few exceptions, any attempts that I made to express my own perceptions and ideas were met either with bewilderment, suspicion, hostility, or ridicule, or were simply dismissed. Of equal inapplicability were most terms relating to what I perceived to be the traditional, upper-middle-class, American Christian theology. Therefore, "Jesus," "Christ," "Holy Spirit," and other such terms were equally inappropriate for my own personal experiences, if for no other reason than the contradictory and unfavorable associations I had attached to them in my mind. Furthermore, I had no real proof that what I had encountered at the lake was God, anyway, although I felt that it was. Similarly, if I had seen Christ, or the Holy Spirit, or some force specifically related to them, it was not evident to me. Thus, "Negoya" came into being.

This first poem that deals with Negoya was an attempt to express the interrelationship and oneness between Negoya's spirit and consciousness, and the phenomena of nature, which was, I realized even then, his body, his metabolism; the physical, dynamic expression of his being. Thus, expressed through a naive but deliberate symbolism, when he smiled, the sunlight danced in the trees; when he sighed, a summer wind stirred their leaves; and where Negoya lingered, the birds came and sang.

I remember being impressed by the figure of Orpheus, with his lute and his magical powers over nature. In Orpheus, I was struck by the analogy between him and the entity, Negoya, who likewise was a being that exercised some kind of magical or mystical control over the forces of nature. I was also taken by a piece of music entitled, "A Song of Orpheus," composed in 1960–61 by William Schuman. This work, a fantasy for cello and orchestra, is based upon the song, "Orpheus With His Lute," composed in 1944 by Vincent Persichetti for a production of William Shakespeare's *Henry VIII*. The words of this song are written in the cello part of Schuman's piece to enable the cello soloist to perform the melody in a manner that reflects the clarity of a singer's projection. Schuman has also requested that William Shakespeare's text be printed in the concert program books, or, if this is not possible, recited before the performance of the work. I often read Shakespeare's text and spent much time pondering over it, and I am sure that I listened to Schuman's piece many hundreds of times during the years of my early experiences at Lake Geneva. I have reproduced Shakespeare's text below.

Orpheus with his lute made trees,
And the mountain tops that freeze,
    Bow themselves, when he did sing:
To his music plants and flowers
Ever sprung; as sun and showers
    There had made a lasting spring.

Everything that heard him play,
Even the billows of the sea,
    Hung their heads, and then lay by.
In sweet music is such art,
Killing care and grief of heart,
    Fall asleep, or hearing, die.
                    —William Shakespeare
                    Henry VIII

Just as the being and emotions of Negoya profoundly and intimately affected nature, likewise did the music of Orpheus sway the powers of nature. Negoya did so by his very breathing and by his emotions, whereas Orpheus did so with his lute. Plants and flowers sprung to the music of Orpheus as if by a lasting spring, and even the billows of the sea hung their heads and then lay by. Negoya smiled and the sunlight came. He sighed and the winds flourished, and the birds came to sing near where he lingered.

However, although I perceived some interesting analogies between Orpheus and Negoya, my concept of Negoya and my ideas about him originated well before my introduction to Orpheus. Negoya had come to embody the idea of God in nature, and this is why I had developed interests both in the ideas of pantheism and transcendentalism. But my experiences at the lake came first, and my research and study afterward. In August 1964, I had never heard of Orpheus, nor of pantheism or transcendentalism, nor of any other such ideas.

As the years passed, my need to use the term, Negoya, diminished. When I stopped writing about Negoya, my inner references to him also lessened, and I do not believe that the term was thereafter much a part of my consciousness.

Previous to a poem written during of winter of 1970–71, my last poem in which Negoya is mentioned, I wrote a poem dated fall 1969. This work, which shows a great stylistic contrast to my other poems, is a series of eight separate images woven together freely in kaleidoscopic fashion. The passage and sequence of time melts into a fluid unity, or collage, of images, experiences, and memories. It is the eighth and final section of this poem that also refers to Negoya, and I have quoted below the passages from it in which his name appears. Many of the lines are directly inspired by images from the Point, and there are allusions to certain perceptions I encountered in the practice of yoga.

light and shadow on the old brick
        washing the bunches of flowers in
afternoon ancient Yellow sunlight
        oh, primeval light   soft diffusion of gold
                through the foliage...
                        negoya...
                shining threadlike Beam hallowing
the cathedral of the mind
        the mind's searchlight spiraling, om.
                its Beacon diving down
                        and down...
The light in one leaf   all the leaves of eternity,
oh, Negoya you who make things to live in all times at once,
        Glory be to the Father
        Oh, silent cathedral in me...
                light filtering through the
                stained glass windows of my eyes...

Although this poem does contain two references to Negoya, they are brief, and in this instance, they are not as central to the overall content or structure of the work as is the case with the references to him which appear subsequently in the poem that I have previously mentioned, dated winter, 1970–71, which is the next and final time that I refer to Negoya in my writing. I reproduce it below in its entirety.

In the blue translucence
        of early morning,
Above the moving waters,
        hovering,
Negoya moves
        in the shining mist.

In the trees and grasses
        and glistening mosses,
Tossed about
        by the lapping waves,
In all the shining
        world of morning,
The light flows forth
        from Negoya's Being,
Illumining
        the sparkling haze.

Atoms of sunlight
    in the sparkling waves,
Flashing diamonds
    in a coruscating sea,
Merged with the brightness
    of billowy clouds,
Silent, floating
    realms of ivory,
Silvery kingdoms
    in a saffron sky...

Eddies of wind,
    His subtle breathing,
Whipped the swelling
    ivory billows,
In a dancing sea
    of celestial brilliance,
Resplendent in the beams
    of the aureate afternoon sun.

Clear and deep,
    ineffable lays the silence,
On the far-off
    verdant shores.
Lulled, hushed lays the lake
    in dusk,
In hues of muted
    pink and crimson.

In the afterglow of day,
    the bright kingfisher soars,
Taking its flight
    from shining birches,
Into the flaming
    depths of Heaven,
A pellucid realm
    of orange and rose...

                  Winter 1970–71

Negoya is not mentioned again in any of my subsequent writings. Although I am not certain why, I am sure that my disuse of the term was in no way intentional or calculated. Rather, that it was due to the direction and character of the quest that dominated my life after I first went to the lake in 1964. From that time until the early 1980s, I explored many different philosophical systems in an attempt to introduce more light and metaphysical knowledge into my life, and to find, if it existed, an already established school of knowledge that might truly embrace and explain the experiences I had found at the lake, and with which I might therefore align myself. Yet I became progressively more removed from the essence of my personal experiences with reality. The clarity of my own visions became clouded because, rather than defining my experiences in my own terms from the beginning, I sought to define them within the contexts of other pathways. Because of this, I became confused and temporarily lost, and less identified with my own experiences, and with certain aspects of them that had contributed to their unique and individual identity. It was in this process, I feel, that "Negoya" fell by the wayside.

Although I gained invaluable knowledge and experience during my searches, and found sources that were partially analogous and supportive to my own perceptions, I was never totally successful. Although I committed great effort and time to various systems and immersed myself deeply in many of them, I have become neither absolutely nor permanently committed to them. Indeed, it has only been since the early 1980s that I have begun to fully formulate and articulate my own perceptions as unique experiences. I am not the only human being who has undergone such things, but I have come to regard this body of experiences as independent and individual, and demanding expression.

On December 4, 1980, an amazing event occurred in my life that provided me with additional impetus to write a book and to further formulate my ideas, and to shed light on the significance of "Negoya." These developments came about through my contact with a psychic. He was the second of two such individuals whom I had seen in my life, who gave readings through the vehicle of their own psychic powers, in conjunction with the use of various kinds of cards. I believe that consultations with bona fide and legitimate individuals who do this kind of work can be both enlightening and valuable if approached in a sane and healthy manner. The psychics whom I have consulted have been upright, honest, and fair individuals who have added insight into my life and perspective, and who have enriched the tone of my life.

Thus in the late fall of 1980, word came to me through friends and acquaintances about a psychic of rather amazing ability who was visiting friends in Louisville, where I was living. I telephoned him and made an appointment for a reading, the results of which were quite astounding, as well as extremely fulfilling and fruitful. Because of this, I decided that it would be worthwhile to have one more consultation with him before he left town, and two weeks after the first session I saw him again the evening of December 4, 1980. I could not possibly have been fully prepared for the incredible impact of this second reading.

I shall refer to him simply as "Robert," for this was the only name he used. The accuracy and depth with which Robert revealed and explored numerous aspects of my past, present, and future, as well as many of my most intimate psychological traits was astounding. But I was yet to experience the impact and significance of this reading. I had told Robert nothing of my metaphysical experiences or quests, and we had never touched upon these aspects of my life.

At one point in this five-hour session, Robert looked at me quizzically and said, "You are working on a book, aren't you?"

I replied that this was true. The impulse to write the book had come during my last visit to Lake Geneva in August, four months earlier. His statement aroused my curiosity, which was further quickened by his next statement.

"Why have you stopped writing?" he asked.

Before I could utter a word, he motioned for me to be silent as he scrawled some words on a pad of paper he always kept nearby. When he had finished, he asked me to continue. I began to explain that my life was filled with a deep and persistent longing, and I felt that I had lost something which was, even though I could not clearly identify it, deeply beloved, and of great value and importance in my personal life—a cherished and longed for "something" that, when it was not present in my life, left an irreconcilable emptiness, a loss of identity and ultimate meaning. This in turn led to feelings of hypocrisy and inadequacy that made me feel unworthy of writing a book about "spiritual" things.

Robert took the piece of paper he had written on and, tearing it from the pad, shoved it in front of me. Never in my life had anything I had ever read produced such a jolt. I became speechless and dumfounded. Tears of emotion welled up in my eyes as I stared in disbelief at the following words:

> Nagoya is the loss.
> Write, not live.

There in front of my eyes, over fourteen years since I had conceived of him, was Negoya. The poetry I had written over the years had been shown only to a trusted handful of individuals. And indeed, within that fairly extensive body of poetry and related writing, Negoya had appeared only a few times. Furthermore, I had never mentioned Negoya, nor his presence and meaning in my poetry, to another living being. I had come to keep my experiences private, with a few trusted exceptions, and also my writings, which had been created primarily for my benefit only, as a means of preserving those great experiences in my life.

And now, suddenly, Negoya reappeared. Not only had Robert pulled Negoya out from years of dormancy in my subconscious, but he had identified him as the embodiment and symbol of those exquisite and longed for experiences. I had noticed previously that Robert often spelled words as he heard them in his own mind, and thus he had spelled the term as "Nagoya" rather than "Negoya." As far as I was concerned, this was inconsequential. In fact, I realized that one could spell "Negoya" a number of different ways and still pronounce it so that it would sound either very similar or even the same. Furthermore, Robert had succinctly identified my dilemma over writing about my experiences and had indicated with unmistakable clarity the proper path to follow: namely, write the book, and do not become entangled in fretting over how I was living my life.

But much more was to unfold. On the table before me, Robert had arranged, face down, a pattern of cards all of which were identical on the back. He instructed me to pass the palm of my hand slowly over a row of these cards and to tell him if I received a sensation from any of them. After passing my palm slowly over several, I paused over one from which I received a strong sensation. Robert asked me what I was feeling and I replied that the card seemed to radiate an intense warmth. He then asked me if the warmth seemed centered in any particular area of the card. I could indeed perceive that the sensation of heat originated from one corner of the card in particular.

"This card reflects the conditions around your writing this book," he said, and he turned the card face up for me to study it.

I was astonished to see, on the face of the card, the image of an open book, and on the corner of the card where I had identified the source of heat, was the image of a brightly burning torch, its light illuminating the open pages of the book and the face of the card. Robert indicated to me that this card symbolized the nature and course of events if I wrote the book, and that such a path would perpetuate light, and that I would find success and fulfillment.

He then asked me to repeat the process of trying to pick up an emanation from another card with the palm of my hand. As I again moved my palm across the remaining cards, I paused over one that felt distinctly cold to me, and reported it. As he turned this card face up for me to study, he told me that this card symbolized my state of being should I not pursue the writing of my book. The face of this card presented the figure of a man who was the epitome of defeat. He exhibited the signs of failure and unhappiness. His walk appeared sluggish and his countenance lifeless. His back was bent and his shoulders stooped beneath some unseen burden. Robert proceeded to explain to me that I "must" write this book; that I had no choice if I wanted to find fulfillment and peace. He was adamant. It was only as the months passed that I came to perceive the full significance of his statements.

The impact of these developments had overwhelmed me, and so at Robert's suggestion we interrupted the reading and adjourned to another room to relax. As we talked, several other ideas came to Robert's mind, which he relayed to me. Since he knew absolutely nothing about my past, I was again astonished by his statements. He looked at me and said, "What do you know about Wisconsin Indians?"

I had never said anything to him that would even vaguely have indicated the geographical base for my experiences. The next thing he said provided me with an impetus and a clue that was to greatly influence my spiritual search over the next many months.

Robert continued. "Negoya means 'Father,'" he said. I did not really understand this, and he asked me about my relationship with my father. I replied that he had died when I was twenty. My spiritual experiences had first occurred when I was fifteen, and I knew intuitively that in whatever sense or role Negoya meant "Father," at least it did not refer to my physical father in this life. I therefore assumed that it must then have meant "Father" in some spiritual sense, perhaps like "God the Father," or something similar; at least that the word might be some kind of designation, along those lines, for the being I envisioned as influencing my own experiences at the lake.

Robert assured me further that Negoya was an American Indian word. Never once in all the passing years had such a possibility even occurred to me. Robert also said to me that by writing this book I was, in effect, "reorganizing a religion."

We returned to the other room and again sat across the table from each other. Robert told me that my book would write itself, so to speak. I assumed from this statement that the process of writing the book would be relatively free of stumbling blocks and would proceed fairly smoothly and automatically. Although in a sense this was true, only the passage of time revealed the meaning of Robert's statement.

It is interesting to note that the other psychic reader whom I had seen occasionally during that preceding summer in 1980 had also mentioned to me, after my trip to the lake and my subsequent decision to write, that I had begun work on a book. She, too, accurately foresaw that I was to interrupt this process temporarily for several months, after which time I would resume the work and eventually realize its completion.

Robert had two further contributions to make. Although still in the preliminary phases of organization and writing, I pondered over an appropriate title. After some consideration, I found none that I felt to be satisfactory. All of the possibilities I had considered seemed either inadequate, unimaginative, or clumsy. Robert told me that he had the title for the book. He again wrote something and handed me the sheet. I was startled and delighted when I read the following words.

Darkness Is Light Enough

I found the title interesting and provocative. But what amazed me was that, in an ironic and accurate way, this title succinctly embodied the character of my metaphysical experiences over the years, at Lake Geneva. Those times of special perceptions at the lake had held great beauty and light for me, and had filled my days there with an exuberant and unending joy. Through them, I bathed in a living fountain of joyous perceptions, and I touched a truth that gave me great solace and peace.

And yet, ironically, I had had another side of those experiences with which to deal. During my visit to the lake in August I had found those worlds of perception more evident and accessible than they had been for some period of time. But despite the great beauty with which I was always confronted, I felt there was more, if I could only reach it, and that the innermost source that engendered those moments of expanded reality was still veiled from me and just beyond my grasp. I always knew that there was still more to be experienced, a more nearly total and final union, or reconciliation. I had never established any objective definition of the nature of those experiences. In spite of their depth and the degree to which they had evolved in my life, they remained enshrouded in mystery, or in "darkness." Thus, I felt that "Darkness Is Light Enough" was so ironically appropriate a title that it would be impossible to improve upon it.

After some discussion with Robert, he supplied me with the following prologue.

When you need this book the most,
you will find it.

This brief thought appealed to me, although I felt that it might have been suitable for a great many books. But because I liked it, and because it represented one facet of a very significant body of information which Robert had given me, I decided to seriously consider using it, and I eventually included it as part of the book.

The sudden reappearance of Negoya in my life was startling, and it was to have much influence in shaping the nature of my search for light regarding my experiences at Lake Geneva. It occurred to me immediately that, particularly if I could find some kind of objective information to verify the nature of the word, "Negoya," it might become the focal point of my book. I had planned to write about my experiences several months before these developments had occurred, but had I never met Robert, the role of Negoya would have been minor indeed. Now, however, my perspective was changed. My immediate thought was to explore and to demonstrate that during my experiences at the lake I had somehow psychically picked up vibrations from another civilization, or from an individual who had once dwelt on or near Lake Geneva. I could imagine various possibilities. For instance, I remembered the conversation that I once had with my spiritual teacher from India, with whom I had studied yoga. We had been discussing my experiences at Lake Geneva, and he made the comment that perhaps some American Indian saint or sage had inhabited that area at one time and had, by his presence, endowed it with special vibrations.

Robert left Louisville shortly after my second reading. I had no more contact with him, and I was left to determine a plan to research Negoya. My life was busy with other matters as well, for I was working at the design firm during the day and holding down my evening work at the restaurant. Making a living was taking much of my time, and my research into Negoya, as well as my efforts in general toward writing the book, came in segmented spurts that were influenced by variations in my schedule, my energy, and my enthusiasm. I began researching Negoya in December 1980, after my second reading with Robert, and although it was characterized by lengthy interruptions, my research continued up until August 1981, when I returned to Lake Geneva for a week.

I had begun my search by exploring the resources of the local university libraries and by contacting the professors in their language and anthropology departments to see if they could point me in some relevant direction. My first task was to determine what Indian tribes, if any, had lived on Lake Geneva or in that area. After some research, I felt that I had narrowed the field of possible tribes down to four. Although I was subsequently proven to be mistaken, I felt that I was dealing with the Illinois, the Winnebago, the Kickapoo, or the Fox.

I was quickly awakened to my state of naiveness by discovering that I could not walk into a library and pull a Kickapoo or Winnebago dictionary off the shelf and look up my possible word. Such collections were much more difficult to locate than I had envisioned, or they did not exist. After wading through quantities of transliterated Indian literature, widely scattered magazine articles, and rolls of microfilm, I realized that I had undertaken a difficult and perhaps even impossible task. Early in my research, it occurred to me that even if my word had once actually existed in some Indian vocabulary, the possibility of verifying this might be lost forever. Furthermore, my spelling of the word was in some manner most likely phonetic, and even Robert had introduced a variation in its spelling. Therefore, I realized that if I was lucky enough even to find it, it would probably look somewhat different.

During my months of sporadic research between December 1980 and August 1981, I pursued leads that put me into contact with numerous universities, anthropologists, linguists, archaeologists, scholarly societies, and research groups, in several areas of the United States. The results were inconclusive.

I contacted Kenneth L. Miner, Associate Professor of Linguistics at the University of Kansas in Lawrence, who had formerly taught at the University of Wisconsin in Milwaukee, and was knowledgeable about certain Wisconsin Indian languages. He pointed out that the Indian language from that area of Wisconsin in which Lake Geneva was located would certainly be of the Algonquian family, and that the various languages in this family exhibited strong similarities. Of particular interest to me was his statement that both "na" and "ne" were possessive forms. I had quoted both Nagoya and Negoya to him. "Na" was an Algonquian form, and "ne" was Menomini. Although Miner did not recognize the word "Negoya," he assured me that he would try to research the matter, and I subsequently received an interesting letter from him in January:

January 12, 1981

Dear Mr. Lishka:

Regarding the item, "Negoya," or "Nagoya," we discussed on the phone: I have worked with Menomini, Potawatomi, and Winnebago in Wisconsin and do not recognize the word or anything very much like it (although of course if you "stretch it" far enough you can get it to look like anything). The other languages in Wisconsin are Oneida and Ojibwa. This word could be

Oneida, a language for which I have no lexical materials. However, the Oneida came late to Wisconsin and are up near Green Bay.

The nearest thing that I can find is Ojibwa, *nagweyaab,* meaning "rainbow," which could be pronounced *nagoyaab,* which matches your word except for the final consonant.

The trouble is that the Ojibwa in Wisconsin were and are in general nowhere near Lake Geneva.

Now Ojibwa and Menomini are closely related, so Menomini *could* have a very similar word for "rainbow." The Menomini word for "rainbow," strangely enough, has not been recorded, and if this correspondence has done nothing else, it has decided me to get the Menomini word for "rainbow."

If your word were Menomini it would make sense, since that's the tribe that controlled the Lake Geneva area; at least all the place names around there are Menomini.

Sorry I can't be of more help.

Yours,

Kenneth L. Miner
Associate Professor of Linguistics

This was enough to ensure my determination to pursue my research. I realized there were various phonetic spellings that could closely approximate the pronunciation of my word.

Since my visit to the lake in August 1980, I had planned to return during the following summer to explore more fully my experiences and perceptions there. I had eventually fixed the date for a week in late August 1981. During the interim, many changes had occurred in my life. In September 1980, I met Suzanne, who would eventually become my wife. I met Robert in late November, and among other things that he told me during my first reading with him, he foresaw that Suzanne and I would marry. Then, on December 4, during my second reading, he confronted me with the startling information about Negoya and my experiences at the lake, and the circumstances concerning the book which I was writing. Then, toward the end of February 1981, I left the design firm for which I had worked since the end of the previous summer and started a new commercial interior design business with Suzanne, who was an experienced designer. In April, I ventured briefly up to Lake Geneva with Suzanne. We were there for only two days, and had gone primarily for the purpose of a rest and a change of scenery. And although, as always, I was happy to be at the lake again, there were no significant developments or changes while I was there. Later in April, I received a phone call from Jerry Alber, from whom I had not heard since the previous April, and whom I had not seen since he left Louisville, in October 1978. He came to visit me for five days in early July, when our relationship truly resumed. We remained close after that, and I told him that I would make every effort to stop by South Bend, Indiana, and visit him in August on my way back from Lake Geneva. Around July, shortly after Jerry had returned home, Suzanne and I moved into the house we had rented, and we were subsequently married on August 1, 1981.

In late August 1981, I ventured alone to Lake Geneva. Every trip that I ever made to the lake was meaningful. The times I have spent there have sometimes brought experiences which were hoped for or expected, and at other times have engendered unforeseen or unanticipated developments. But that trip was possibly the most rewarding, and yet the most unsettling, of all my trips there.

I went to the lake expecting to have certain kinds of experiences. During the intervening year I had become deeply involved with the knowledge that, if one could "turn off" the constant clamor of internal dialogue one uses to define and continuously maintain the world for one's self, and which in reality tells one absolutely nothing about the real nature of the world, but rather, works to further mislead one, then one could begin to apprehend things in a deeper and more profound manner. The idea that our knowledge and perception of things and phenomena in the universe around us was shallow, incomplete, and incorrect, and that it could be corrected and renewed through certain nontraditional modes of thought and perception, became relevant to all facets of my life; to my own body and mind and essence; to their true nature, and to that of all other things—the trees and rocks, the earth, the sky and the stars; time and dimensionality, and all else. I knew that our so-called "knowledge" served only to blind us, and if we could but get beyond the prison of our traditional methods of thinking and perceiving, we should encounter and embrace a universe of endless mystery, whose essence and manifestation embodied the purest beauty and the most fathomless truth, and whose glory would infinitely outstrip the limitations of our objective consciousness.

I had contemplated my trip to Lake Geneva with this mind set. And although what I found there was indeed a new and deepened knowledge, it was not the kind I had expected. I arrived at the lake on Friday, August 21, 1981. From the beginning of that visit my feelings were characterized by sensations that were familiar to me. This time, however, I was struck with the singular intensity of the wonderful and yet disturbing feeling that I was home—truly home. I particularly remember the first few evenings there. I traveled that familiar and beloved path along the shores of the lake to the Point, which was my special place of power. That path, too, was home for me, and I trod it with great gladness, and listened with joy to the familiar talk of the waves splashing along the boulders. I savored each precious moment as I walked the shore. Its dear sights and sounds washed away my cares, and made me buoyant and full of light. I was truly alive, and all the world around me vibrated with that life. The wind filled my lungs, and my whole being was renewed.

When I walked to the Point, I was greeted by the familiar sight of the huge boulder on its shore, and as I stepped out onto the open ground, my soul came fully to rest. No other sensations on earth could restore me so quickly. I was one again with my beloved, and she spoke to my weary being and gave me rest. With reverence I surveyed the beauty of her being. And after wandering here and there to renew in my mind every inch of that place, I settled at the edge of the water, surrounded by the rocks and boulders, as close as I could get to the wonderful earth which, in various places, revealed the roots of the shimmering birches that rose above me.

As evening approached, the lake was serene, and yet ever shifting and breathing, and full of life. Day faded and mellowed with that delicate and gradual mutation which was almost imperceptible, but rather felt, or sensed. The sun traveled beyond the darkening hills, its light cooling and softening, as the world transmuted to evening's exquisite hues. I felt protected by the power and beauty of the living spirit of that place. I was safe, happy, and at peace. I reflected contentedly that I never spent much of my time at the lake brooding over my life away from there and its many problems. There at the lake, it was another universe. My problems seemed nonexistent. They were part of another world, another time, another existence, which seemed so alien and far from me that I could hardly relate them to the being that I became when I was there.

When Monday arrived, I was able to get into the town of Lake Geneva to the public library and establish a plan for continuing my research concerning the Indians who may have lived in that area. It seemed logical, as a first step, simply to consult with the local librarians and ask them to what sources I might go to learn about Indians who may have once inhabited the locale of the lake. I was immediately referred to several sources, and among those which I found to be particularly interesting and which I read in their entirety were the following:

History and Indian Remains of Lake Geneva and Lake Como, Walworth County, Wisconsin: Part I—Historical by Paul B. Jenkins, and *Part II—Indian Remains* by Charles E. Brown (Williams Bay, Wisconsin: Geneva Lake Historical Society,1930)

Lake Geneva Before the Pioneers by Paul Richard Cowen (Williams Bay, Wisconsin: George Williams College, 1969)

The Book of Lake Geneva by Paul B. Jenkins (Chicago: Chicago Historical Society, 1922)

Wau-Bun by Mrs. John H. Kinzie (Menasha, Wisconsin: National Society of Colonial Dames in Wisconsin, 1948)

Among the sources I read, these were the most informative and interesting, and during my several visits to the library that week, I referred back to some of them numerous times.

I realized the need for caution and discrimination in assessing the accounts of local historians whose approach to recording the history and language of other cultures might not be as professional as that of a trained anthropologist. While maintaining this attitude, I sensed the need for particular care in the area of recording vocabulary of so-called nonliterate cultures. In my research at Lake Geneva, as well as in other instances concerning my research about Negoya and Indians in general, I sometimes found that my information was suspect. I became tentative about accepting as accurate and final both the written and oral information that came my way. Nevertheless, I was able to gain a sizeable amount of valuable knowledge.

The *History and Indian Remains of Lake Geneva* immediately identified for me the Indian tribe I was searching for, or at least the tribe whose history was most recently and intimately bound up with Lake Geneva; namely, the Potawatomi. They were of the Algonquian language family, in accord with Kenneth Miner's information about certain tribes in that general area, and they had come eventually to the Lake Geneva locale from their ancestral home in central New York. They were known as the forest Potawatomi, as distinguished from the prairie Potawatomi who had migrated somewhat further south. They were at one time one with the Ojibwa and the Ottawa. The name, "Potawatomi," means something like "blowers of the fire," "those who keep the council fires going," or Fire Builder Nation;" in other words, the builders for the sacred fire for the three Indian nations of the Potawatomi, Ojibwa, and Ottawa. The course of the Potawatomi history was forever and, to me, tragically changed with the coming of the white men, as indeed was true for many, many Indian tribes.

The first recorded visit by white men to Lake Geneva occurred in 1831, with the arrival of John H. Kinzie, his wife, Juliette, who was the author of *Wau-Bun,* and their party. However, the white men certainly had a knowledge of Lake Geneva and the Potawatomi living there well before this date. At the time the Kinzie party visited the lake in 1831, the Potawatomi were living in three principal settlements around the lake.

1. In the area which is now the site of the town of Lake Geneva, at the east end of the lake

2. On the northwest shore of Williams Bay, now the site of the town of Williams Bay

3. At their principal settlement at the west end of the lake, now the site of the town of Fontana

Their chief at that time was called "Maunk-suck," or "Maung-zet," by the Potawatomi, meaning "Big Foot," a nickname given to him by his brother-in-law on the occasion of his noticing the size of the chief's footprints in the snow, when he retrieved the partially frozen carcass of a deer, that had been chased by wolves onto the ice of the lake and trapped and partially imbedded there. Thus, the lake was often referred to by the Potawatomi as "Maung-zet-ne-biss," or "Big Foot

Lake," and it was therefore called "Lac Gros Pied" by the French trappers and traders. I found the designation, "Maung-zet-ne-biss," of some interest and speculated that, with reference to the possibility of the syllable, "ne," functioning here in the role of a possessive form, in accordance with the information furnished by Kenneth Miner, a literal rendering of the term, "Maung-zet-ne-biss," might be something like "Big-Foot-His-Lake." I was to learn later, however, that "nee-bee-sh" meant "water," and thus one might render "Maung-zet-ne-biss," or "Maung-zet-nee-bee-sh," as "Big Foot's Water." I pondered over such matters in considering the possibility of building a case that my term, "Negoya," or "Ne-gaw-yuh," might exhibit traits that were indeed related to the style and functionality of the Potawatomi language.

I further learned that the lake was known to the Indians by the Potawatomi name of "Kishwauketoe," meaning "sparkling water." The lake was known, even then as now, for the singular clarity and purity of its spring fed waters.

Another linguistic matter immediately caught my attention. I found recorded a number of related terms which apparently functioned as the designation for head chief of the tribe. They were as follows:

O-nan-ge-sa	Oh-ne-gas-sun
O-non-gee-say	Ne-gas-sun
O-nan-guis-se	Ne-gau-sim

I did not know the reasons for these variations, although I attributed them in part to discrepancies arising from their having been recorded by amateurs, which I suspected to be the case with other related materials I was studying. Nevertheless, I was struck with the similarity, for instance, between the terms, "Ne-gas-sun," and particularly "Ne-gau-sim," and my term, "Ne-gaw-yuh." The first two syllables of "Ne-gau-sim" and "Ne-gaw-yuh" were virtually identical. I speculated that "Ne-gaw-yuh" might be yet another variation of the term in question, or that it might very possibly pertain to someone or something that, in terms of its function or role, was similar to that of a head chief; that is, some kind of figurehead or authority or leader, or possibly a spiritual entity or figurehead, or even a deity.

Thus, I was assessing the relevance of assembling these various terms, along with my own term, into a collection or family of terms that were related through their structural similarities, and which might function as a class of words denoting various entities of spiritual significance, whether embodied in the form of a physical chief, or in the forms of various spirit beings. And I pondered once again the idea that whomever or whatever I had seen out over the waters of Conference Point, seventeen years earlier, must have been Negoya, or somehow related to my concept of him. I reflected also over the fact that I had always denoted Negoya as "him." For just as I had always conceived of the lake as "female," in some deep metaphysical sense, I had always intuitively known that Negoya was male.

Of further interest was the fact that, among the numerous sites on the lake that had served various roles in the lives of the Indians who had lived there, some were of particular spiritual significance, and I was eager to learn about them. They were of the nature of local shrines connected with the supernatural forces in that locale and were designated by the term "Shin-ga-ba-sin." One such place was located within several hundred yards beyond the western end of the lake, near Fontana, on what is now the Big Foot Country Club. Located there are seven lovely spring-fed pools that must once have been surrounded by lush forests. The Indians called these pools the "Seven Sacred Springs." They were a gathering place for councils, and no important act of hunting or war was undertaken without propitiating the spirits believed to dwell there, and invoking their guidance. The underground sources for these springs have now been tapped in artesian fashion and piped so that there are fountains in the pools. The surrounding grounds have been cleared and landscaped, but still retain a provocative beauty.

The second site of special interest to me was located, according to the reference in the *History and Indian Remains of Lake Geneva*, on Cedar Point, which comprises the eastern tip of Williams Bay, and which was a prominent feature of the landscape as I viewed it from Conference Point, my special place, the western tip of Williams Bay. There on Cedar Point, according to this 1930 account, were located "spirit stones," two large granite boulders situated several hundred feet east of the tip of Cedar Point and fifty to sixty feet inland from shore. There also, as at the site of the Seven Sacred Springs, the spirits were invoked and propitiated.

On Memorial Day, May 31, 1929, Chief Simon Kah-qua-dos, who was born May 30, 1851, and who was the grandson of Chief Big Foot and the last hereditary chief of the Potawatomi tribe, visited Lake Geneva to advise the Centennial Committee, and visited the two sites discussed above, where he performed the traditional tribal dances and rites. These sites were subsequently revisited on June 27, 1931, by the Potawatomi Indians on the occasion of the one-hundred-year centennial celebration of the first recorded visit by the white men to Lake Geneva.

My special place, Conference Point, was also a unique site that possessed significant power. And even though I was deeply involved with that particular place, and although I realized that my perceptions and feelings about it were a combination of objective observations and also intensely subjective perceptions, I was certain that it held a power of its own, beyond my attachment to it. I was seeking some kind of evidence that might support this. I had not as yet found anything to substantiate my feelings, but the *History and Indian Remains of Lake Geneva* did cite the Conference Point area as one in which various stone tools had been unearthed, and above which, where still stand many magnificent trees indicating the area's former character, were located some of the Potawatomi burying grounds, extending northward into what is now a residential area of Williams Bay.

There was another site in Williams Bay that I did not have the opportunity to visit, which was the burial place of two of the wives of Chief Big Foot. Regarding the various traces of Indian influence still to be detected in the area of the lake, perhaps the most obvious was the trail along the shores of the lake, which I walked so often, and which was so beloved to me. It was blazed and travelled long ago by the Indians. About thirty miles in length, it is a continuous trail which encircles the entire perimeter of the lake and one of the most beautiful walks one could ever take. I will always remember the time I walked around the entire lake on this trail with Nancy, during the summer of 1972, and I can still clearly call to mind the awesome and enchanting beauty of that day.

From *History and Indian Remains of Lake Geneva*, I also learned the following facts, which were of special interest to me:

1. The Potawatomi had a special regard for fire. They regarded it as an entity which had life in and of itself. They referred to it as "our grandfather," and believed their fire to be purer than the white men's fire. It was considered a grave insult if a visitor or guest spit into the fire of his host.

2. The Potawatomi had a legend of a water monster, perhaps an eel or a serpent, that lived in the lake.

3. They believed that various areas of the lake were characterized by both "good" and "evil" waters.

4. They believed in the *nampé-shiu,* or *nampéshi-k,* a water panther spirit that was an evil power in the water and which occasionally drowned people, who were subsequently found with their eyes, ears, and mouth stuffed with mud. This evil spirit travelled through the earth as well as the water, and if it appeared to a man, he became a warrior. These evil spirits were seen to engage in battle with the mighty thunderbirds, great, eagle-like heavenly spirits who dwelt in the empyrean realms of the sky, and from whose eyes flashed forth lightning.

From *Lake Geneva Before the Pioneers* by Paul Richard Cowen, I established further information about the Potawatomi; for instance, that they were, historically speaking, relatively late arrivals to the Lake Geneva area, according to this source. Preceding the Potawatomi was a culture whose people are described as "effigy mound builders," whose burial mounds were constructed in the forms of various animals and other figures. There is evidence of their activity later than the fifteenth century. It is apparent that the other cultures which followed theirs affected various changes in the evidences that the effigy mound builders left behind, and these changes have been researched and studied in modern times. The presence of man in the Lake Geneva area is being pushed back several thousand years, and thus one finds represented a series of cultures ranging from the so-called "primitive," a term which grows increasingly distasteful to me, to the more advanced.

The thought occurred to me that, if the word, "Negoya," had come from a culture whose existence had ceased at some point in the distant past, then my chances of verifying its authenticity were virtually nonexistent.

Another highly interesting work which I studied was *The Book of Lake Geneva* by Paul B. Jenkins. Of some sentimental interest to me was the dedication, which I have reproduced below:

> Dedicated to the memory of my beloved father, Herman Dutilh Jenkins, D.D.,
> A Soldier of the Republic, Lover of Nature, Minister of the Gospel, and Among
> the First to Appreciate the Beauty and the Message of Lake Geneva.

I sensed from this, as I did from other such testaments that I had found, that perhaps there were other individuals, like myself, who had experienced a profound love for the lake, and who may have sensed something very unique and special in its character. I also found particularly relevant the prologue which Jenkins had included, and which I also reproduce here:

> Nothing is more inspiring than a lake,
> and no environment has more character.
> Professor A.S. Pearse
> University of Wisconsin

According to this work, the Potawatomi migrated to Lake Geneva about 150 years before the first visit there by the whites, perhaps during the latter portion of the seventeenth century, from the Green Bay area, where they were encountered by Jean Nicolet in 1634. They were seen to be peaceful and hospitable, as has always been fairly characteristic of them. The Potawatomi had claimed to have inhabited the Lake Geneva area for a good number of generations before the 150-year period preceding the arrival of the whites in the early 1830s.

In terms of their implements, the Potawatomi were a Stone Age culture, and survived principally through hunting and fishing. This book also describes the circumstances under which the Potawatomi left their lake paradise forever. As I stated earlier, the first recorded visit of the white men to Lake Geneva occurred in 1831. Although generally of a more peaceful predilection, the Potawatomi were planning to take part in the Indian uprising of 1832, but were betrayed to the whites by Shabonna, the chief of another tribe, and thus deterred. In 1833, the United States government "purchased" their lands, and in 1836 the last Potawatomi were expelled from the area and sent off to a reservation in Kansas. Their people were so unhappy and discontent, and understandably so, upon seeing what awaited them in Kansas, that many wandered off to spend the rest of their lives seeking a more fit place to live, and others walked the long distance back to Wisconsin and settled in the northern part, which was relatively unsettled at that time, and where some of their descendants can still be found today.

Needless to say, they had been bought out cheaply, and much of their money was drained off by opportunity-seizing traders. There were also other questionable aspects of this transaction. But this describes briefly the tragic demise of their lives and culture. The Lake Geneva Potawatomi were the last of their people to be expelled, and I truly felt sick in my heart when I read this account. Before leaving, Chief Big Foot commended the burial site of his two wives to the care of the local Indian agent, with the request that, when the time came and the bodies had decomposed to their proper state, they were to be interred in the ground. I have read of this chief, standing with his arm around the council pole of what had been his village, surveying for the last time the scene of his home, the lake, with its encircling hills and forests, and I have tried to imagine what his feelings must have been.

I have since pondered over the fact that when we in the United States refer to the takeover of the lands and cultures of one people by another people, we usually refer to the aggressors as invaders, marauders, or conquerors. We, in our own history books, manage to avoid such designations in relation to ourselves, but rather, call ourselves pioneers or settlers. How ironic that we, the pioneers, who opened up new lands, destroyed myriads of cultures—uprooted them, stole their land, poisoned and forever destroyed their way of life.

The Book of Lake Geneva contains an interesting story that also should be mentioned here. In 1833, John Brink, a surveyor for the United States government, discovered near the Fontana Potawatomi village an Indian coffin fashioned from a butternut log. It had been split in half lengthwise, and the two halves had been hollowed out to accommodate a body. A hole had been carved into one of these halves so as to access the face of the corpse. This log coffin was then fastened upright to a bur oak tree, near to the shore and overlooking the lake, in such a way so that the face-hole was directed toward the lake. This coffin contained the body of Chief Big Foot's son, who had died between the ages of fourteen and eighteen. This youth had loved the lake so deeply that he had expressed the wish to his father that even in death he should like always to be able to see the lake. In order to realize his son's wish never to be deprived of seeing his beloved lake, the chief buried him in the fashion described above. In 1836, I presume after the departure of Chief Big Foot and his tribe, a local doctor stole the body, and for a long time kept the skull on his office desk and the skeleton in his closet. Some time later these items unaccountably disappeared, and it is thought that they were perhaps reclaimed by Potawatomi who had returned to the area.

Besides the data which I was able to compile from *The Book of Lake Geneva*, I was touched by its testament to the beauty and message of Lake Geneva. I also recorded from it some brief facts about the geological history of the lake. Its bed was formed into its final shape by the last glacial retreat which took place some twenty to sixty thousand years ago. More recent dates within that span of time are favored. It is a spring fed lake whose outlet is the White River, located at the northeast end of the lake. This outlet was dammed up in 1936, the result of which has kept the water level of the lake seven feet or more above what it would otherwise be. Due to erosion, some of the cliffs around the lake have receded as much as sixteen feet in ninety years.

Wau-Bun: The Early Days in the Northwest (1830–1833) was written by Mrs. John H. (Juliette A.) Kinzie in 1856, but it was not published until 1948. Written more than twenty years after the fact, it was an account in diary form describing the travels and adventures of the Kinzie party in the early 1830s. The title, *Wau-Bun*, is an Ojibwa word which means something like "the dawn," or "the break of day." During the course of this narrative, the passage of the Kinzie party through the Lake Geneva area is briefly touched upon, and Mrs. Kinzie describes their short contact with the Potawatomi village which was located on what is now the site of the town of Fontana, at the west end of the lake. In a colorful way, she outlines various features of this settlement, and includes in her description a mention of Chief Big Foot. It is Mrs. Kinzie's account of this encounter with Lake Geneva in 1831 that is considered to be the first recorded visit to the lake by white men. And although this work is, in general, somewhat romanticized and perhaps suspect here and there in its accuracy, it nevertheless did provide me with another small facet for my overall concept of the history of the Potawatomi of Lake Geneva.

I felt a profound empathy for those Indian people, a disturbingly intense sense of identification with them. Even from the personal standpoint of my own seventeen years of experiences and associations with the lake, I could imagine the tragedy of alienation from that place of beauty and power, and I felt that such a thing would be like death itself. For every time I left the lake after a visit, I experienced an intense feeling of having left something precious and beloved, of having gone away from my home. Although I had not as yet fully absorbed and digested all the material I had studied, I began to feel intuitively that perhaps my feelings of identification with the Indians and their experiences there were rooted in something deeper than mere empathy. As I read those various accounts, I experienced a fascination and an intensity of interest that I did not characteristically experience when studying historical matters. It was almost as if an unknown and forgotten self inside of me quickened to life. The things I had read had an unexplained yet unprecedented sense of meaning for me. It was as if I had made a profound discovery, and yet its full message and meaning had not revealed itself to me.

I felt more strongly than ever that, through my experiences and perceptions at the lake, I had psychically touched another culture or another time, or possibly experienced the modes of perception of other minds. I had not yet identified "Negoya," but in the process of searching, a whole new world was opening up for me. I recalled, for instance, the unusual perceptions of fire that had characterized my consciousness during my first visit to Lake Geneva in August, 1964, on that strange night that I later went to the Point and had my vision of the shining being there, out over the waters.

As was characteristic of all my experiences surrounding my first visit to the lake, there had been no precedents or analogous experiences in my earlier years with which to compare and measure those new ones, which were startlingly unique. Now, I see it as if I had suddenly happened onto a strange yet wonderful new set of perceptions. I recalled that experience with the fire and my various accompanying feelings, and my perception of it as having had a life and being of its own, when I read, in the *History and Indian Remains of Lake Geneva,* of the Potawatomi view of fire. I assumed that this view, described on page 96, was typical of many Indian cultures.

My experiences at the lake had another side, or aspect, also, for which I have difficulty in finding or grasping suitable and appropriate words to characterize it. And even though in its own way it was strangely beautiful and made me feel uniquely alive, I shall call this aspect of my experiences the "dark side." It is even hinted at in my descriptive account on page 1 of this book, regarding my perceptions of the fire, in which I sensed an alluring, compelling, yet almost sinister presence. I sensed that same presence in other phenomena as well, and which in my opinion were noumenally related; for instance, the voices of the insects and the murmuring of the waves, all of which seemed to summon me. It was as if I was not only being drawn to some being, or power, but also as if I was being introduced into an entirely new world of multifaceted perceptions. I was initiated into a new set of perceptions that were different and alien from what I had considered to be my own, but which, having once found them, I instantaneously and naturally embraced as mine. When I did so, it was inevitably a shock.

There were many times during my first visit to the lake, and indeed, which were also characteristic of many subsequent visits, when certain spots, like the Point, for example, particularly in daytime, seemed not only incomparably beautiful, but even, in some deep, meaningful sense, sacred ground, so close to God that to tread upon their hallowed ground demanded reverence and care. These spots made me feel that I was separated only by a thin veil from the full and direct presence of a divine consciousness. I experienced this feeling of holiness and light more fully at certain moments than at others, although it was almost always present to some degree, and it was engendered more easily and profoundly by certain spots than by others. These feelings could be catalyzed by various aspects of the natural world; among others, the movement and sound of water, the play of sunlight over its undulating surface, the dancing of the waves and the endless expression of energy that flowed through them.

If I had psychically touched upon the perceptions of an Indian culture that had once existed upon the shores of the lake, then it was possible that, at least to a degree, my experiences there were reflective of this. I had come to embrace not only a profound love for the natural world and a true intimacy with it, but also a whole repertory of vague but disturbing apprehensions relating to the mysterious side of that environment. Was it the spirit world of the Potawatomi that was the root of these fears, touching some dark aspect of my mind? I considered the accounts I had read of the various spirit beings they believed to inhabit the lake, and I thought of the instinctive fears that sometimes gripped me when I approached the shores of the lake alone at night. I remembered the vision which I had encountered one night at the Point during my first visit there in August 1964. Was it, after all, some force from the spiritual world of the Indians which had "initiated" me that night? And through that encounter, had I become available to the darker side of that incredible world there, as well as to its exquisite light and shining beauty?

Even as a baby and as a young child, and into my early teens, I had never had any fear of darkness. Indeed, I had seemed to welcome it, and even as a small child sleeping alone in the upstairs of my parents' house, I was always eager to have the lights shut off because their brightness bothered my eyes. It seemed in fact as if my acquired apprehension for the darkness at certain times was an element, or component, of the new set of perceptions which I had embraced at Lake Geneva, one manifestation of which was that, on various occasions, I avoided certain areas of the lake during the night.

One night during that first week at the lake in 1964, I was walking alone along a paved roadway above the lake, on my way toward the Point. By that time during my first visit, I had been thoroughly initiated into the lovely perceptions of that world. And yet, as I walked along that road, I acutely sensed the presence of something that seemed threatening and malevolent. But it was different from the hideous, demonic malevolence and evil I uncovered during my experiences with the occult, many years later, in my early twenties. Rather, the feelings I got at the lake seemed to be of an elemental nature. They seemed to arise out of my contact with certain forces or powers that existed in the world and in nature, and which I feel were of two kinds.

1. Those of a more mechanical nature and which did not possess, at least as we would understand it, a volition of their own

2. Those which did possess some kind of volition and personalized consciousness, whose abodes were in the realms of nature and in the astral worlds, and which, in occult terminology, are designated as "elementals"

Such forces may be sensed by those who are truly intimate with the consciousness of nature, and it was possibly those forces to which the Indian consciousness, and indeed my own, were sensitive. At any rate, those "forces" were of a somewhat different character from those which I associate with the true occult and with magic. Unlike true demonic forces, they were not, I feel, in any way "deliberately" destructive or debilitating. But rather, in some mysterious way, they were yet a dynamic aspect of my overall body of experiences at the lake. My fear of those forces there, and my sensations of malevolence, or evil, were manifestations of my sense of alarm and self-preservation, rather than a reflection of the presence of something truly and willfully malevolent. Whence came my sensations of danger? Did they arise from a source that was consciously evil, or were they engendered by the presence of a power which was simply to be met with respect and caution? I can recall many incidences in which the source of my apprehension was clearly one or the other. And with regard to such kinds of nonordinary experiences, I feel strongly that there is an important point to be made; namely, that in such instances one must be able to discriminate between the various powers that exist, and the emotional reactions and sensations they can produce.

Gravity is a powerful and immutable force in our lives. It does not possess a volition bent on doing us harm, but if we foolishly violate this law, we will surely suffer, and perhaps pay with our lives. This was the kind of situation in which I found myself at Lake Geneva. I was surrounded by gigantic and powerful forces that I did not understand, and I was frightened by them. In time, all of these things would be explained to me, but at that time I had no conscious idea of what was really happening. However, when one has touched forces that are truly demonic, they are thereafter immediately recognizable, because there is nothing more terrifying than facing those monstrous powers.

Thus, as I walked toward the Point, the very sounds of the insects and tree frogs, the dark foliage, and the splashing and murmuring of the water along the shores seemed to voice and to catalyze in me a real feeling of danger, an imperative need for caution and discriminatory action.

At times, while sitting on the shore and meditating on the water, I would turn now and then and look over my shoulder with a feeling of vague apprehension, real rather than imagined, as if I sensed something there that was a threat to me. At times I could almost visualize it—a kind of animal perhaps, yet not merely a brute, but something with a more evolved mind; something like an embodied spirit. Were these sensations which the Potawatomi had once experienced concerning some elemental being there? Was I picking up vibrations of those thoughts out of the past? And was there even now a real presence there which I had intuited?

In light of the unusual nature of the things I am describing, I can identify with the skepticism some might feel. Nevertheless, they were real to me, and I sought answers that would make them more coherent to me, even though they would always be of a somewhat incredible character.

Since I did not always get the same feelings from the same places, I reasoned that this might be due to one of two things. First, either my perceptions of things were shifting and fluctuating, or second, some psychic force around me might be shifting or fluctuating, in which case my relationship to it would fluctuate. Although I was certain that my own states of mind were subject to variations that influenced my receptivity, I felt intuitively that the latter factor also played a large role, and perhaps a dominant one. But was this "noumenal movement" around me due to the interaction of blind, inanimate forces, or to something which was, in some more graspable sense of the word, alive? Again, I felt intuitively that, although the influence of both factors probably played a role, the latter was strongly active. The total explanation was rather complex, and represented the interplay of various forces. I had begun to feel that, viewed from a perceptual level inaccessible to many people, there was nothing in the universe that could be called truly inanimate. Everything that existed manifested a kind of consciousness, although in our limited view of things we would not define it as such, and all things were enveloped in a universal mind, which imbued life even to rocks and clouds. Indeed, these and all the other things in the manifested world represented the body and metabolism of an all-pervasive Spirit.

Thus, as I had come to contemplate and reflect on all of the world around me, and to interact with it, I had gained the knowledge that I was surrounded by a Life and Consciousness which was incredibly different and vastly more expansive than what my culture traditionally recognized as being alive and as having consciousness. In fact, everything that my culture had taught me about the nature of life and consciousness was inadequate. Its concepts were so warped that they were useless. The forces around me were indeed alive and possessed a consciousness, but which was very different from my own, or from the part of me that, until that first week at the lake when I was fifteen years old, I had mistakenly regarded as the totality of my being. Since then, I had grown to realize that my being was greater than I had imagined, and possessed facets that, even though they had for a time been unknown to me, were incredibly real. I came to see that it was indeed these unfamiliar facets that enabled me to perceive the awesome world around me and its inexplicable forces, and that this was the part of me that was interacting at this heightened level of perception.

The Indians who had lived at Lake Geneva centuries before I arrived perceived the universe in a way that was far more similar to my own than that of the culture in which I was living. There was much to suggest that I was in touch with a set of perceptions that, although they were intimately mine, were yet also a vital aspect of the way of life of a race or men from another time and culture. It was as if I had actually experienced a revelation, and I embraced the knowledge in my inner being that, through the working of some mystery of time and space, the path of my being had intersected with the paths of others.

I had witnessed things that were inaccessible through ordinary techniques of investigative research. I had overthrown the tyranny of the labels and suffocating definitions that had limited my views of reality. There was much more to the world than the description which my own culture had given me. I had come closer to becoming one with the essence of things, with the reality around me. The process of samyama comes to mind. Through this complex yoga technique, one becomes one with the true and ultimate essence of things; he achieves a union with them and thus perceives them in their true nature.

I experienced an intensifying distaste and repugnance for the materialistic arrogance and insensitivity of our culture, and for our view of so-called primitives. We had blundered through universes of beauty and mystery, and had never sensed what was there, or what we had missed and had not seen. We were suffocating in our own spiritual poverty, wandering insane and rootless through our own spiritual desert because we had turned our backs on our greatest inheritance and had lost our love for the beloved being that was the living world.

After some reflection, I decided that the next step in finding Negoya might be to locate some living descendants of the Potawatomi. I conferred with one of the librarians, and she suggested that I seek the guidance of her next-door neighbor. Alice Hackett was a local city historian and a member of the Lake Geneva Historical Society. I went that very day, Monday, August 24, 1981, to see if I might find her at home. I encountered her at her house, an elderly lady with sparkling eyes and an immediate friendliness. I sensed that she was an individual who would be open and empathetic to the nature of my search, so that the first thing I said to her was, "Are you a religious person?"

After a moment of surprise and reflection, she replied to me that, in her own way, she was. I began immediately to outline to her my relationship to the lake and the nature of my search. As I proceeded, I was much encouraged by her comments and interest, and I provided her with a brief, overall view of my experiences, including my readings with Robert, the psychic, and my search for Negoya.

She corroborated and amplified much of the material I had read, and discussed the visit of Chief Simon Kah-qua-dos to Lake Geneva in 1929 and the subsequent visit of members of the Potawatomi people to Lake Geneva in 1931, on the occasion of the one-hundred-year centennial celebration of the first recorded visit by white men to the lake. We also talked about the various historical Indian sites around the lake, including the spirit stones and the Seven Sacred Springs visited by Chief Kah-qua-dos in 1929, the burial site of Chief Big Foot's two wives, and the site where the body of Chief Big Foot's son had been laid to rest overlooking Lake Geneva. This story of Chief Big Foot's son held a special interest and fascination for me, and I listened with even increased attentiveness as she recounted it for me, even though I had already read it.

Alice Hackett first suggested the possibility that the intensity of my feelings for the lake, and my identification with it and with the Potawatomi people who had lived there, might strongly suggest the possibility that I had been reincarnated there in a past life.

I immediately had the distinct sensation that a mass of vague feelings and thoughts that had been floating adrift in a loosely related manner inside of me had, like pieces in a puzzle, suddenly fallen into place. If I had lived one or more past lives at the lake, it would go a long way in explaining my love for it, my empathy with the Indians who had lived there, the nature of many of my perceptions, and the fact that I had found in my own mind an Indian name, Negoya, to designate some spiritual aspect of the power there, if I could verify its origin. Alice Hackett did not try to convince me of anything, but rather pointed out that these were ideas that I should mull over in my mind. And as to the present location of any Potawatomi Indians, she suggested that I might do some research on Forest County, which was, as I later came to discover, almost the same longitude as Lake Geneva, except that it was in the extreme northern part of Wisconsin. When I returned later to the library, I noticed, in the *History and Indian Remains of Lake Geneva and Lake Como*, mention of Forest County and a town there called Blackwell. This was an area where some of the Potawatomi had gone after deserting their reservation in Kansas.

Alice Hackett also suggested that I should contact the Wisconsin State Historical Society in Madison, as they might be able to give me some additional information and leads, and she further encouraged me to go visit the Seven Sacred Springs on Big Foot Country Club in Fontana. My conversation with her had been so stimulating that I found myself overflowing with energy, and I had hoped that we could continue talking at length. But much to my disappointment, our visit was abruptly cut short when she noticed that the time had slipped away, for she was expecting some lunch guests from Ireland. I will always remember her encouraging comments to me about not being discouraged or deterred in my search by those who had no empathy for my feelings, and she admonished me not to "waste my neural energies" on such people. She really understood my love for Lake Geneva, and she even suggested that I might think some more about Chief Big Foot's son, who had also had a similarly passionate attachment to the lake. It would indeed be a romantic exercise to ponder over the possibility that I had been that boy. Time drew short, so promising to stay in touch with her, I said good-bye.

The time between my visit with Alice Hackett on Monday, August 24, and my anticipated departure from the lake midmorning, Thursday, August 27, seemed like little space to do all the work I wanted to do. Even if I had decided to go to northern Wisconsin to look for Potawatomi, the time factor would have been severely prohibitive, if not impossible. I decided that if I were ever to make that trip, it would have to be another time, because there was simply too much I needed to do at Lake Geneva.

On Alice Hackett's advice, I made some calls to the Wisconsin State Historical Society. The most concrete recommendation they could offer me was to contact James Clifton at the University of Wisconsin in Green Bay. He was not able to offer any help, although he did point out that the Potawatomi in Forest County were not descendants of those who had been inhabitants of the Lake Geneva area. I made contact with a dedicated amateur archaeologist named Pete Oehmen who lived in Williams Bay, with whom I compared notes and discussed my research. Although he was supportive, he could offer little help. However, he did refer me to a text entitled *The Winnebago Tribe* by Paul Radin (Lincoln: University of Nebraska Press, 1970). This material had been originally published as part of the Thirty-Seventh Annual Report of the Bureau of American Ethnology, Smithsonian Institution, Washington, 1923. Oehmen felt that its listings of terminology, including terms of address, clan names, and other vocabulary, and its collections of songs, religious beliefs, and other related materials, might be of some help. I examined his copy, and purchased one for myself when I returned to Louisville.

In terms of providing linguistic clues, this book proved to be of no help, inasmuch as I subsequently learned that the Winnebago language, which belonged to the Siouan language family, had little to do with the language of the Potawatomi, which was part of the Algonquian language family.

It was a remarkable coincidence that I met some people at Lake Geneva who were from Riverside, Illinois, just outside of Chicago, and who, besides being neighbors to Sarah's family, the girl whom I had dated in college for a year and a half and lost after becoming involved with Nancy during the summer of 1972, knew someone in Riverside whose father was a retired professor and an authority on the Potawatomi. This was Burt Anson, who had formerly taught American Indian history and culture at Ball State University in Muncie, Indiana. I learned, however, that Mr. Anson was not at home and that I would not be able to reach him until Labor Day.

I had very much wanted to talk with Alice Hackett again before leaving, and I telephoned her to ask if this would be possible. Her commitments to her out-of-town guests made another visit impossible, but she assured me that she would write me a letter. I received a letter from her at George Williams College Camp. Her promptness in replying to me was extremely helpful, because she retraced many of the major points of our previous conversation, and supplied me with more information, including the names of other individuals I might wish to contact, and some other literature that might prove helpful. She again advised me to visit the Seven Sacred Springs, which I had already done, but I decided to visit them once again before leaving the lake.

Of particular interest was an addendum that she had included at the end of the letter, apparently almost as an afterthought. She had included several items of vocabulary, among which were the words *negaunee* and *ishpeming,* which she said that she had heard long ago meant "heaven" and "hell," respectively. A couple of weeks later I discovered quite accidentally that Neguanee and Ishpeming were also the names of two small towns near each other, located far up in the northern part of Michigan, about fifty miles from a Potawatomi Indian reservation. I also could not help but immediately notice some similarity between Negaunee and Negoya, or Negawyuh.

What really caught my attention in Alice's addendum was that, according to Indian tradition, a thunderbird had once been sighted on Conference Point. The Point was a place of steep cliffs. Directly behind the several hundred square feet of land whose shore was graced by birch trees at the water's edge, there rose a steep slope of land, covered with trees and dense shrubbery, and which at a certain height leveled off to become a gently rising knob covered with grass and majestic trees. It was in this dramatic setting that the Indian legend told of a special happening.

Someone else, in another time and culture, had seen something there that perhaps was as extraordinary as what I had seen. Every culture and every religion has had different symbols that express realities which are otherwise inexpressible. The

Indians had the thunderbirds, eagle-like spirits whose eyes flashed lightning and who dwelt in the heavens. Christianity still employed angels, man-like spirits with long robes and wings on their backs. Some Christians believe in literal angels. Perhaps others do not. But this is not what is of central importance, any more than whether or not the Indians believed in literal thunderbirds. With respect to the Indians, I would be cautious in underestimating their sensibleness.

Conference Point was a place where someone else had also witnessed something that was spiritually significant. They had come into contact with some kind of noumenal reality, perhaps a power or some kind of entity. Perhaps this manifestation they saw came from the astral world or from some higher plane. And whatever its true nature, it was seen in the mind of the person who witnessed it as something that was a part of their religious view, and which fit the pattern of their concepts of the higher worlds. They had called it a thunderbird. Likewise, I had witnessed an event of a similar nature and had become part of that event. It had changed my life. I had seen what looked like a man, enshrouded in brilliant white light and suspended above the waters of the Point. He appeared to have manifested through some kind of hole or warp in space. At the time I had witnessed that event, I did not know if what I saw was really a man, or if he was actually clothed in such a manner. But that is how my conscious mind received the impressions of whatever was out there, as they were transmitted to my personal awareness through some inner faculty of cognition. And any student of the occult knows that the astral plane is conceived of as a kind of medium that is fluid and which, unlike the more dense material plane, is constantly in a state of change and susceptible to the vibrations of thought. It is therefore malleable in the sense that the fine matter which comprises it is capable of assuming the shape and image of the thought forms which one projects into it. This is the mechanism by which one can see and interpret visions in a way which makes them comprehensible to the conscious mind.

I had determined that I would visit two of the sites described in the *History and Indian Remains of Lake Geneva and Lake Como*. One was the Seven Sacred Springs on Big Foot Country Club in Fontana, and the other was the site of the spirit stones on Cedar Point. Big Foot Country Club presented no problem to locate. The site of the seven pools, although I am sure that it was vastly different in appearance from what it had been one hundred fifty years ago, due to the clearing and modern landscaping which had taken place, was nevertheless enchanting. The natural topography had created the pools in such a way that they were graciously spaced and beautifully terraced at different levels. In spite of the fact that they were now surrounded by a golf course and near a clubhouse, I immediately experienced a sensation of delight in being there, near to them; a strange, yet intensely pleasurable fascination and profound peacefulness. Whatever the reason, I again experienced that unique feeling of coming to rest.

The site of the spirit stones proved to be elusive. I made three separate trips to find them, one on foot in the driving rain, and two by car. I was finally forced to assume that the stones had been moved to another location, probably as the result of some landscaping or development effort.

I was also interested in visiting the site that was reputedly where Chief Big Foot had placed the body of his son to rest. Although I went to Fontana and questioned a number of people, I was not successful in locating it. But even though I failed, I am convinced that the site was in the general area where I had searched. There was supposedly a plaque commemorating the spot.

Negoya had still remained unidentified, but in searching for him, I had encountered a whole new world of possibilities I had never imagined a year ago. Although as yet I had no conclusive proof, the idea that I had spent one or more past lives as an Indian in the Lake Geneva area was provocative. But it was more than that. It was unsettling, because I was experiencing that nervousness which is characteristic of one who feels himself on the verge of a momentous discovery. I realized that I had possibly found a clue to the thread of my existence as it wove its way through a chain of successive lives, meeting more and more experiences. It felt exactly right, and as I said before, something inside of me seemed to settle into place, to find resolution. So much of the emptiness and feeling of loss I had known seemed to have been reconciled. Had I found myself?

Who was Negoya? Was my longing due to some feeling that I had lost contact with him, at least for a time, in this life? Was he a god, a force, some elemental being, or perhaps a man? Had he been my physical father in another life, or perhaps my teacher or guide? I felt close to a great truth, yet I had a host of unanswered questions over which to ponder. These thoughts filled my mind as I savored my remaining time at Lake Geneva.

Whenever I visited Lake Geneva, it was almost always my custom to visit Conference Point just before departing. My final day at the lake arrived, and I found myself at the top of the concrete steps which led down to the Point, and after pausing there for a few moments I descended part of the way, to the small brick alcove in the side of the hill where I paused to sit down and reflect further on the sights and sounds of the Point, and to absorb its power.

I eventually arose from my seat and descended the rest of the way to the bottom of the steps, where I stepped out onto the ground of the Point and slowly approached the water. I sat for a bit at several different locations along the edge of the water, and briefly stood atop the large granite boulder a few yards down the shore path. I breathed deeply and repeatedly the invigorating air from the lake, and listened intently to the voices of the waves, hearing their messages with my body as I stood motionless near the swaying birches and glistening rocks. I told the Point and the lake of my everlasting love for it. I asked for its guidance and protection, and I prayed that it would draw me back to it as it had always done. I asked it never to let me go, and thanked it for the matchless gifts it had bestowed upon me. I released the totality of my being to be filled by it, and as I surveyed its beauty one last time, I said farewell to that shining Being and turned away.

Without looking back, I approached the concrete steps and slowly made my ascent. As I made my way to the top and started away, I felt so much sadness in leaving there that I became almost physically ill. I felt very hot, and it was as if there was a great weight pressing down upon me. But I knew that there was no way to avoid that inevitable moment, so I continued on to my car and was soon gone.

Thus it was that I left Lake Geneva midmorning on Thursday, August 27, 1981, for South Bend, Indiana, to visit and consult with Jerry Alber, who was living there. When he visited me in Louisville a few weeks previously, in early July, I had agreed that I would try to stop and visit him on my way home from the lake in August. I had soon passed through the town of Williams Bay, where I caught a final look at the lake, and then through the town of Lake Geneva, and I found myself driving east, in the direction of Lake Michigan. I had only to drive a distance of a few miles in order to perceive a dramatic change in the environment and in my perceptions and feelings, and I had no way of knowing then that I would finally be given the answers to the reasons for this familiar state of mind within a couple of weeks. As I drove farther from the lake, I felt surrounded by death, and I experienced a suffocation within my spirit which profoundly affected even my physical body, making it feel like a dead weight. Everything around me, the trees and fields, the sky and the clouds, the farmhouses, and all else seemed characterized by a horrible inertia, an absence of motion, or vibration; a lack of energy, an absence of psychic life. It was ugly, and I felt sick inside. Everything around me became pale, dimensionless, lifeless phenomena in comparison with the living fountain of consciousness from which I had just come. I found myself moving through a sterile and meaningless dream that had none of the magic of a dream.

As I drove south, into and through Chicago, it was as if what I perceived around me was an enormous funeral. The people were dead. The buildings and automobiles and endless acres of roadway, steel, and concrete, all were monuments of this vista of death, draped with a heavy, lifeless sky, stifled by chemicals and filled with filth and stench. The air was worse than being merely unfit to breathe. It was, as was all else around me, the very antithesis of life. I tried not to focus my attention on any of it, but instead to center my consciousness somewhere inside of myself. Strange, how often in the past I had visited that city and enjoyed its life and found it exciting. But such perceptions were all relative, and I had come from a world of true life and power.

I arrived that afternoon in South Bend, Indiana, to find it completely typical and representative of the abortion known as the large, midwestern town. It could easily have been any one of a thousand such towns. Its name was completely irrelevant. Its one and only redeeming attribute was the fact that my friend, Jerry Alber, lived there, and during my brief visit with him he listened patiently as I told him of my perceptions and feelings with regard to Lake Geneva, and I was comforted by his understanding and empathy. For I know very well that, among all the souls in my life, he was one of a very few who would really come close to understanding what was inside of me. I reluctantly left him the following morning, Friday, August 28, 1981, although I looked forward to being reunited with my wife, Suzanne, and I drove south toward Louisville, Kentucky.

Late in the afternoon I could see Louisville ahead of me, just across the Ohio River, and as I got within a short distance of crossing the river into Kentucky, my senses were assaulted with another wall of stagnant filth and heat. My frame of mind deteriorated even more. I crossed the river into the center of the city, and as I sat at a red traffic signal light, I looked at the faces on the street corner. As I surveyed those blank, lifeless countenances, with their empty, lusterless eyes, the tears welled up in my eyes. The desolation seemed complete. This was hell.

Although many of my returns from the lake were characterized by similar feelings, they were particularly acute that time, and I spent the next several days pursuing what seemed like meaningless and frustrating routines, while trying to make some kind of emotional readjustment to the traumatic impact of my return to that poisoned and lifeless world. Concerning my writing, I was not sure which direction to pursue first, but I knew that I must somehow keep working at it at all costs, if I was at least going to remain "alive" inside. Again, I remembered Robert's admonitions about my pursuing the goal of writing this book, and I understood then in an even deeper way the truth in what he had said to me.

I had been trying to conceive and assess all possible ways in which I could go about furthering my research with respect to the nature and identity of Negoya. I listed all of the other avenues of investigation I could think of. I had even considered having another reading with Robert, the psychic, to see if he could furnish me with more definite information, but all of my attempts to locate him were unsuccessful. He had discontinued his answering service in Chicago, and all of his acquaintances in Louisville and Chicago were unable to help me. *The Winnebago Tribe* had proven useless in any linguistic sense, because the languages of the Winnebago and the Potawatomi were remote from each other. The extent of facilities and personnel in Louisville seemed to make any systematic research there highly improbable.

My wife knew of an extraordinary psychic in California, who did readings under the name of Lazaris, and who did consultations by telephone as well as in person. I was considering availing myself of his services if nothing else materialized, although I had come to view any psychic assistance as a last resort, certainly not because of any lack of faith on my part, but because I felt that to acquire the information I was seeking through more traditional and documentable means would make my case more tenable and strengthen its credibility. I also had the option of trying to locate some of the living descendants of the Potawatomi with the possibility of interviewing them, which seemed a more viable course of action, although I was not sure where to start and realized that this avenue of research would probably entail some extensive efforts. When I had stopped to visit Jerry Alber in South Bend, he had shown me a book written by a woman who had performed and documented hypnotic regressions on many individuals to enable them to recall aspects of their past lives, and I was also assessing the feasibility of undergoing this kind of process.

As far as identifying Negoya, I decided that my next immediate step was to make contact with Burt Anson in Muncie, Indiana, and although I telephoned his residence every day after returning from Lake Geneva, I was fairly certain that I would not be able to reach him until at least September 7. In the meantime, I worked primarily on updating my accounts of my searches for Negoya, from the time of my reading with Robert, the psychic, up through my last visit to Lake Geneva.

On September 8, I reached Burt Anson by telephone, and after waiting for over two weeks to speak with him, I was disappointed that he had virtually nothing to say. In fact, I did not have the opportunity to explain what I was looking for. I did manage to learn from him that he had been working on a book about the Potawatomi, and that after his retirement he had ceased to pursue this endeavor. He had turned all of his notes over to Dr. Elizabeth Glenn, an anthropologist at Ball State University in Muncie, and knowing that I was interested in learning about the Potawatomi, Mr. Anson referred me to her.

I was able to reach Dr. Glenn that day. She listened patiently as I explained to her that, both for personal reasons and for the purpose of writing a book about my experiences, I was intent on learning about the Potawatomi Indians, particularly their language and religion. I found her very kind and interested, and she talked for some time, supplying me with a list of references and the name of a man who lived in Fort Wayne, Indiana, who was a Potawatomi and, as she referred to him, a "Medawinne," or someone who actively practiced their religion. In speaking with Dr. Glenn, I realized again the need for caution in accepting as truth the information which I was compiling as a result of my contact with various individuals and with numerous written sources. For instance, she rightly commented on the erroneous notion which I had previously held that the language of the Potawatomi was "closely related, almost virtually interchangeable with that of the Winnebago." The Potawatomi language was a member of the Algonquian language family, and the Winnebago language was far removed, falling into the Siouan language family.

Dr. Glenn had taken my address, and a couple of weeks later I received an extensive list of references pertaining to the Potawatomi that she had kindly obtained for me. Early that same evening, Tuesday, September 8, 1981, after having gotten his telephone number, I was able to reach the Potawatomi in Fort Wayne. Although the last name he used was French and although he had an American first name, I shall refer to him as "Shupshe," which was his Potawatomi name.

I introduced myself and told him very briefly about my background. I spoke about my deep interest in the Potawatomi language and religion, and about my experiences at Lake Geneva, including the shining figure I had seen there many years earlier. I felt that he immediately understood the meaning of everything I said. I asked him if he might know a word like "Negoya," and to my surprise he replied that he knew what it meant and to what it referred. He did not elaborate, but he said that it was related to the term, "Negale," or "Neegal," which in turn was related to the term, "nagual," which is found frequently in the books by Carlos Castaneda that I have frequently mentioned, and which describe his relationship and experiences with a Yaqui Indian sorcerer named don Juan Matus. As I have said, I had studied all of Castaneda's works as they had appeared over the years, and I had found much in them that seemed to be along the same lines as many of my own experiences. In fact, the system of knowledge Castaneda had described in his accounts had been the one with which I could most closely identify, out of all the various systems of thought I had studied. Therefore, I was quite familiar with the term "nagual." Don Juan was often referred to as the nagual by those who were his apprentices in sorcery. He was their teacher, and the key, or the embodiment of the world of the nagual, which was that mysterious and undefinable part of existence whose power lay beyond the reach of the "tonal," that aspect of our mind and being which was concerned with objective knowledge and labels.

Shupshe went on to speak about his ideas concerning reincarnation and the nature of time and the universe, and that it was possible for me to have come into contact with another world, or dimension. Although I cannot recall everything we talked about, partly due to my state of excitement, this was the general content and tone of our first communication. He also provided me with the name of Joseph Migwanabe, who lived in Wilson, Michigan, a Potawatomi who taught the language and who was an expert in it.

I was very impressed with Shupshe. Here was an individual who was descended from an American Indian tribe and whose English was in its structure and enunciation far superior to the sloppy speech habits of most individuals. He was of high intelligence, and a man of unusual directness and honesty. But as impressed as I was with his obvious refinement and knowledge, I did not realize or even suspect the far more unique and amazing aspects of his being until we met face to face.

It was not always easy to get interviews with Indians, and I had asked Dr. Glenn if she felt that Shupshe would grant me one, to which she replied that she was not sure, and that it would depend upon the circumstances. So it was to my surprise and delight when Shupshe introduced the idea of my coming to see him and talking "man-to-man." In fact, he seemed to regard my visit as a foregone conclusion.

He explained that he was a "Medawinne;" that is, one who practices the "Medae," or "Midé," according to the French version. The "Medawinne," or "Midewiwin," as it is often referred to, although Shupshe was clear in his assertion that the former version was more correct, was the "Grand Medicine Lodge." "Winne" referred to action or doing, and the "Medae" was the context or framework within which the action or doing was performed. As a practicing Medawinne, Shupshe was, in other words, a "medicine man." He himself was a Medawinne of the fourth, or highest, degree. Only when I talked with him face to face was I able to perceive the implications and manifestations of this fact.

I wanted to see Shupshe as soon as possible, and drove to Fort Wayne, Indiana, on the morning of September 11 to meet him at his home. I estimated him to be in his mid-sixties. I learned from him later that he had worked for a railroad company for over forty years, and that he was now retired, so he must have been at least that old. If he was older, his appearance certainly did not indicate it. I had coffee with him and his wife while they ate breakfast, after which he wasted no time in ushering me into his den. We talked for five hours without any break. His den, where we first sat and talked, had a large window that looked out into his back yard, where there was a vegetable garden. There was also another "garden" there, which was comprised of various plants and carefully positioned stones, and which was divided into four separate sections by two intersecting pathways which formed the shape of an "x," or a cross. I observed another area in his back yard which he referred to as his "altar."

The altar was comprised of two shallow pits positioned on an east-west axis, several feet apart, and which were designed to accommodate small fires. Rounded stones of various sizes were arranged in piles near the fire pits. On at least one of these piles was placed a similarly rounded stone that was somewhat hollow on top. Shupshe explained that he had fashioned the hollow in the stone for the purpose of placing offerings of tobacco there. There were two other structures that comprised part of the overall plan of the altar. One was a sturdy pole anchored in the ground above the westernmost fire pit, along the same east-west axis. Several feet above the ground, another member was fastened to it, parallel to the ground, giving the structure the general appearance of a cross. It was painted white, and was decorated with at least two other colors, which were red and green. I do not remember if there were other colors as well. At the juncture of the two members comprising this structure was hung some kind of colored cloth or ribbon. Below the easternmost fire pit, along the same east-west axis, was another pole, which was shorter and thinner than the other one. I seem to remember the principal colors of this pole as being red and green. Near the top of this pole was a hole, perhaps five feet above the ground, which was designed so that one should stand east of the pole, and look through it to the west. Shupshe told me that if one looked through the hole in this manner it was possible to see the future. One night, several days after I had been to Fort Wayne to visit Shupshe, I had a strange and disturbingly intense dream, or a vision, in which I saw some kind of geometrical forms or figures, comprised of the same three colors which I had seen on the poles of Shupshe's altar; that is, green, red, and white. These colored forms moved about in front of me, in various patterns beyond my ability to understand, but they seemed peculiarly animated, as if, in some mysterious way, they were alive. I awoke abruptly from this vision and was disoriented. I experienced a mildly alarming sensation that there was some kind of presence near me, perhaps trying to contact me.

Shupshe's comments about Lake Geneva itself were of enormous significance. He explained that, both through his involvement in his own esoteric tradition and through the vehicle of his own individual psychic powers, he had personal knowledge that Lake Geneva was a center of great power. Here at last, after seventeen years, was another individual who truly understood what I had perceived at the lake, who not merely empathized with me and lent me his understanding, but who actually knew what I was talking about. Shupshe said that there were many such places of power in the world, and that men often built great monuments on those locations. He cited the impressive structures erected by the Mayans and the Aztecs. He said that the power at Lake Geneva was centered somewhere out over the water itself, and that if anyone had ever figured out how to erect a temple out over open water, they probably would have done so there. He felt that anyone with true psychic development and abilities should be able to go to the lake and sense something unusual there. He explained the manifestation of power around the lake in terms of a combination of conditions and factors, such as the belt of electromagnetic forces which flowed over the earth at that point, the atmosphere and the layer of ozone, and how it interacted with the cosmic and solar rays which entered the atmosphere at a particular angle there and struck the earth. His explanation and comments were more detailed than this, but my memory is not entirely adequate. I further learned that the exact focal point for the concentration of this power would be expected to fluctuate somewhat, perhaps as much as several miles, due to the slight wobble of the earth as it rotated on its axis. I asked him if various geological conditions and other factors would ensure that Lake Geneva would always be a place of power, or for how long. He said that, although the focus of power moved about somewhat, it would be in that area for the duration of this epoch. He did not elaborate as to how much time, according to his thinking, comprised an epoch, but it was clear that he meant it would endure there for a considerable span of geological time.

Shupshe's explanations and descriptions of the manifestations of power in the Lake Geneva area immediately answered some fundamental questions that had plagued me for years. Although, over the years, as my experiences at Lake Geneva had evolved, I had become more intuitively certain that there did exist a real power there, outside of my own mind and emotional ties with the area, I nevertheless found myself confronted at times with the question as to whether or not my experiences and perceptions there were largely or even solely a projection of my own consciousness; that is, if the environment around me was somehow just mirroring back to me the content of my inner being which I was projecting outward onto the world. I was not so much concerned as to whether or not the experiences I found there were ultimately real, as opposed to merely imaginary, although this question occasionally plagued me also, but rather, how much of all of it was coming from inside of me as opposed to there being some concrete, objective causes in the environment.

I had also found another possibility regarding another dilemma. Shupshe had said that the exact focal point of the power in the area of the lake might fluctuate as much as several miles. Reflecting on this, I recalled that there was never an occasion on which I visited the lake without sensing to some degree the forces there, but that from trip to trip, over the years and during different periods of the year, I certainly seemed to experience fluctuations in the intensity and accessibility of that power and its presence. Although I am certain that this was due, at least in part, and more so at certain times than at others, to the instability of my own psychic receptivity and mental states, I am also convinced that, at least on some occasions, I truly did perceive fluctuations of power. I realized that this was due to the fact that the power moved about to a degree. Thus, I remembered that during one short visit which I made to the lake the presence there seemed to be almost totally veiled. I felt it, and yet I was cut off from it. At other times I would go to the lake and my sensations of the power and presence would become apparent even several miles from the lake, and by the time I got close enough to the lake to catch my first glimpse of its waters, I felt as if I were witnessing a world of pure and limitless magic. Thus, from trip to trip, I might understandably sense power as much as several miles from the lake, as well as close to it. Because of my contact with Shupshe, I had thus obtained answers to some significant questions.

I sometimes marvelled over the circuitous course of events that had finally led me to Shupshe. Had I not found him, I might never have learned all that I did, and he himself said that I could have talked with anthropologists and linguists and even with Potawatomi Indians for the rest of my life and possibly never learned anything about Lake Geneva or Negoya. I reasoned that, had I not gone to Lake Geneva during precisely the week that I did, I would not have met with people there who were visiting friends from Riverside, Illinois, and I would not have gotten the lead to telephone their friends through whom I was guided to Dr. Elizabeth Glenn, and finally to Shupshe. For that matter, none of it would ever have happened if I had not met Robert. And yet Shupshe told me that he believed I was led to him, and that had I not found him in the manner which I did, I would have gotten there through some other set of circumstances.

In order for me to present Shupshe's explanation in its fullest light, it will first be appropriate for me to go back to my initial visit to Lake Geneva, in August, 1964, when I was fifteen years old, and recapitulate my experiences there. My life was forever altered that week. Until that time, my life could have been characterized as fairly ordinary. And then one day, at the lake, I had simply overheard a fragment of a conversation spoken by Margaret Patton, that very new acquaintance of mine, to another person. They had not even been talking to me, and I have absolutely no idea what the rest of their conversation was about. But I had picked up something about "God in nature," and that was all. By hearing those few words, my world had been changed forever. I had experienced a sensation that was literally as if a light had been turned on in my head. I wondered continuously at this new idea, and I talked about it often with my friend, Margaret. I asked her how I would go about finding this great Presence in nature, and she told me to go off by myself, perhaps along the edge of the water or among the trees, and to be very quiet inside myself; to ask for guidance, and to listen and wait.

That is exactly what I did. I went off alone and sat on the rocks by the edge of the water, near the Point, and within my mind I had called out, very calmly, for something to guide me. One might have called my act of reaching out a prayer, although I did not then, nor do I now, necessarily think of it as such. And reaching out from within myself, I had simply asked for truth. I was totally intent on knowing Reality, whatever it might be. And if I were to find that Reality was ugly, or hideous, or evil, I still wanted it. If Reality was despair and emptiness, or Hell itself, I still wished to know it, because above all I did not want to be deceived. I did not want to believe something that was not real. I wanted truth, whatever it might be, and I was prepared for anything.

I used all of my free time to meditate, usually near the water. Each time I had done so, my perceptions were opened more. I was a serious pianist by the age of fifteen. My training as a pianist and musician, and my love for music, were instrumental in providing me with an approach to listening to the world around me. This was true not only in terms of listening to the world, but also in terms of "feeling" it deeply within myself, and seeing its every movement and variation. As the days passed, there was a truth which was progressively revealed to me, a great and inexpressibly beautiful truth. For when I had asked to know truth, and reality, there was opened and shown to me a world of the purest and most unimaginable beauty. I had found, within the great being of nature, the Eternal Being, and I came to know a love of measureless dimensions. I had perceived the creation and my own small being to be enveloped in it, to be moving and breathing upon a boundless sea of it.

Each time I meditated, I found more, and my joy deepened. I perceived the order and harmony and the infinite variety in the rhythms of nature. I sensed the eternally unfolding expression of cosmic law, through the endless rolling in of the waves upon the shores, and through the procession of day and night; through the infinite facets of the pulsing, breathing metabolism of nature. I saw the harmony and brotherhood of all things; how the trees and grasses and waves and the distant stars were all brothers, and how they perpetually rejoiced in the expression of the one great Presence in all things. And I came to know that the world and the universe were truly and fully alive. Creation was a living and conscious thing, dancing, vibrating in time and space to the cosmic rhythm, and expressing the incredible love which permeated it.

My perceptions of the phenomena in the universe around me became progressively more profound, as if my mind was penetrating into deeper and deeper aspects of the manifested world. The labels of things gradually melted away, and I learned that the artificial definitions of things I had previously accepted had obscured the true nature of everything in the world. Trees and rocks and all else became pure being. In relationship to the manifested universe, the concept, "inanimate," lost all of its meaning, because I saw that everything was alive. My joyous perceptions of objects and phenomena deepened, and I came to see beyond or through them. Thus, I found myself moving in an ocean of consciousness, enveloped in a love which was dimensions beyond all the kinds of love that I had ever known.

Those experiences during that first week at Lake Geneva culminated on the evening of those mysterious and dynamic events that brought me to the Point and opened my being to its highest and most intense perceptions, when I witnessed the presence of that shining figure over the surface of the lake.

I learned from Shupshe that this shining being was Negoya. As Shupshe had known about Lake Geneva and its power, he had likewise immediately known, during our first telephone conversation, the identity of Negoya. As was true of his knowledge of the lake, he had also recognized Negoya and understood his significance both through the context of his own particular esoteric tradition and through his own individual psychic powers. The being whom I had seen at the Point was an Indian; that is, he had been an Indian during his physical lifetime, before he had died and passed on to a higher world. I was somewhat surprised to learn that he had not been a Potawatomi, but rather an Ojibwa. The Potawatomi, the Ojibwa, and the Ottawa were once one people, which was confirmed by Shupshe. Thus, the Potawatomi were the "Fire Builder Nation," of the "Builders of the Sacred Fire," for the three Indian nations; that is, the Potawatomi, the Ojibwa, or Chippewa, and the Ottawa. Although they are classified as three separate Indian nations, Shupshe stated that even in these times they thought of themselves as one people. Thus, the close interrelationship between these three tribes made it of no great difference that the being which I saw had been an Ojibwa, rather than a Potawatomi.

Like Shupshe, Negoya had also been a fourth degree Medawinne, or medicine man. Shupshe did not tell me exactly where he had lived, but I believe that it would not have been around the area of the lake, but probably farther north. It occurred to me that he might have moved about during his lifetime. Shupshe told me that, with respect to his spirit form, his location in the higher worlds would shift in relation to the lake. Shupshe identified his physical life span on the earth as having been around the earlier part of the 1400s, and claimed that the Potawatomi were in the Lake Geneva area at that time. He further told me that he himself had seen and read some of the writings and songs that this Medawinne had written, and that they were recorded on scrolls made of tree bark, and were referred to as the Winna-bow-gah-sh scrolls. When I asked him where these scrolls were located, he said that he dared not answer. Shupshe also confirmed my assumption that the spirit form I saw had died a normal physical death and entered a higher plane of existence, manifesting in that state some five hundred years later.

When I questioned Shupshe about his personal knowledge of this being, he replied that this question required too long an explanation. Shupshe explained that I had heard the name of this Medawinne in my mind somewhat differently than he would pronounce it himself, but he emphatically and repeatedly assured me that this was of no consequence whatsoever, and that I should in no way be concerned about it. He explained that this "distortion" was due to the particular characteristics and idiosyncrasies of the Ojibwas language, such as the fact that the guttural nature of the pronunciation of this entity's name would make it very difficult for me to reproduce accurately. It did not fit the patterns of speech and pronunciation to which I was accustomed, and it was therefore justifiable to conclude that my mind would have reinterpreted somewhat these sounds that found their way into my psyche. I found this to be a tenable explanation, and I reflected further that the singularly dramatic and turbulent circumstances surrounding my vision might also have contributed to my having heard his name in a distorted manner. I find it interesting to note also that, as far as my conscious mind was concerned, I was not "aware" of this word until some indeterminable amount of time after the actual experience had taken place. The name, Negoya, may have remained submerged in my subconscious mind two years or more before surfacing. Again, considering the impact and intensity of my original vision, and the overwhelming stimuli that simultaneously flooded my being, it is clearly understandable how the psychically perceived term, Negoya, would have entered my mind only at a subliminal level at the time of my experiences.

Shupshe went on to compare the terms Negoya and Negale, the title he himself used for this Ojibwa Medawinne. The first syllable of each term, that is, "ne," was identical. He explained that if the "a" in "Negale" was uttered in a guttural manner which was typical of Indian pronunciation, rather than in the manner typical of English pronunciation, it would approximate the second syllable, or "go," of Negoya, or Negawyuh. This, then, would leave only the third and last syllable of these two terms to consider, the somewhat blurry nature of which he likewise attributed to the guttural nature of Indian speech and to the other factors which I have cited above. He was so certain that it was the spirit of this being I had seen and whose name I had heard that I believe he considered the above explanation not only justifiable, but almost inconsequential.

Shupshe proceeded to explain to me further about Negoya, or, as he wrote my word, Nee-go-yáh. At Shupshe's suggestion, I shall continue to refer to this Medawinne as Negoya, as I have done in the past. Since I had somewhat reinterpreted the term from the manner in which Shupshe would actually have pronounced it, I asked him how I should therefore designate and address this being. He was convinced that I should feel free and right to call him by the name just as I had heard it in my own mind. The name I had psychically perceived was a title given to him by an older member of his tribe, somewhat later during his life and after he had reached a certain level of advancement. Although his title could be interpreted in somewhat different ways, it connoted or carried with it the meaning of spiritual guide, and in this sense it was related to nagual, the term Castaneda used. In Castaneda's works, Don Juan was sometimes referred to as the nagual by his apprentices, and he was their teacher, and the key to the mysterious power which existed in the world. Shupshe stated further that the title, Negoya, could be interpreted as meaning something like "I go before you," or, "I extend my hand to you."

Thus, the sense of a spiritual guide was strongly implied, and I felt that it was in this sense that, according to the assertions of Robert, the psychic, Negoya meant "father." I also recalled the similarity between "Ne-gaw-yuh" and "Ne-gau-sim," a word I had come across that past August at Lake Geneva, which was supposedly a designation for head chief. Again, there seemed to be an underlying connection in terms of similarity of meaning, which conveyed a sense of a spiritual guide with paternalistic overtones. I considered that Negoya might even have been my spiritual teacher in a former life. Had I been an Indian at one time, under his guidance? He had certainly been a spiritual guide to me in my present life. It was even possible that I could have lived as an Indian during his lifetime and known him, and been reincarnated as an Indian again during the period between that time and the time of this present life. I could have had contact with him in one life and still lived another life after that, as a Potawatomi on Lake Geneva.

Aside from these speculations, there were many questions concerning Negoya churning about inside my head. I asked Shupshe if he had also had another name. He replied affirmatively, saying that it was "Esh-gee-bow-gah," but he did not elaborate. How had Negoya heard my call for guidance and for a vision of truth, and how he had come to manifest himself to me? What was the nature of the circumstances under which he had been able to do this?

Shupshe pointed out that I had had my vision of Negoya at a time in my life when I was particularly sensitive and open to various psychic and spiritual influences. My mind and spirit had not yet become encumbered with the multitude of responsibilities and distractions that encroach upon an individual as he enters the world of adult responsibilities. Nevertheless, this is not to say that I had a shallow attitude about life at that time, for I was intensely serious about things. The fact that Lake Geneva was in and of itself a place of unique power was unquestionably an important factor in my experiences also.

Shupshe was uniquely qualified to explain these matters to me, because he was, just as Negoya had been, a fourth degree Medawinne. Therefore, they shared common esoteric traditions. Just as Shupshe had in various ways demonstrated that he possessed psychic powers, Negoya had heard the silent psychic call that I had sent forth as I sat near the shores of Lake Geneva. Shupshe stated that Negoya's realm of existence was in the astral world, and therefore his locale would shift in relation to Lake Geneva. And yet, he was in some metaphysical sense nearby.

Shupshe explained that his esoteric traditions embodied the concepts of parallel and overlapping worlds and times. His system of beliefs asserted that time, rather than being a "line," as it is often thought of, was rather a "spiral," and that these spirals of different worlds of time sometimes came into contact with one another, and that it was possible to travel from one world into the other and to return. He showed me a wooden Indian pipe, upon which had been carved a series of spirals, which he said were symbolic of these spiral worlds. Anyone who has ever read the works of metaphysicians like P. D. Ouspensky and Rodney Collin would be immediately struck by the similarity between their theories of time and space and the nature of the universe, and the concepts which Shupshe communicated to me. As one's consciousness evolves to a state of being capable of perceiving the world in more than three dimensions, his concept of the nature of time changes dramatically, and he would come to perceive time and the universe much in the same way that Shupshe described it.

Shupshe further elucidated that the tremendous astral energy that would have surrounded Negoya during those dynamic moments would have made him appear to be clothed in an intense white light.

During my intense experiences at the Point, Negoya had clearly accomplished two dramatic things, as well as having stepped across space and time from his world into mine. He was instrumental in altering my consciousness and accelerating my perceptions, and he exercised a powerful influence over the forces of nature. Negoya had appeared to me during the most climactic moments of my perceptions. My consciousness had been accelerated to a tremendously intensified level of vibration.

During those thrilling moments, the natural forces around me became dramatically turbulent. The force of the wind increased to a driving velocity, violently agitating the waters around the Point and dashing the waves against the rocks with escalating force. The trees around me bent and hissed. After Negoya ceased to appear to me, and as my experience subsided and my consciousness returned to a more normal level of vibration, the forces in the physical world around me also became progressively subdued and calm. Negoya's presence catalyzed this occurrence. Shupshe was in total agreement about this, and he told me about certain powers which he himself could and had exercised over the forces in nature.

I also discussed Conference Point with Shupshe, and I cited that portion of Alice Hackett's letter to me which dealt specifically with that place. I have reproduced it below.

Conference Point, Lake Geneva, is "A-ka-do-wa-be-win," referring to a steep rock or cliff. A thunderbird is said to have alighted there (Brown and Brown, 1928, page 199).
    Found in *The Wisconsin Archaeologist,* bound copies of quantities, March-June 1952, borrowed from Milwaukee Library. "Indian Place Names," researched by Dr. Herbert W. Kuhn

Shupshe seemed to feel that the term, "A-ka-do-wa-be-win," and the accompanying commentary, "referring to a steep rock or cliff," were acceptable. Since Conference Point was a place of meditation and extraordinary experience for me, and a domain of real power, I had been most interested to learn also that, allegedly, a thunderbird is said to have alighted there. Again, Shupshe accepted the plausibility of this statement. With regard to this statement about the thunderbird and

Conference Point, I was interested in the fact that it was that spot to which I had always been particularly attracted from the very beginning of my experiences at Lake Geneva, probably through the vehicle of my own intuition and by a combination of other forces. And I was further struck by the fact that Conference Point was the site where I had had my vision of Negoya.

I was also interested to know whether or not the various information I had accumulated pertaining to the Potawatomi language was accurate, for I had learned to be cautious with respect to this. We did not discuss this subject in great detail. However, I did point out to him, for instance, that I had been told that *negaunee* meant "heaven" and that *ne-gau-sim,* as well as *ne-gas-sun,* and *oh-ne-gas-sun,* among other terms, were words which designated the head chief of the tribe, according to the information I found in *History and Indian Remains of Lake Geneva and Lake Como.* After everything Shupshe had told me, I had noted the similarity, for example, between the first two syllables of the terms, Negoya, Negale, *ne-gau-sim,* and *negaunee,* and I had wondered if these latter two terms were indeed accurate and, if so, if some or all of these terms were, as I had conjectured, then functionally related in some way. Shupshe responded by asserting that the word for "chief" was *ogima,* and that the term for "heaven" was *wau kwing.* His assertion, therefore, was that the terms which I had recorded—that is, *ne-gau-sim* for "chief" and *negaunee* for "heaven," were inaccurate. I could only assume either that these terms which I had come across were from some language other than Potawatomi, or that they had been inaccurately recorded or passed down, because of faulty interpretation. I asked Shupshe if he felt that it would be worth my while to consult someone about these matters, and I mentioned Joseph Migwanabe, who lived in Wilson, Michigan, the Potawatomi whom Shupshe had referred me to as a teacher of that language and an expert in it. Shupshe stated that he saw no valid reason for me to carry my research about these linguistic matters any further. And indeed, since I had met him and learned what I had about Negoya, it seemed somewhat irrelevant for me to do so. He listed for me several Potawatomi words and their meanings, which I have reproduced below.

nah-dun-meow	to defend
nee-bee-sh	water
nee-bin	summer
nee-boo	dead
nee-gahn	front
nee-gahn-ah-yah	ahead
nee-gee	friend
nee-gee-wee-dun-ah-wah	I tell him how

I noted the similarity between *nee-bee-sh,* or "water," which was on the list of terms with which Shupshe had provided me, and *maung-zet-ne-biss,* or "Big Foot Lake." It might appear from this that one could, through equating *nee-bee-sh* with *ne-biss,* translate *maung-zet-ne-biss* as something like "Big Foot Water" or "Big Foot's Water." Extremely rigid and literal translations are sometimes inadequate or clumsy, and fail to capture subtleties that are often present. But I think that, with a disciplined imagination and some common sense, one can probably make some intelligent inferences. Nevertheless, I have also realized all along the difficulty of Indian languages, and the inherent danger of absorbing various inaccuracies. I was thus relieved to accept the authority of Shupshe, a Potawatomi Indian, concerning such matters, for I felt somewhat uncomfortable in making inferences on my own, and that such linguistic work was better left to professionals. My work in this area has not always been accurate, but I feel it should be included to convey the nature and scope of the search that I pursued for the purpose of arriving at something conclusive regarding Negoya.

During my interview with Shupshe, I asked him many other questions, many of which related to himself or to the Potawatomi Indians. I was interested to learn whether or not there was a longer version of his Potawatomi name. He explained that his complete name was "Shupshe Wahnah," which means "Vision of a Lion." I was quite interested in Shupshe's ideas about the Potawatomi and their relationship to the Wisconsin area, which included Lake Geneva. I was surprised to learn that he traced his descendants around the Wisconsin area as far back as five thousand years. When I asked him if they were called something else then, his only reply was, "no."

We had been talking about various behavioral traits and attitudes of the white men, and he commented that another Indian had once made the following observation; namely, that the white men had managed to absolve themselves of all responsibility by means of three inventions: government, religion, and the flush toilet.

I offer below portions of the letter I wrote to Shupshe on Saturday, September 12, 1981, the day after I had visited him in Fort Wayne, Indiana.

Dear Shupshe:
Since my visit yesterday, I have allowed my thoughts to settle some, and I realize that there is a need to write to you. I wish to thank you for the time which you spent with me. I, too, feel that our meeting was meant to be. Otherwise, I might have been wandering around for another seventeen years without finding these answers. I want to thank you also for extending to me the hand of brotherly spiritual love and empathy, and inasmuch as I have anything to offer you, I extend to you the same.

Power works in strange ways. You saw, of course, that when I visited you my being had been exhausted and depleted by worry, and I was weak. Perhaps we will meet sometime when I am more complete and myself. Because of the fact that I was somewhat in a state of depletion, I think that I reacted to you in a way that I have reacted to Lake Geneva when I have gone there, in a weakened condition, seeking power. Or perhaps I should say that this is how power reacts to me, when I am weak. At any rate, for a long time when I was there with you at your home, I did not sense much. But by the time I left I was almost incoherent, in a sense. My mind was burnt out, "fried." After I drove away from your house, I wandered around for about fifteen minutes, aimlessly, in circles, not having any idea where I was going, nor caring. Finally, I pulled off the road to have something to eat and to let my mind settle and reorient a bit, and I thus got myself aimed in the proper direction and headed home. I spent the night with an ice pack on my head, with a migraine headache. I am feeling much better this morning.

Although I listened to every word you said to me with great intensity, my head was swimming, and when we sat at your altar, although I felt a bit relieved, I had some very peculiar sensations indeed, including the strange feeling that the features of your face were changing shape somewhat. What I am saying is that, since I did not have the opportunity to write down a single word, I need you, if you would be so kind, to clarify some things for me. I understand completely what you say about my not getting bogged down in Indian lore and history. It would be wasteful, unnecessary, and probably even damaging. But I need you only to reiterate some of the basic things which you have already told me. I know that I must have asked you some of these questions several times when I was with you, and I just could not get them straight. I was much more disoriented by the presence of energy there than I realized, until I left, and then the full impact really hit me like a ton of bricks. I feel that I need a better grasp of a few facts in order to write them coherently and understand them within myself. The state of perception which Negoya opened to me and the knowledge which he communicated to me was exquisitely beautiful. But what is also beautiful to me is the wonder and mystery of how he led me to that state of perception and knowledge, because that is also an integral and meaningful component in the dynamics of my experiences. Thus, I want to understand these things clearly, for they are important to me. I beg your indulgence in explaining and clarifying these matters.

[At this point, I listed an entire page of questions dealing with the material which I have already discussed, and to which Shupshe responded in writing.]

Since I am asking all of these questions, you might think that I am as dense as Carlos Castaneda has sometimes represented himself as being. I have a firm intuitive grasp of what you said to me, and the more I ponder it, the more wonderful it becomes, as another facet of the infinite and beautiful mystery which surrounds us, who are for the most part unaware and blind to it. Thus, I need once again for you to give me a brief but clear description of the nature of the circumstances, or the "metaphysical mechanics," so to speak, of my experiences, so that I can grasp them within myself and incorporate them into the book. I will not dwell on these matters, but it is of vital importance to me to know the things which I have asked you. Otherwise, I cannot be content. I might never know whether or not I was an Indian in a past life. You do not seem to have any positive feelings that I was, and, after all, it is not in any way essential to my experiences, although it would be interesting to know if there were some momentum or karma or relationships from past lives involved. I have considered the possibility of trying to find a qualified individual who could give me a hypnotic regression in order to explore some of my past lives. Would you know of anyone who does this? [Shupshe's written reply was, "No. Look in your own mind."] This could add an interesting facet to the book, although I will not get caught up in it. Where would my quest begin or stop? Five hundred years ago, or fifty thousand? It could become endless. But the facet of the mechanics of reincarnation and the manner in which they may have affected my experiences in this life would be enlightening if it could be demonstrated as relevant, and it could add depth to the book. However, in comparison to the immediacy and reality of what I have experienced at Lake Geneva, these concerns are relatively minor to me, and, I suppose, basically and ultimately unessential. What I really need is simply a clear understanding of the questions which I have asked you in this letter.

I am including some poems about Negoya and the lake, if you might be interested in reading them. If not, just throw them out, as I have many copies. I know that you are one whose time is important to him. Likewise, I am sending a rough, handwritten copy of one of my first experiences at the lake, which must be rewritten and cleaned up. I know that it is crude right now, and much in need of work. Regarding the poems, I ascribe no literary merit to them. I am sending them because of their content and meaning.

I am most grateful for your time and help, and I hope very much to hear from you at your convenience. I will certainly stay in touch with you, and assure you a copy of my book.

With love,

Gerald Lishka

P.S. You have given me both comfort and courage. Thank you.
P.P.S. As the days go by, I realize more and more the strength you have given me to follow my convictions.

Shupshe gave me a special strength and comfort and courage. For the moments have been scarce in my life when I have encountered those rare and valuable individuals who have truly perceived and understood the nature of my perceptions and experiences, and who have been able to bestow upon me the peace which can only come when they can say to me that they truly understand. Those moments always remain vividly in my memory, and they have the power to sustain me through years of existing without seeking further understanding or recognition.

Shupshe Wahnah became one of those people. He drove into my being a new courage to pursue my perceptions and experiences. He gave me a feeling of comfort and of deep peace, and a renewed and clarified sense of resolution, not only about the validity of my ideas, but about the unalterable necessity for me to develop them and write about them. Just as Robert, the psychic, had been, Shupshe was adamant in his assertions that this book must be written. I was compelled to ask him what he felt would happen if I did not do so, and he replied with the following words.

"Let me put it this way. The book will be written, and if you do not write it, someone else will. And in the meantime, you will have lost an irreplaceable opportunity. If you do not share this knowledge, you will always be miserably unhappy, and you will probably go crazy. This knowledge was given to you for a reason. You cannot just carry it around secretly all the time like something in your shirt pocket to peek at once in a while, when it suits you."

Shupshe gave me another piece of advice which, as yet, I have not acted upon. He suggested that I move as close as possible to Lake Geneva, that I find any kind of job there, and continue the writing of the book. Perhaps, one day, I will move in order to be very close to the lake always. To do so is my greatest desire. But during the period of time in which I visited Shupshe, such a course of action seemed simply beyond the realm of feasibility. In my mind, my personal and material circumstances were just not of such a nature as to allow for such a move. Nevertheless, I paid serious attention to his remarks concerning my writing this book, and I worked on it intently and diligently until I had completed it, several months later.

From the very first moment I talked with him on the telephone, Shupshe was convinced of my sincerity, and he was shortly thereafter equally convinced of the reality and validity of my experiences. He remarked to me that, just from shaking my hand when he met me, he had perceived that I had been drained of a certain amount of psychic energy and ability by my recent years of progressively accumulated material responsibilities. He was, without my knowledge, "testing" me. I particularly sensed this when he pointed out his "garden" to me, something to which I know he attributed special powers, and I also sensed it later when we moved outdoors to his altar, where we continued our talk, and at which time he explained the significance of the altar. He had reserved the entire day to talk with me, but he informed me early in the afternoon that it would be necessary for us to finish up our talk, as there were some things which he had to attend to. Granted, I had arrived there very early, and we had talked continuously for many hours, and yet I had this feeling, about our meeting, that he was ending it earlier than planned because of some perception which he had had. I did not feel that it was appropriate to ask him about it at the time. I felt that he knew best, and besides, I was mentally exhausted, which I am sure he noticed. It is not so much, I feel, that I simply "failed" some test, but rather that, for reasons known only to him, it was appropriate that we should end our meeting at that point. He had certainly perceived clearly that, for some time prior to our meeting, I had been experiencing considerable mental and emotional stress, and that I was weakened from it.

Nevertheless, he was encouraging in every way to me, and at one point he said, "You had a teacher once, and now you have another," referring to Negoya, and to himself.

I had been speculating with Shupshe about whether or not I might ever again encounter Negoya at Lake Geneva. He acknowledged that it could come to pass, although he made some interesting comments about which he seemed to prefer not to elaborate. But he did intimate that there were some things about Negoya's past life as an Ojibwa Medawinne which probably indicated that he would be reborn into another physical body, rather than remaining free of rebirth and existing on a higher plane of existence. Shupshe's statements implied two things. The first was that perhaps there was something a little dark in Negoya's past that Shupshe knew about but which he did not reveal. For in the philosophy of reincarnation, one must have attained supreme perfection in order to be free from the cycle of birth and death. And even though Negoya had been an adept of high psychic development, he could still have possessed certain traits that would have prevented him from such final freedom. The second implication was the possibility that, even during my physical lifetime, Negoya might thus at some point reincarnate into another earthly body. Indeed, he may even have already done so, since the time that I had had my vision of him at Lake Geneva in August 1964. If this was true, I would not see him in the same form again. However, Shupshe stated that, even if this subsequently proved to be the case, I might very possibly encounter another guide at the lake at some point in the future.

Shupshe's personal power had acted upon me in an unexpected manner. Rather than noticing it immediately, I had become aware of it only gradually, the longer I was with him. Its full impact did not register with me until I left him. My typical experience with such individuals usually was that I was immediately aware of their power upon coming into their presence. Shupshe had really thrown me, however, and I am left with no doubt that he was an individual of considerable power, to say nothing of his knowledge and wisdom. When I left him, I was already looking forward to a time when I could come back to see him once again. In parting, he offered me his continued help and friendship, and he invited me to return. He conveyed his support and brotherly love to me, and asked that he might receive a copy of my book when it became published.

Regardless of how events fell into place, I felt that another visit with Shupshe could be very instrumental in helping me to determine the nature and course of my future relationship to Lake Geneva. I had discussed this with Shupshe, and he had readily agreed to set aside a day for me to come and visit with him during my anticipated trip to the lake the following summer. I remember that, with respect to my trips to Lake Geneva, Shupshe said to me, "Do not always go to the lake with great or specific expectations. Rather, go there empty, with openness, so that you can be filled."

I will always be grateful to Shupshe Wahnah for the things which he gave to me. I will always respect him and his counsel, and I will always carry inside of me the courage and faith which he imparted to me. He helped me to clarify my motives for writing about my experiences, one of which is to do for others what he did for me: to encourage others to pursue their visions, and to struggle against the inexorable tendency of the world to obscure and obliterate those unique moments in their lives when they touched Reality.

Places of Power

I have referred to Lake Geneva and its surrounding hills as a place of unique and exquisite power. From the very beginning of my experiences at Lake Geneva, it was a place of great power for me, and because of everything that has happened to me as a result of my relationship with the lake, I have always regarded it as unique. I have never claimed that the lake and its surroundings were unique, however, from the standpoint that it was the only such place on the earth that expressed special power and consciousness. Indeed, I imagine that there are a very great number of such places which, through their own particular energy and magnetism, would fall into the category into which I have placed the lake. Some of these places I have only heard about, and some I have visited. However, Lake Geneva has always been unique for me, and cannot be replaced by any other place.

For the term, "place of power," I acknowledge Carlos Castaneda, and his works based upon the teachings of don Juan Matus. However, out of due respect both for myself and for Castaneda, I should strongly assert that the perceptions and experiences which I have had at Lake Geneva, and the other inner processes which I have undergone as a result, are uniquely and totally mine. I have perceived distinct differences between my experiences and Castaneda's, but in the cases where I have found similarities which I feel are meaningful, I have related them, with the end in mind of establishing a fuller knowledge about such kinds of experiences, which Castaneda has very appropriately classified and designated by the term, "nonordinary." I must say that, when I finally discovered *The Teachings of Don Juan: A Yaqui Way of Knowledge* (New York: Simon and Schuster, 1968), and as I subsequently read Castaneda's other works, despite the obvious differences between his experiences and mine, I found, possibly for the first time in my life, a context into which many of my perceptions and experiences at Lake Geneva could properly fit without being warped or censored.

My experiences began some time before I had ever heard of Castaneda. My vision of Negoya, and all of the experiences that accompanied it, occurred during my first trip to Lake Geneva. I first picked up a copy of *The Teachings of Don Juan* sometime around April 1974, almost ten years after my initial experiences at the lake, although this first book of Castaneda's was copyrighted in 1968, and deals with his experiences which began during the summer of 1960.

By the end of November 1974, I had read all four of Castaneda's books then in print. Between April and November 1974, I began to think of Lake Geneva as a "place of power." Nothing had changed in terms of my experiences there. But Castaneda's works had given me an enlightening new perspective, and had caused me to focus on something which, although in a sense it had always been a part of my experiences at the lake, had now become more concrete in my mind; namely, the concept of a "place of power," a term that I found to be functionally useful and descriptively accurate. This concept has grown with me as my experiences have grown and evolved, and is one that I still use quite extensively today. Thus, during the ten years between my first experiences at the lake and my discovery of Castaneda's writings, the lake was most certainly a marvelous place of power for me, but I did not refer to it specifically as such. Rather, the lake was simply a mysterious and wondrous and special place, where incredible things had happened to me, which, apparently, could not happen anywhere else.

Although I have always intuitively known that the lake expressed a special power, it was not until I talked with Shupshe that I was able to share my perceptions with another individual who also had a personal knowledge of the lake as a place of power. At that time I thus received some outside reinforcement for my own views, which therefore furnished them with a more objective aspect. And Shupshe himself had told me that he had come to this knowledge of the lake both through his own personal psychic powers and through the esoteric tradition of which he was a part.

Thus, through him I learned that there were various physical factors that made the locale of the lake special. Although his explanation had been more detailed, he had explained its power in terms of a combination of things, such as the belt of electromagnetic forces which flowed over the earth at that point, the atmosphere and the layer of ozone, and how it interacted with the cosmic and solar rays which entered the atmosphere at a particular angle there and struck the earth. He had explained that there were many such places on earth, and that men had sometimes built special structures and monuments upon these spots. Citing the obvious problems involved in building such a structure out in the middle of a lake, he went on to express his feeling that anyone with any true psychic power should be able to detect something unusual in that geographic area. Thus, Shupshe helped to substantiate my knowledge of Lake Geneva as a place of power by sharing his own knowledge, a contribution that lent more of an overall objective aspect to my own views. I am quite sure that, in terms of the objective factors which made the lake unique, there was a deep and complex unseen world of forces which made it so. There was a reality outside my own subjective consciousness which characterized the lake as a place of power. This book only scratches the surface in terms of offering insights as to the true and ultimate nature of the forces operating there. Therefore, I know that part of the path that awaits me in the future will be to look more deeply into myself and into the mysteries which express themselves through the being of the lake, in order that I might confront more fully the unexplored and incredible facets of my own mind, and those of the living consciousness which we call the world. For surely, there is an awesome and extraordinary realm which awaits those who have transcended the restrictions of ordinary perceptions.

My relationship to Lake Geneva as a place of power was a complex one, when considered from a subjective aspect. Although my relationship to the lake is supremely real to me, I do not even begin to understand it fully, and I cannot offer any complete or final explanations as to the ultimate nature or purpose of this relationship. I can only convey, to the best of my capabilities, what I have experienced there and how I feel about it. I have experienced other places of power, or other places where I have detected the presence of power. The power in one of those places responded to me by giving me something I very much wanted in my life, a specific thing I asked for, and which ultimately played an important role in the direction of my life. That particular place of power was an area located in a wild section of the country, hundreds of miles from Wisconsin. There was a river that flowed through the forest. Its waters fell gently over the terraces of giant boulders, where they filled a beautiful pool which was surrounded by high rocks, before continuing their course through the woods. I had not been immediately aware of something there during my first visit, but as I began to notice more and more the nature of certain things that happened there each successive time I visited that spot, it gradually and finally became quite clear that that area had special power for me and that it could help me.

There was something I deeply desired at that time, and I had not been able to attain it. I knew that if I could find the courage to go to that place of power alone at night and ask the power there for this thing, I would have it. I found it within myself to do so one night, and not without a considerable exertion of will. It was so dark that I had to locate the pool by listening for the churning water that descended into it from above, and by feeling my way to it through the trees. I stood there and simply and straightforwardly asked for the thing I wanted. The power there seemed to ask me if I was really sure that I wanted this thing, and it told me that my desire might have far-reaching consequences. But I knew that I wanted it, regardless of whatever else it would bring, and I asked for it. Because of the deeply personal nature of my reasons for seeking out the power in that place, I am not free to say what it was that I sought from it. But I can say that, after I had turned from that spot and left it, although I had waited for over two years to obtain that particular thing, it came to be mine in a most remarkable way within twenty-four hours after I had left that place of power. This incident took place during July 1978, and the realization of my desires catalyzed a series of decisive events which were to bring about sweeping changes in my life over the next three years.

I really do not care for the term, "psychic." There is something about the connotations attached to it that I do not like. When I hear this word, I somehow think of minds that are not really balanced and healthy because of a preoccupation with various specific and peculiar mental powers. I also feel that terms like "psychic" and "clairvoyant," just like "genius" and "talent," are rather useless words. A lot of people who use them do not know what they are talking about. The term "psychic" tends to create erroneous notions about perception by giving the impression that the mind is compartmentalized and that its various abilities are separate and segregated. I do not feel that this is true, at least in terms of myself. I have also noticed that many psychic people are not very happy. Furthermore, I tend not to think of the perceptions and experiences I have had at the lake as psychic, except for one or two isolated exceptions, and those experiences had nothing to do with Lake Geneva. They might have happened anywhere. I regard everything that has happened at Lake Geneva simply in terms of an expanded and deepened consciousness, through which I have seen further and more clearly into the wondrous and infinite world of power that waits to be witnessed and embraced. Furthermore, the term "psychic" does nothing to explain the awesome mystery that has confronted me there. It is for the same reason that I do not care for such terms as "lofty" and "spiritual," in connection with my personal experiences, and I try to use other words that will convey my meaning without engendering misleading associations.

I have shared a profound love with the being of the lake and its surrounding hills. It has been unique from the standpoint that, of all the places on the earth where I have been, it is home to me.

I have felt for many years that the lake and its surrounding hills, and particularly the Point, "belonged" to me. I hasten to make a very clear distinction between this and any feeling that I "owned" it. I did not feel that the people who had property there and lived there, and who had probably paid very large sums of money for that land, owned it either. I regarded it to be conscious and alive, and I do not feel that one can ever own another living thing. One may acquire certain legal rights to it, but in an ultimate sense, it does not belong to them. For example, I have pets, and I love them. When I accepted them, I assumed a sacred trust to care and provide for them. I will protect them. But they are living beings, not objects, and I do not own them. In that sense, I have no right to control and usurp their identity in order to gratify my own egocentric territoriality and instincts for dominion. They are living beings with whom I have a relationship. I know that true places of power are "alive," and for that reason, I can never, in any sense, own any part of the lake of its beautiful hills, but because of the nature of my relationship to it, it truly belongs to me, and I to it.

Thus, as I have said elsewhere in this work, the lake was my beloved. It was a being with which I had a passionate relationship, a place of power with which my life shared a strong tie. And when I went there, I experienced many extraordinary things. I have also said elsewhere that I experienced a unique sense of identity when I moved within the world of the lake. And again, I must stress that I use the term, "identity," as it has been defined in that realm of power, in a much deeper, noumenal, expansive sense. There was a profound rationality behind something I experienced at the lake that, at first glance, might appear to be a contradiction. When I was there, I experienced a clearer and more lucid sense of identity than at any other time. At the same time, I also had a very strong and intensely pleasurable feeling or anonymity. These feelings of identity and anonymity were actually two harmonious facets of a single, unified perception.

Although there were several elements which went to make up this overall perception, the real key to it lay in this; namely, that rather than realizing *who* I really was, I came to grasp more deeply *what* I was, and to understand who I was not. First of all, I clearly recognized that, in that world of power, I was someone different from the person whom I felt I was when I was away from there. The world was different at the lake, and so was I. I expanded to move in new modes of perception there, to embrace far more beautiful and expansive states of feeling and knowledge. The petty and constricting preoccupations that generally cluttered my mind fell away, and I became free of the energy-draining machinations in which my ego ordinarily indulged in order to protect and maintain itself. The worries and fears that ordinarily sought to devour me ceased to exist. But the change in my state of being went far beyond the cessation of many of the major psychological deterrents that normally interfered with my peace of mind. When confronted with the mysteries of the lake, I became totally still. I was utterly silenced. I became pure perception, without thought. I knew indescribable peace. The identity with which I ordinarily associated myself, with its mannerisms and idiosyncrasies, was forgotten, left behind in some other distant universe.

Thus, as I had abandoned the dead weight of the empty and sterile labels and definitions that were traditionally used to represent the world, I had, without any conscious effort, attained the realization that all the notions I had had about myself were equally limiting and ridiculous. The lake taught me this, that I was something far more mysterious than the repertory of roles I had been playing out within the framework of the stage erected by my culture. Consequently, within the sweeping framework of boundless power that confronted me at the lake, my thoughts focused on the question of who I really was, and as I came to grasp more clearly and directly the undefinable nature of the world, I came to ponder this enigma more in terms of what I was. Words became meaningless when I became perception and flowed out into the unknowable identity that moved within the world and animated it. The more fully I apprehended it, the fewer attributes were apparent that seemed to define what I was.

During the course of my life, when I had at one point become free, to an extent, of the various roles I played out in everyday life, I was able to say that I was simply and foremost just a human being. But the perceptions of the lake took me far beyond even this. I was consciousness. The term, "human being," was just another lame word. For when I considered all the great multitudes of attributes that identified and defined men in their own eyes, I knew that the conscious perception through which my essence expressed itself was infinitely more. There was a tremendous, inconceivable freedom in this. For rather than spiritually starving to death, imprisoned and deluded in a dry wasteland of glib and myopic notions about the nature of the world and of life, I shed all this garbage with which my mind was encrusted, and soared into the living reality.

I became Mind without thought, yet I did not become lost in it. I was self, but without boundaries; I moved freely, without limits. The more fully I realized that I really did not know anything about the true nature of the world or of myself, the more I came to embrace the world as it actually was, and the more clearly I truly saw the incomprehensible thing that I really was, freed from the delusions of knowledge. This, too, is why I have rightly called the lake and its hills a place of power, for this was one of the great gifts which it bestowed upon me, this enormously liberating, joyous perception.

I did not spend all of my time at the lake in the abstract states which I have described. I walked, ate, slept, thought, conversed, wrote, and just looked and enjoyed. I sailed, went exploring, and occasionally ventured into one of the little towns there. I would describe it as a kind of relish or enthusiasm that pervaded all my activities, an almost disproportionate delight I felt in everything I did. At times, this feeling simply became an overflowing joy, a deep gratefulness just to be alive and existing in that marvelous place. I tended to focus on my movements, and to experience, consciously and deliberately, my responses to everything around me.

It was marvelous to be in a world of such living power. Nothing was ever boring, and so I wanted to be as alive and alert as I could possibly be. I thought of this in contrast to the kind of "life" which I ordinarily experienced through the slant of my own culture, where the horizons were so bleak that in order to survive many people either indulged in things that were grossly unbalanced and overstimulating, or lapsed into a death of semiconsciousness, robot-like automatism, a kind of premature senility. The possibilities for self-delusion, and for impeding one's own evolution, were endless.

In that world of power lay the ever-present possibility of the impossible being realized. I would say that it was a world of magic, but it was not the magic of fantasy, but rather of a superreality. Things could happen to me there that apparently could not happen anywhere else. And they did, every moment.

The lake filled me with personal power, and if I acted intelligently, and consciously, all of my actions there were characterized by a kind of strength; that is, they were the harmonious expression of a wisdom which gave my actions an efficiency and impeccability. This power seemed to come simply from my being there and being open and accessible. I allowed my being to expand and I breathed it in through every pore. This power was not some vague or abstract state of being I sought to attain. It was a tangible energy that pervaded the very air I breathed, which animated the lake, and every rock and tree, and which fed my body and made it strong and happy. In fact, this energy and power I found there was so tangible that I thought of it as materiality. I perceived it as such. And yet it was a feeling. It was as if something within me reached out and grasped the world, an undefined but clearly present and active inner faculty which, although it seemed associated with the senses, was distinct from them and extended beyond them. Through some inner vehicle of knowing that I had not yet come to understand, but which used the physical senses as instruments of perception and worked in conjunction with them, I was able to experience a whole spectrum of perceptions of things not normally considered to be within the scope of sense perception.

Although I have consistently used the terms "phenomena" and "noumena" as pertaining to manifestations of the seen and unseen world, I have done so to indicate the direction from which certain perceptions and experiences have come—from what level of reality. The universe is not divided down the middle, with the phenomenal world on one side and the noumenal world on the other. This is a distinction that is arbitrary and, in an objective sense, nonexistent. There is only one incredible and mysterious world. We have chopped it up into sections only to accommodate our limited and compartmentalized perceptions, which we have imposed upon ourselves, and which happen not to be in accordance with reality. I have found it difficult not to become aggravated when I hear the kinds of experiences I have described referred to as otherworldly. We have elected to entertain a severely limited spectrum of perceptions, and have created a flat, constricted, inanimate world, divided into spirit and matter, life and death, spiritual and profane; the physical world and the other world. We may persist in this until we drop dead, but it will not alter reality. There is one Unity, one enormous and awesome world, and to divide it into the comprehensible and the incomprehensible only reveals our ignorance, because we do not comprehend any of it. The only real comprehension is to dump the garbage notions we have about things and open our beings to embrace the limitless Reality around us. This was what the lake taught me. This was one of the gifts of a place of power.

At the lake, I became restored. I found sustenance. Some vital aspect of my being was nourished, relieved of a hunger which only that power could appease.

I had been given a place of wondrous power, an endless path to follow. And although this power was not yet something that I was able to sustain continuously, it had nevertheless been given to me that I was able to avail myself, at various times, of the opportunity to search out the mysteries of a great place of power and beauty, and open myself to its matchless gifts, and, through it, to experience a supreme and unbounded love.

In light of what I have just said, I now express again, as I have earlier, that, although there were many features of my experiences which distinguished them from those described in the works of Carlos Castaneda, I nevertheless found in those writings, far more than in any other system of thought which I had previously explored, a meaningful context into which many of my perceptions at the lake fit in a clear and logical way, and within which were accounts that I identified with

readily and powerfully. I had come to know an incredible love for the lake and for
the earth, and the power of this love carried me beyond the emptiness and direc-
tionlessness which seemed to characterize my life. Because of this, when I read the
passages from Castaneda's *Tales of Power** reproduced below, I felt the message
they expressed. They were an eloquent expression of my own feelings.

The passages quoted below are part of a dramatic scene in which Castaneda
and another apprentice named Pablito are preparing for an awesome excursion
into an unknown world of perception and experience. Also present are another
apprentice named Nestor, who is witnessing the scene, and don Juan and don
Genaro, two sorcerers who have trained and guided the apprentices, and who are
now expressing their final thoughts to Castaneda and Pablito. The passage speaks
for itself. Its message is clear. The first speaker is don Genaro.

> "It's almost time for us to disband like the warriors in the story," he said.
> "But before we go our separate ways I must tell you two one last thing. I am
> going to disclose to you a warrior's secret. Perhaps you can call it a warrior's
> predilection."
>
> He addressed me in particular and said that once I had told him that the
> life of a warrior was cold and lonely and devoid of feelings. He even added
> that at that precise moment I was convinced that it was so.
>
> "The life of a warrior cannot possibly be cold and lonely and without feel-
> ings," he said, "because it is based on his affection, his devotion, his dedication
> to his beloved. And who, you may ask, is his beloved? I will show you now."
>
> Don Genaro stood up and walked slowly to a perfectly flat area right in
> front of us, ten or twelve feet away. He made a strange gesture there. He moved
> his hands as if he were sweeping dust from his chest and his stomach. Then
> an odd thing happened. A flash of an almost imperceptible light went through
> him; it came from the ground and seemed to kindle his entire body. He did a
> sort of backward pirouette, a backward dive more properly speaking, and
> landed on his chest and arms. His movement had been executed with such
> precision and skill that he seemed to be a weightless being, a wormlike crea-
> ture that had turned on itself. When he was on the ground he performed a
> series of unearthly movements. He glided just a few inches above the ground,
> or rolled on it as if he were lying on ball bearings; or he swam on it describ-
> ing circles and turning with the swiftness and agility of an eel swimming in
> the ocean.
>
> My eyes began to cross at one moment and then without any transition
> I was watching a ball of luminosity sliding back and forth on something that

*New York: Simon and Schuster, 1974, pp. 283–6. Reprinted with the permission of
Pocket Books, a Division of Simon & Schuster Inc. from *Tales of Power* by Carlos Castaneda. Copyright ©1974 by Carlos Castaneda.

appeared to be the floor of an ice-skating rink with a thousand lights shining on it.

The sight was sublime. Then the ball of fire came to rest and stayed motionless. A voice shook me and dispelled my attention. It was don Juan talking. I could not understand at first what he was saying. I looked again at the ball of fire; I could distinguish only don Genaro lying on the ground with his arms and legs spread out.

Don Juan's voice was very clear. It seemed to trigger something in me and I began to write.

"Genaro's love is the world," he said. "He was just now embracing this enormous earth but since he's so little all he can do is swim in it. But the earth knows that Genaro loves it and it bestows on him its care. That's why Genaro's life is filled to the brim and his state, wherever he'll be, will be plentiful. Genaro roams on the paths of his love and, wherever he is, he is complete."

Don Juan squatted in front of us. He caressed the ground gently.

"This is the predilection of two warriors," he said. "This earth, this world. For a warrior there can be no greater love."

Don Genaro stood up and squatted next to don Juan for a moment while both of them peered fixedly at us, then they sat in unison, cross-legged.

"Only if one loves this earth with unbending passion can one release one's sadness," don Juan said. "A warrior is always joyful because his love is unalterable and his beloved, the earth, embraces him and bestows upon him inconceivable gifts. The sadness belongs only to those who hate the very thing that gives shelter to their beings."

Don Juan caressed the ground with tenderness.

"This lovely being, which is alive to its last recesses and understands every feeling, soothed me, it cured me of my pains, and finally when I had fully understood my love for it, it taught me freedom."

He paused. The silence around us was frightening. The wind hissed softly and then I heard the distant barking of a lone dog.

"Listen to that barking," don Juan went on. "That is the way my beloved earth is helping me now to bring this last point to you. That barking is the saddest thing one can hear."

We were quiet for a moment. The barking of that lone dog was so sad and the stillness around us so intense that I experienced a numbing anguish. It made me think of my own life, my sadness, my not knowing where to go, what to do.

"That dog's barking is the nocturnal voice of man," don Juan said. "It comes from a house in that valley towards the south. A man is shouting through his dog, since they are companion slaves for life, his sadness, his boredom. He's begging his death to come and release him from the dull and dreary chains of his life."

Don Juan's words had caught a most disturbing line in me. I felt he was speaking directly to me.

"That barking, and the loneliness it creates, speaks of the feelings of men," he went on. "Men for whom an entire life was like one Sunday afternoon, an afternoon which was not altogether miserable, but rather hot and dull and uncomfortable. They sweated and fussed a great deal. They didn't know where to go, or what to do. That afternoon left them only with the memory of petty annoyances and tedium, and then suddenly it was over; it was already night."

He recounted a story I had once told him about a seventy-two-year-old man who complained that his life had been so short that it seemed to him that it was only the day before that he was a boy. The man had said to me, "I remember the pajamas I used to wear when I was ten years old. It seems that only one day has passed. Where did the time go?"

"The antidote that kills the poison is here," don Juan said, caressing the ground. "The sorcerer's explanation cannot at all liberate the spirit. Look at you two. You have gotten the sorcerer's explanation, but it doesn't make any difference that you know it. You're more alone than ever, because without an unwavering love for the being that gives you shelter, aloneness is loneliness."

"Only the love for this splendorous being can give freedom to a warrior's spirit; and freedom is joy, efficiency, and abandon in the face of any odds. That is the last lesson. It is always left for the very last moment, for the moment of ultimate solitude when a man faces his death and his aloneness. Only then does it make sense."

There is much in this passage that reflects my own feelings about Lake Geneva. In spite of the power that I found there, it was a long time before I willingly went there alone. I was afraid of becoming lonely, and I think that I felt even more that such would be the case, given the "isolated" character of my experiences there. Many times, I had wanted companionship in the world of the lake, someone to share the experiences with me. It took a long time for me to become convinced that this was not possible. I think that I really knew that this was so, that the experiences that confronted me there were ones of solitude, but I was unable to acknowledge this for many years. I had felt lonely for most of my life, and I did not want to do anything to make that loneliness more acute. So, on the occasions when I could have gone to the lake alone, I sometimes did not. And yet, whenever I was accompanied by someone else, whether a friend or a lover, I realized that their presence held me back. For in trying to avoid one kind of isolation I created another. I had provided myself with the human companionship that I needed in order not to be lonely, but in doing so I had made myself less than totally available to the exquisite power there.

Thus, when I did not travel to the lake alone, I was not always able to be alone there when I wanted, and what was worse, I sometimes experienced another, more alarming kind of isolation. Because although I was well aware of the lovely power there, calling to me, I felt separated from it. That was truly agonizing, to sense its presence and yet be "outside" of it, by having not come alone and by having remained entangled, by my own choice, in affairs which separated me from it. And I could feel every precious moment of that magical time there slipping away with alarming speed. Then, when the inevitable moment of departure came, and even before, I experienced the quiet but agonizing feeling that I had not wisely used an opportunity to become available to that wondrous power, and that I had wasted precious time that was gone forever. It was as if I had damned myself. And yet, I often viewed loneliness for human companionship almost as death itself.

It must seem like quite a contradiction that I could be capable of opening myself to the incredible forces in that place of power and yet be so afraid that I might be lonely. There had been times when, in order to go to the lake, I had gone with large groups of people out of necessity, and had ended up feeling empty. This was of course because I was splitting myself between my need for human companionship and acceptance and my longing to embrace whatever existed there. Fortunately, I came to realize this in the course of time. And certainly, on the occasions when I went to the lake with other people, whether with a large group or with just one other person, those trips were not fruitless. But sometimes it was as if the power there had withdrawn from me, as if I was separated from it by a kind of veil. I then felt as if I was peering into a memory that had once been supremely real, but which had become obscured or partially lost, and I found myself even wondering if it had really been as I had thought. And after returning from such visits, I would experience doubts as to whether or not it had ever been real at all. But despite such frightening doubts, the beautiful memory of that place and the knowledge it had brought to me, and my longing to be one with it, could never be extinguished. In spite of everything, including an almost total lack of support from other people, my desire for that supreme experience persisted.

> In memory's echoing chambers,
> Through imagination's filter,
> Glows the spirit
>   of a memory,
> Lost somewhere in
>   Time's vast ocean.
>   August 1971

Happily, a time came in my life when I overcame my fear of loneliness in the face of the power of the lake. I admit that it was not through any conscious decision or noble effort of will on my part. Rather, it was a realization whose time had simply come. It happened during the trip that I made to Lake Geneva during August 1980, and, ironically, it was not a trip that I had taken alone. I was accompanied by a girl whom I had recently come to know, and I cannot but think that her presence must have been a distraction that prevented me from giving my attention wholly to seeking out the power that existed there. Nevertheless, that trip was a decisive one.

For some reason that I do not understand, the power there manifested itself to me in such a way that I was never again to doubt it. Although there would be times ahead of great internal struggle and growth, this was a realization whose impact and conviction would remain with me. Something unexplainable yet decisive had happened to me, and it had engendered within me a certainty of paramount importance in the evolution of my ideas about the lake and its power. I saw that any degree of separation that I had experienced during past visits had been in my own mind. I had created it by allowing my fear of loneliness to hold me back. Any doubts that I may have felt about the reality of the matchless power in the realm of the lake had been due solely to my past reluctance and inability to rise above my fears and insecurities and open myself to it. The incredible reality that breathed there had never abated, nor had it veiled itself from me. I had created the barrier. Naturally, as Shupshe Wahnah had said, there was a slight variation in terms of the geographical focus of the power at the lake that might influence somewhat my receptivity to it. But even taking that into consideration, I had now arrived at a perspective that forever released me from doubt and fear. I would not be alone, because I was surrounded by a limitless power that manifested an extraordinary consciousness.

I had discovered a new freedom. Now, rather than being intimidated by the idea of solitude, I sought it out. For when I opened myself to the loving consciousness that was within the being of the living earth, I was filled with an unsurpassable joy and peace. The earth and the lake and the hills spoke to me. They comforted me and revealed wonderful things to me, and within that marvelous world in which all things were redefined I realized what "home" really was, and all my desires came to rest. I came not only to know the beauty and peace of that exquisite solitude, but to understand clearly that that solitude was an inevitable condition that I must fully accept before I could take the next steps in knowing more fully the power that expressed itself there.

My August 1980 trip to Lake Geneva saw the accomplishment of a major step in the evolution of my relationship to the power of the lake and the growth of my own consciousness—the removal forever of all doubts about the unique consciousness and power that the lake possessed. Another important step remained to be taken, sometime in the future. There would have to come a time when I would overcome my fear of the yet unexplored world at the lake that still lay beyond what I had seen there and that I intuitively sensed. There was a boundary that I would have to cross and confront whatever lay beyond. And, I would have to embrace that power and fuse my being with it so that it would permanently transform and strengthen the rest of my life. All of my existence had to become accessible to that power. Every step and thought and action had to express it. I sought to move forever beyond the weakness and lack of impeccability that still characterized much of my life, and I wanted that beautiful path that I followed at the lake to be one upon which I set my feet every moment. I had wanted that ever since my first vision there. Although I felt supremely fortunate for the great gifts of power that had been given to me, it was my desire and, I felt, my responsibility to accept the challenge of weaving that wondrous power inseparably into the fabric of my everyday life.

The August 1980 trip was also the inspiration for the writing of this book. It would play a role that I did not, of course, then fully understand. But I knew that it was a task of far-reaching importance. Other individuals would also see it as such, and would admonish me to see this task through to its completion.

Thus I came to understand clearly the meaning of the passages from *Tales of Power*, and to see that they expressed truth. I had been no stranger to loneliness. I suppose I considered myself an authority on it. But although my life was not all I wanted it to be, my relationship with the lake had revealed the living power of the earth, and during my stays, my unbounded love for the beautiful being of the earth had removed from me all loneliness; it had soothed me and filled me with peace and happiness. It was as don Juan had said. The earth had revealed itself to me as conscious and infinitely alive, and although I had a long way to travel on the path I was following, power had nevertheless revealed to me an experience of incredible freedom. The world was more than I had imagined, and there was a better way to live than the way I was living. There was an infinity of things I did not understand, and I felt that the path I was following had no final end. I had only begun to walk it. But the direction was unmistakably clear. I could not have failed to discern it. An unfathomable power had indicated it to me.

I thought of all the people for whom, as don Juan had said, life had been much like a Sunday afternoon which, although not entirely miserable, had been rather boring and uncomfortable. And I thought of those whose entire lives had passed by them almost unnoticed, and were suddenly over. Living this way might not have been so alarming and grim if I had never encountered the lake. Many things had contributed to awakening me to the reality that my life would be over quickly, and that I had better consider carefully how I would spend the time allotted to me. I had been aware of this even during my mid-teens. But it was the power of the lake that brought home to me most dramatically that I could never be satisfied with an ordinary life. My time on earth was too precious; I could not just let it slip by. Not only could I never be satisfied with this, but, as I had learned when I strayed the furthest from the truth the lake had revealed, I could not endure such a life; I could not survive intact under such conditions. It was this kind of realization that drove me to complete this book. I had seen too much. I was hooked by something incredible which I had seen and experienced, and, although I went through periods of confusion and depression and lethargy at various points, I could never let that vision go. It was not possible for me to do so. I was compelled to reject the death of an ordinary existence, and to search out that which had given me real life.

I was constantly confronted with the challenge of overcoming the inertia of everyday life. It required a continual struggle for me to focus my attention on my own evolution and the quality of my consciousness. It demanded enormous effort and sustained will to neutralize the comfortable but fatal tendencies toward lethargy and laziness. At times, when I succumbed, I would experience moments when I felt as if I were dying, and it made me very sad. I would become aware that there had been a gradual process of anesthetization in my spirit which I was often unaware of, and at such moments, which were often the results of my thoughts turning unexpectedly to the power of the lake, I experienced a despondency that often escalated to a kind of mute, inner alarm. These feelings, along with others with which I often struggled, were the payment I made for living in a culture which was so far removed in character from the world of the lake. Thus, the loneliness, and confusion, and lethargy, and despondency, and all the other negative forces with which I struggled at various times were the poison that dragged me down and encumbered my life, and sapped my strength. I had not yet made that step which would enable me to remove that poison entirely from my life and being by embracing in a deeper way the power at the lake. As I have said, I saw that as part of the challenge which lay ahead of me. And yet I knew that there was truth in the following words, if I could possess it as my own.

> "The antidote that kills the poison is here," don Juan said, caressing the ground...
> "Only the love for this splendorous being can give freedom to a warrior's spirit; and freedom is joy, efficiency, and abandon in the face of any odds..."

There is another passage, in Castaneda's *Journey to Ixtlan*,* which, because of its relevance to my own experiences, I have quoted here. The chapter from which this passage is taken is entitled, "A Warrior's Last Stand," and relates some of Castaneda's experiences while hunting power with don Juan. This scene takes place on the top of a hill, which is a very special place of power. Among the portions omitted is one that deals with "dreaming." This is a phenomenon that appears to suggest astral projection, and yet it seems to involve more than that. The quote begins at a point where Castaneda is recounting his experiences.

> I sat up. Don Juan was not anywhere in sight. I had a sudden attack of fear. I thought he may have left me there alone, and I did not know the way back to the car. I lay down again on the mat of branches and strangely enough my apprehension vanished. I again experienced a sense of quietness, an exquisite sense of well-being. It was an extremely new sensation to me; my thoughts seemed to have turned off. I was happy. I felt healthy. A very quiet ebullience filled me. A soft wind was blowing from the west and swept over my entire body without making me cold. I felt it on my face and around my ears, like a gentle wave of

---

*New York: Simon and Schuster, 1972, pp. 182–9. Reprinted with the permission of Pocket Books, a Division of Simon & Schuster Inc. from *Journey to Ixtlan* by Carlos Castaneda. Copyright ©1972 by Carlos Castaneda.

warm water that bathed me and then receded and bathed me again. It was a strange state of being that had no parallel in my busy and dislocated life. I began to weep, not out of sadness or self-pity but out of some ineffable, inexplicable joy.

I wanted to stay in that spot forever and I may have, had don Juan not come and yanked me out of the place.

"You've had enough rest," he said as he pulled me up.

He led me very calmly on a walk around the periphery of the hilltop. We walked slowly and in complete silence. He seemed to be interested in making me observe the scenery all around us. He pointed to clouds and mountains with a movement of his eyes or with a movement of his chin.

The scenery in the late afternoon was superb. It evoked sensations of awe and despair in me. It reminded me of sights in my childhood.

We climbed to the highest point of the hilltop, a peak of igneous rock, and sat down comfortably with our backs against the rock, facing the south. The endless expanse of land towards the south was truly majestic.

"Fix all this in your memory," don Juan whispered in my ear. "This spot is yours. This morning you saw, and that was the omen. You found this spot by seeing. The omen was unexpected, but it happened. You are going to hunt power whether you like it or not. It is not a human decision, not yours or mine.

"Now, properly speaking, this hilltop is your place, your beloved place; all that is around you is under your care. You must look after everything here and everything will in turn look after you."

In a joking way I asked if everything was mine. He said yes in a very serious tone. I laughed and told him that what we were doing reminded me of the story of how the Spaniards that conquered the New World had divided the land in the name of their king. They used to climb to the top of a mountain and claim all the land they could see in any specific direction.

"That's a good idea," he said. "I'm going to give you all the land you can see, not in one direction but all around you."

He stood up and pointed with his extended hand, turning his body around to cover a complete circle.

"All this land is yours," he said.

I laughed out loud.

He giggled and asked me, "Why not? Why can't I give you this land?"

"You don't own this land," I said.

"So what? The Spaniards didn't own it either and yet they divided it and gave it away. So why can't you take possession of it in the same vein?"

I scrutinized him to see if I could detect the real mood behind his smile. He had an explosion of laughter and nearly fell off the rock.

"All this land, as far as you can see, is yours," he went on, still smiling. "Not to use but to remember. This hilltop, however, is yours to use for the rest of your life. I am giving it to you because you have found it yourself. It is yours. Accept it."

I laughed, but don Juan seemed to be very serious. Except for his funny smile, he appeared to actually believe that he could give me that hilltop.

"Why not?" he asked as if he were reading my thoughts.

"I accept it," I said half in jest.

His smile disappeared. He squinted his eyes as he looked at me.

"Every rock and pebble and bush on this hill, especially on the top, is under your care," he said. "every worm that lives here is your friend. You can use them and they can use you."

We remained silent for a few minutes. My thoughts were unusually scarce. I vaguely felt that his sudden change of mood was foreboding to me, but I was not afraid or apprehensive. I just did not want to talk any more. Somehow, words seemed to be inaccurate and their meanings difficult to pinpoint. I had never felt that way about talking, and upon realizing my unusual mood I hurriedly began to talk.

"But what can I do with this hill, don Juan?"

"Fix every feature of it in your memory. This is the place where you will come in dreaming. This is the place where you will meet with powers, where secrets will someday be revealed to you.

"You are hunting power and this is your place, the place where you will store your resources.

"It doesn't make sense to you now. So let it be a piece of nonsense for the time being."

We climbed down the rock and he led me to a small bowl-like depression on the west side of the hilltop. We sat down and ate there.

Undoubtedly there was something indescribably pleasant for me on that hilltop. Eating, like resting, was an unknown exquisite sensation.

The light of the setting sun had a rich, almost copperish, glow, and everything in the surroundings seemed to be dabbed with a golden hue. I was given totally to observing the scenery; I did not even want to think.

Don Juan spoke to me almost in a whisper. He told me to watch every detail of the surroundings, no matter how small or seemingly trivial. Especially the features of the scenery that were most prominent in a westerly direction. He said that I should look at the sun without focusing on it until it had disappeared over the horizon.

The last minutes of light, right before the sun hit a blanket of low clouds or fog, were, in a total sense, magnificent. It was as if the sun were inflaming the earth, kindling it like a bonfire. I felt a sensation of redness in my face.

"But now you must focus your attention on everything that exists on this hilltop, because this is the most important place of your life."

He look at me as if judging the effect of his words.

"This is the place where you will die," he said in a soft voice.

I fidgeted nervously, changing sitting positions, and he smiled.

"I will have to come with you over and over to this hilltop," he said. "And then you will have to come by yourself until you're saturated with it, until the hilltop is oozing you. You will know the time when you are filled with it. This hilltop, as it is now, will then be the place of your last dance."

"What do you mean by my last dance, don Juan"?

"This is the site of your last stand," he said. "You will die here no matter where you are. Every warrior has a place to die. A place of his predilection which is soaked with unforgettable memories, where powerful events left their mark, a place where he has witnessed marvels, where secrets have been revealed to him, a place where he has stored his personal power.

"A warrior has the obligation to go back to that place of his predilection every time he taps power in order to store it there. He either goes there by means of walking or by means of dreaming.

"And finally, one day when his time on earth is up and he feels the tap of death on his left shoulder, his spirit, which is always ready, flies to the place of his predilection and there the warrior dances to his death.

"Every warrior has a specific form, a specific posture of power, which he develops throughout his life. It is a sort of dance. A movement that he does under the influence of his personal power.

"If a dying warrior has limited power, his dance is short; if his power is grandiose, his dance is magnificent. But regardless of whether his power is small or magnificent, death must stop to witness his last stand on earth. Death cannot overtake the warrior who is recounting the toil of his life for the last time until he has finished his dance."

Don Juan's words made me shiver. The quietness, the twilight, the magnificent scenery, all seemed to have been placed there as props for the image of a warrior's last dance of power.

"And thus you will dance to your death here, on this hilltop, at the end of the day. And in your last dance you will tell of your struggle, of the battles you have won and of those you have lost; you will tell of your joys and bewilderments upon encountering personal power. Your dance will tell about the secrets and about the marvels you have stored. And your death will sit here and watch you.

"The dying sun will glow on you without burning, as it has done today. The wind will be soft and mellow and your hilltop will tremble. As you reach the end of your dance you will look at the sun, for you will never see it again in waking or in dreaming, and then your death will point to the south. To the vastness."

Much within this passage was akin to my perceptions at the lake, which substantiated my view of it as a place of superb power. At the beginning of the passage, Castaneda describes feelings strongly aligned to my own. He experienced an unexplainable sense of quietness and well-being. His thoughts ceased, and he felt an unprecedented happiness and sense of health. He was filled with a quiet joy that made him weep, and yet he did not understand it. And he felt as if he would like to remain there forever. These feelings were a mystery to him, and yet he experienced them with profound intensity. They were engendered entirely by his surroundings, by some power on that hilltop. His peace and joy were unprecedented, and yet they were completely unexplainable. How well I knew those sensations!

Don Juan gave that land, and particularly that hilltop, to Castaneda. It became his beloved place, uniquely his. It was his to care for, and in turn, it would care for him. Everything there, every rock and bush, occupied a position of significance. He would return throughout his life. It was intimately bound up with his evolution. This was exactly the relationship I shared with the lake. It was, as that hilltop was for Castaneda, a place saturated with unforgettable memories, where powerful events took place that would forever alter the course of my life, where marvelous secrets were revealed to me, and where I sought power. And every activity which I pursued in the locale of the lake was, as was true for Castaneda on his hilltop, a peculiarly exquisite sensation.

I possessed the lake in some deep, inner way. By some process he did not fully understand, Castaneda had found that hill himself, and therefore it was uniquely his. And by some design or combination of forces equally mysterious, I had found the lake. It had become a dominant feature of my life, and, just as Castaneda had discovered about his hill in relation to his own experiences, I found no parallel to the lake in the turmoil of my everyday life. There was nothing with which the lake could compare. It was a unique and inexplicable world. There had never been precedent for it in my life. With what could I equate it? In all my experience, it was strangely singular.

Castaneda had come to that hill to hunt power whether he liked it or not, and it was pointed out to him that not only was this not his decision, but that it was not a human decision. I had often viewed my relationship to the power of the lake the same way. It had always seemed that there was more involved than my own will. Many years ago I had set forces in motion by making a simple decision that I wanted to know what truth was. I had uttered this desire at the lake. But why had I done it there, and what had guided me there? Was it some karmic force? Had I lived other lives there? Were there other volitions, perhaps nonhuman ones, involved in the evolution and development of these circumstances in my life? I could never have imagined what this naive desire would set into motion. As the years passed, I had become a deliberate hunter of power, but was this really my choice to make? Was I about to turn and walk away and forget what I had seen at the lake? Was I not compelled to write this book, and to see it through to its completion? I had become a hunter of power because I had first been hunted. It was as if I had sprung a trap on myself. I was led there, and I had participated in a design of power by uttering that desire. And when I did so, I became the prey. This had been evident ever since my first visit.

It was true that man had the potential to exercise a tremendous force of will over his life, but few people had any idea of its true nature. I had never been either a determinist or a fatalist. But I intuited that there was far more involved in the determining of direction in one's life than one's own hopes and actions. Karma could not explain it all. There was much truth in what the pagans believed: that there were innumerable forces in the world around us which, although unseen and incomprehensible, exercised tremendous influence over our lives. I was open to astrology. I saw that man was deeply affected by a whole array of celestial influences, but I felt that it went much further than this. The world was full of mysterious volitional forces, entities, modes of being, which affected our lives. And where, indeed, would they act upon one more that in the setting of a place of power, or a "place of one's predilection," as don Juan would express it?

Perhaps science would eventually resurrect the idea of a living world. It had removed a dimension from the world that mythology had provided, and had rendered man's view of the universe inanimate. Even though there were rationalists who would concede to a certain credibility in astrology, it would be from the standpoint of a blind, dead mechanicalism; that is, mindless, whirling celestial bodies, whose inanimate masses exerted pressure on us as they pursued their courses through space. And indeed, merely by virtue of their enormous masses, they do have profound effects upon life on earth, including men. But is that all there is to it? Hindu cosmology tells us that these celestial bodies are the vehicles, one might say the "bodies," through which the evolution of enormously advanced modes of consciousness takes place. Anyone who has studied G. I. Gurdjieff is familiar with the unsettling idea that, not only are the various planetary and solar bodies, or entities, alive, but that psychic life on earth, including that generated by men, provides a kind of food for them. And since this is one of the immutable conditions within the enormous design of nature, there is nothing man can do about it, at least from the standpoint of the overall conditions of his race, although there is room in the scheme of things for a small percentage of individuals who possess the necessary will and intelligence to evolve beyond such conditions.

Such ideas are not uncommon, nor are they irrational. They compel us to consider the possibility that we are not so free and independent as our egocentric nature would delude us into believing. They suggest a condition which, although disturbing, would nevertheless seem logical: that everything which exists is both a consumer and something which is eventually consumed. We prey upon and eat many things, whether it is the meat we obtain from animals to feed our bodies, or the minerals and energy we remove from the earth to feed our cars and homes and factories. In turn, we accept that our bodies die and become food for other forms of life. But Gurdjieff suggests that there are other such cycles, psychic ones, and that, just as we derive psychic energy from the world around us, the psychic energy we produce is food for forces greater than we are. To deny this or to maintain that our will is completely our own and that we do what we please is nothing but ignorance, a foolish attempt to deny reality. We feed, and we are fed upon. This is not necessarily bad. It means that there is the possibility of relationships in which one experiences a condition of mutual sustenance between himself and other forces and powers around him, and surely there are many such powers.

The idea of places of power strongly suggests that our wills are not always our own, and that our relationships to other things are symbiotic in a sense that exceeds the physical. Thus don Juan indicated to Castaneda that the decision to hunt power was not a human one, that everything on the hilltop was under his care, and vice versa, and finally, that, just as he could use everything on the hilltop, he also could be used by all that was there.

After don Juan gave the hill to Castaneda, the question arose as to what could be done with it. I have thought about how difficult it would be for me to describe to someone exactly what I did at the lake. It was the place where I hunted power. But how many would understand what I meant by this? I have referred briefly in the following chapter to my "techniques" for exploring my perceptions at the lake and seeking power there, but beyond this, there is not much that I can say. In a sense, I really had no techniques. Whatever else this might indicate, it was ironic, at least in the case of an individual like myself, because for the greater part of my life I had been deeply involved with techniques of every kind. I had been seriously involved with the piano for over twenty years, a discipline which had called for many different aspects of technical proficiency. And certainly, the yoga disciplines with which I had been involved required, as the piano had, the constant practice of various techniques to attain a degree of mastery. During the years that filled the period from the time that my relationship with my guru came to an end, during the fall of 1968, until the beginning of the 1980s, I was preoccupied with techniques; that is, with various practices that would enable me to acquire more knowledge. It was really with this end in mind that I explored so many occult and metaphysical schools. I was searching for ways that would enable me to have control over my life. And in doing so I compiled a large repertory of techniques for affecting my own consciousness and the world around me. It was a valuable experience, but it did not bring happiness. This preoccupation seemed sometimes to separate me more from the fulfillment and happiness I was seeking. I eventually realized that these techniques were not really my goals, but that what I really desired was a true relationship with the power which had now and then touched my life through the lake.

I had no overall, set methods for my encounters with power at Lake Geneva. Everything was very fluid and characterized by a certain sense of spontaneity. What I did there depended on the world at that moment, and how I perceived the power within it. I somehow knew exactly what I was doing. My actions arose from a deep intuitive awareness of the forces around me, and because I was flexible, I had control. This control lay in my being profoundly aware of myself in a non-egoistic way, and aware of the movement of power there, and open and sensitive to it. True control lay in knowing what I could fully control and in doing so, and in knowing, on the other hand, how to flow with forces which were under the control of other volitions. Yet it was not a kind of wisdom I could take credit for in the sense that I had struggled and worked in some arduous way to attain it. It was the result of the one most consistent and deliberate technique, or course of action, which I followed at the lake; namely, to be available to the power there. This was the key that unlocked the door. I could not define it or predict its outcome, but I knew unmistakably the feeling and the direction. I wanted it very much and I was aware that I was hunting it. During the course of my life, my searching had been born out of something simple and pure, and had become very complicated. But eventually, my search had again become simple, although its implications might seem rather complex and far-reaching, and although its present character was the outgrowth of many years of questing and experimentation.

As Castaneda has said of his experiences on that hilltop, so I have said of my experiences at Lake Geneva; that is, that eating, and resting, and walking, and every other action which I executed at the lake brought a unique and indescribable pleasure to me. As perplexing as it may sound, even the experiences of apprehension and fear which I sometimes encountered there were not, in my mind, of a negative character. They were charged with energy, and they made me incredibly alert. Through them, I became more attuned to the power around me, and they even had a pleasurable aspect. I saw even those experiences as positive. They, too, were part of the power at the lake, and through them, as well as through the experiences of light, I approached the reality which I was seeking.

I studied every minute detail of the lake and its hills, particularly the Point. Nothing was too small to be worthy of notice. The awareness of the position of every rock and pebble was a means to focus and enhance my consciousness, and the movement of every cloud in the sky held meaning. I was intent upon being as acutely aware as possible of everything at the lake. I sought to compress all the experience I could into every second I was there. The more fully I absorbed every aspect of that world and stored it in my memory, the more it became an indelible part of my being, both at the lake and away from it.

I mention astral travel because, although I once practiced it for various reasons, one of the most important motivations was that it could potentially enable me to return to the lake in nonphysical form. Although it is possible for a person to will himself to travel astrally to a location he has never seen nor previously been to physically, in cases where one is trying to send his astral consciousness to a locale physically known to him, a clear and detailed memory of that place cannot but help him achieve that goal. When don Juan spoke to Castaneda about dreaming, a concept that strongly suggests astral projection, he made it clear that, when traveling to a place in dreaming, it was most helpful to have committed specific objects there to memory, and also that, in dreaming, it was easier to focus on a place of power. I refer to don Juan's reference to dreaming which is part of the passage from *Journey to Ixtlan*. He is speaking to Castaneda about the hilltop.

"Fix every feature of it in your memory. This is the place where you will come in dreaming. This is the place where you will meet with powers, where secrets will someday be revealed to you."

Don Juan instructed Castaneda to look at the sun without focusing on it until it was gone from sight, beyond the horizon. What is most significant here is not that it was the sun that was the object of attention, although it was indeed important at that moment, but rather that Castaneda was to look at it "without focusing on it." Although it would be very misleading to imply that this was all there was to detecting power, it is an important aspect of it because looking without focusing enables the eyes to perceive something in a manner differently than they ordinarily would. It permits a wider range of sensory phenomena to reach the observer's consciousness without undergoing the normal degree of selective censorship to which one's impressions are ordinarily subjected, and at the same time it helps to make the mind more clear and open by inhibiting its natural tendency to be cluttered by a constant stream of useless thoughts. This helps change the nature of the perception, and enables one to receive things about phenomena in the surrounding world that would not ordinarily be apparent, although very real. One might say that this technique helps one allow the power in some outer aspect of the world to enter him by permitting him to step from behind those aspects of the mind that ordinarily shield him from such perceptions.

For some time, I felt that I did not understand what was meant by returning to a place of power, either by walking or dreaming, in order to store power. But as time passed, it seemed that that was exactly what I had been doing, without really realizing it, for many years. Tremendous changes immediately took place when I went to the lake; that is, the transfiguration that came about in my consciousness, and the nature of my perceptions and feelings, and the dramatic contrast in the environment that surrounded me there, in comparison with the ordinary environment in which I lived. And I had noticed that, particularly in the last few years when my relationship with the lake seemed to unfold more dramatically and many interesting, related events began to take place in my life, I had experienced even more profound perceptions and realizations there. The power there seemed to be growing. It was becoming more apparent. Although I was still experiencing inner struggles, I was gradually undergoing a kind of crystallization within myself, a growing conviction about what I found at the lake, which became ever more indispensible to my life. I felt compelled to search for the meaning of those experiences.

Why? It became clear that I had been storing power there during all those trips. And the more focused I became about the lake, the more power I stored. I had not gone there in dreaming, by astral projection, for a long time. It was not something that had occupied my thoughts and energies. But my trips there were becoming more and more deliberate in their purpose, which was, specifically, to become available to the mysterious power there, to explore it, and to realize the potential of my own consciousness. I was acquiring a kind of momentum that was inexorably growing. I was accumulating power. All the signs of it were there. I simply had not thought of it as such. In don Juan's terms, I was becoming saturated with the lake and its power, until it was oozing me. I was looking for that time when I would be filled with it. I intuited, in don Juan's words, an implication of a kind of finality, a crystallization on a certain level of consciousness I had not yet attained. This was part of that important step that remained to be taken; that is, to go beyond certain fears I had and discover what waited in the world beyond them, and to embrace that power and fuse my being with it in such a way that it would permanently transform and strengthen the rest of my life.

Finally, don Juan spoke of a place of power as the site of one's death. This was not something I had thought about very much, but in studying that passage, certain things I had thought about in the past became much clearer. I understood don Juan's statement that the location where one was actually physically dying was of no importance. Still, I had not thought of experiencing my death within the realm of power at the lake. I had, however, often pondered the possibility of some kind of personal identification or fusion with that power after my death. It was not something I sought, at least not yet, because I was not fully aware of what lay in that direction. Death seemed like an awesome thing, and the nature of whatever experiences lay beyond it also seemed to be something not to be taken lightly or thought about carelessly. Thus, I felt that it would not be wise to desire something so incredibly final and yet not fully understood.

Don Juan said that a warrior's last dance was a kind of movement, the nature of which was determined by his personal power. This dance was reflective of the nature and scope of the personal power which he had stored during his life, and recounted the warrior's encounters with power. Many years after I had originally read this, I discerned a meaning in it that related to the growth of my own experiences at the lake. Everything I did at the lake was creating my own personal form, or posture, of power. My relationship to the power of the lake was growing and I was indeed accumulating a power there that reflected itself in the increasing expansion and momentum of my perceptions and experiences. I knew that I was developing my own form, or posture, of power.

I clearly understood then, more than ever before, why it was really impossible to fully share and explain my experiences with anyone else. I also saw why it was so that I must always seek those experiences alone, and why it had been absolutely necessary to overcome my fear of loneliness at the lake and embrace its ultimate solitude. My quest for that power and my relationship with it was a profoundly personal affair, and it was thus that I had developed, over the years, a personal relationship with the lake. How could I ever hope, in a few moments or even in an hour or two of conversation, to express to someone else the state of power and awareness and perception that had taken me a lifetime to develop? When I realized this, the frustration I had often experienced in the past over not being able to articulate my experiences in a clearly graspable way greatly diminished. I had expected something that was really not possible, and to have agonized over it was unnecessary. In the past, I had undergone a great deal of uncertainty about the nature and validity of what I had experienced at Lake Geneva, particularly about how I could characterize it all in terms of its subjective and objective aspects. Because of the difficulty I had in communicating those experiences to others, I had somehow felt at times that perhaps my experiences had, after all, been exclusively subjective in character—that they had come entirely from within my own being, and that there had been no objective, exterior circumstances or forces involved in my perceptions. It was not so much that I feared that my experiences had been only imagined, but rather that I found myself wondering if there were really a power and consciousness at the lake, independent of the forces that moved within my own personal psyche. All such doubts were eventually put to rest, and my encounters with individuals like Shupshe Wahnah had greatly helped, and had deeply strengthened my convictions about my perceptions and experiences. Still, it was almost a revelation when I finally embraced the realization that my experiences at Lake Geneva were ultimately inexpressible not particularly because of any uniquely subjective aspects, but rather because they were intensely personal. They were incredibly so, and they were the result of years of effort and searching. They were the testimony of an intimate relationship with a unique and lovely place that was developing over a lifetime—a lifetime whose character and direction had been touched and forever altered by a contact with a place of exquisite and incomprehensible power.

Meditations and Reflections

O how I love Thy law!
It is my meditation all the day.
—Psalm 119:97

In Whose waters, here, I lie,
In Lake Geneva's deep blue realms,
Where willow fronds bend down to touch
The wavering reflections of the sky—
Its silent, meditative heights, where
Great vaulted walls of vibrant cyanine
Arch, to make a roof, for floors
Of moving waters.

This Giant Room—
Mansion Celestial,
Whose Tapestries are leaves of green,
Filigreed to weave and blend;
Whose colors never find their end,
In the whispering, shifting
Breathing of the Day...

Lake Geneva
July 19, 1972

The world that surrounds us holds infinite possibilities for new perceptions and experiences. There are no boundaries for those who have discovered how to release their consciousness so that it may soar into expanded modes of awareness. It is possible to perceive the awesome power and mystery within the being and consciousness of the world by means of certain powerful senses that are subtler than physical ones, and which are capable of extending into realms of experience that are traditionally viewed as inaccessible. But these finer instruments of perception can enable one to grasp the world in new and profound, nonordinary ways; for example, to feel it with the eyes, and to receive extraordinary sensations from it through the solar plexus. How does one identify and define these mysterious mechanisms of perception? Do they function through the vehicles of certain psychic or spiritual organs unknown to modern physiologists?

I am deeply aware of the power of many phenomena in nature to evoke various distinct and profound states of consciousness. Certain sounds that are found in the natural environment can produce intensely animating effects within my inner being. Are they stimulating certain specific psychic or astral centers, or chakras? The evocation of specific states of consciousness through the effects of sound upon the nervous system is a science that has been known in the East for thousands of years, and I perceive a strong relationship between the theory behind such practices and the effects which many sounds in nature have had upon me. For sound and vibration are intimately interrelated with consciousness, a fact utilized in many different cultures and in many schools of knowledge. It is for the purpose of affecting consciousness that mantras are employed, and striking results can be similarly attained through the use of various Eastern musical instruments.

As with sound, there are various visual phenomena in nature that are capable of inducing remarkable psychic states of awareness. In a similar way, the vast multiplicity of the auditory, visual, and even olfactory and tactile aspects of nature are capable of engendering intense emotional reactions. It is thus that, in various religious and occult contexts, one finds the extensive use of diagrams, images, icons, colors, incense, sounds, music, and other sense-directed devices for inducing desired states of consciousness.

In my experiences with the natural world, I have found that certain sounds in particular have compelled my attention. These sounds include those produced by the cicadas, and other insects, and those of the tree frogs; bird calls; wind; and particularly water. These and other sounds, and also certain visual elements in nature, including the play of sunlight on water, the motion of waves, the depthless blue sky and its shining processions of clouds, and the deep shadows among dark green hills, can produce immediate changes in my consciousness. In the world of exquisite power at Lake Geneva, these diverse manifestations of nature assumed an unparalleled potency and spoke to me with awesome eloquence. I have experienced again and again a mode of consciousness at the lake, a state of acute awareness, in which every manifestation and movement within the conscious being of nature communicated a message to me.

The Water

I have sat for hours upon the rocks along the shores of Lake Geneva, enthralled in the ever-changing movements and sounds of the water. Contemplating the surface of the lake, gazing at some distant point on the sparkling, undulating surface, and then refocusing on the water a few feet in front of me, I have witnessed one of the greatest and most exhilarating expressions of the spirit and psychic life of the earth. Rising suddenly above the undercurrent of countless patterns and rhythms of the waves, exploding joyously above the confluence of gurglings and splashes and sloshings, the water would break against the immovable boulders with a sharp and percussive sound it often makes, and my consciousness would be instantly galvanized into an acute and vibrant alertness. For in that sound, that explosion, or *éclat* (burst, explosion, peal, outburst), there seemed to be expressed all the limitless joy of nature, a spontaneous outburst, a celebration of infinite life that constantly renewed itself and manifested countless new facets.

Others have perceived this spontaneous celebration of life, not only through the medium of water, but in other aspects of nature, as well.

For you will go out with joy,
And be led forth with peace;
The mountains and the hills will break forth into shouts of joy before you,
And all the trees of the field will clap their hands.
—Isaiah 55:12

O sing to the Lord a new song,
For He had done wonderful things...

Shout joyfully to the Lord, all the earth;
Break forth and sing for joy and sing praises...

Let the sea roar and all it contains,
The world and those who dwell in it.
Let the rivers clap their hands;
Let the mountains sing together for joy
Before the Lord...
—Psalm 98: 1, 4, 7–9

Let the heavens be glad, and let the earth rejoice;
Let the sea roar, and all it contains;
Let the field exult, and all that is in it.
Then all the trees of the forest will sing for joy
Before the Lord...
—Psalm 96: 11–13

The floods have lifted up, O Lord,
The floods have lifted up their voice;
The floods lift up their pounding waves.
More than the sounds of many waters,

Than the mighty breakers of the sea,
The Lord on high is mighty.
                                        —Psalm 93: 3–4

Although these references to nature are symbolic, they refer to the reality of the consciousness and expressiveness of nature, and to the fact that, even though this knowledge has been largely cast away and forgotten, the being of the universe is the manifestation, the body, the expression of an infinite and eternal consciousness, and is intimately and inextricably bound up with it.

The passages from Isaiah 55 and from Psalm 98 both employ the term "clap." Here I refer back to the French term *éclat,* whose infinitive form, *éclater,* means, among other things, "to clap," and also "to burst," "to explode," "to break out." I was attracted by the similarity and general resemblance between the two terms, and noted with delight their obvious connection to the joyous sound made by the water. Whenever I heard this sound, I experienced inner joy and happiness, and fell in step with a creation that was reflecting back its exuberance toward the power that engendered it.

Because I made my living for several years as a pianist in the professional worlds of ballet and modern dance, I have observed the performances of various African dance companies and listened to the ensembles of African percussionists who accompanied them. I have never heard any other manmade sounds which were more joyous or exciting. They were characterized by an infinite variety of complex and subtle rhythms, timbres, and intonations, and exhibited an inexorable force. At various intervals, one particular drummer would suddenly rise above the driving ostinato of the rest of the ensemble and break forth spontaneously into an ecstatic explosion of breathtaking syncopation and intensity. The percussive power of such sounds not only reached me through my ears, but I could feel them throughout my entire body. Those waves of sound struck gently yet detectably against my solar plexus, and seemed to penetrate and arouse my inner being, creating a kind of intensely pleasurable agitation. I perceived a direct affinity between the ecstatic rhythms and timbres of the drummers and the expressively articulate sounds of the water.

It is also interesting to note that the syllable, "aum," which is familiar to anyone who has studied yoga or Hindu philosophy, is often compared to the sound of rushing water. Aum, also written, "om," is the most sacred word of the Vedas, symbolizing both the Personal God and the Absolute. Patanjali said that this is the word which manifests God. It is the basis of all sounds, and denotes the entire range and possibility of all the words which can be uttered. It is the Logos, the Word. It is the most universal of all word-symbols that expresses the nondual Brahman, the Akhanda Satchidānanda, whose essence is undivided existence-knowledge-bliss. When I studied yoga, my spiritual teacher told me that, when one came to hear this sound, it was like hearing the roaring of the ocean. Many people are aware of how relaxing and revivifying it is to be near water, and of how cleansing and beneficial the effects of its voice can be upon a troubled mind. Similar benefit may be derived from meditating upon the symbol *aum,* the fundamental vibration upon which the entire manifested universe is based. Everything in the Creation is vibrating, and the infinite variety of vibratory rates derive from the one fundamental vibration, aum. When I sat quietly at the shore of the lake and meditated upon the sounds of the waters for even a short period of time, I derived as much benefit as I would have experienced from a considerably longer period of yoga meditation. Diligent meditation upon aum can even lead one to cosmic consciousness.

Aum is the Word spoken of in John 1:1–4.

> In the beginning was the Word, and the Word was with God, and the Word was God.
> The same was in the beginning with God.
> All things were made by him; and without him was not any thing made that was made.
> In Him was life; and the life was the light of men.

In the book of Revelation, in 1:12–18, John describes his vision of the great being who calls himself "the first and the last, and the living One." It is most interesting and significant that John describes the voice of this being as "like the sound of many waters." The passage is given below.

> And I turned to see the voice that was speaking with me. And having turned I saw seven golden lampstands;
> And in the middle of the lampstands one like a son of man, clothed in a robe reaching to the feet, and girded across His breast with a golden girdle.
> And His head and His hair were white like white wool, like snow; and His eyes were like a flame of fire;
> And His feet were like burnished bronze, when it has been caused to glow in a furnace, and His voice was like the sound of many waters.
> And in His right hand He held seven stars; and out of His mouth came a sharp two-edged sword; and His face was like the sun shining in its strength.
> And when I saw Him, I fell at His feet like a dead man. And He laid His right hand upon me, saying, "Do not be afraid; I am the first and the last,
> And the living One…

I have seen many bodies of water, large and small, and I have lived on a number of them. I have seen many other beautiful northern lakes, and I lived for three summers at the Interlochen Arts Academy in northern Michigan, on a charming little lake a few miles from Traverse City, which itself is situated upon the shores of Lake Michigan, whose waters, for many miles up and down its eastern shores, are clear and beautiful and, to all appearances, unpolluted. But none of those waters drew me like Lake Geneva, not even the great oceans. The oceans and many other bodies of water manifest their own beauty and magnetism, and I have seen and enjoyed the things they offer.

But Lake Geneva was different. It was a place of visions, where I had been spiritually reborn. There had been revealed to me there, and only there, a new and awesome universe. And, since I had come to know Shupshe Wahnah, I had been provided with evidence that, in terms of its geographic locale and various related characteristics, Lake Geneva was indeed a place of special power.

My experiences at the lake began in mystery. I spent many years trying to understand those mysteries in the wrong way, in a roundabout manner, by studying things, by accumulating masses of information and data, and by entertaining all kinds of theories instead of looking directly to the lake and its experiences for the answers. I will never regret all those years of searching. They gave me greatly expanded and enhanced insight and appreciation into various schools of thought and discipline, and they helped me construct a proper sense of perspective about where I stood in relation to the universe of thought and philosophies.

But I became aware of a remarkable duality in my quest. For years, I had been digging for more and more knowledge, yet what I really longed for was not knowledge, but oneness with the mystery that expressed itself through the waters of Lake Geneva. I did not really need to define that mystery; indeed, I could not. I needed to become one with it, and in doing so, I would come to know it in a different manner, in a deeper, more living way.

I learned from Shupshe Wahnah that the mystery there was real. It had an objective reality. It was known by someone besides myself. In addition to this knowledge, I was helped and gratified by Shupshe's comments concerning the nature of the forces at the lake, and I was deeply affected and fulfilled by his knowledge which he had shared with me about Negoya, his identity, and the manner in which he had appeared to me. These were all things which were of paramount importance. But beyond that objective sphere of knowledge, any other true knowledge concerning the essence of the power within the waters of the lake would come only through direct experience, through my own perceptions. Thus, in warning me against becoming bogged down in American Indian research, reincarnation, and other such things, Shupshe had wisely directed me in such a way that I would not repeat my tendencies of earlier years.

There are no explanations I can give for what lives within Lake Geneva's waters. There is only that sublime reality which exists and breathes there, and which can be known only through experience and direct perception. In that world, to have knowledge means to become alive, to flow out into something else and become one with it. In the face of what I have seen at the lake, all explanations and labels, scientific and otherwise, are destined to be nothing but meaningless, dead weight, only so many pointless and empty words. To present some groping philosophical explanation as to what those living, breathing waters really embodied and expressed, or the trees, or the rocks and hills, or anything else there, would be doomed to failure. It would only render the reality flat and sterile, and it would only be creating yet another barrier between ourselves and that glorious identity which animates the world, and which can only be comprehended through love for it, through striving to become one with it.

My initial experiences when I was fifteen released within me a flood of spiritual yearning. I wanted to return to those waters again and again. I loved them deeply, and the reality which they expressed:

> Such a long time ago, since I sat
> upon the glistening rocks, drenched with
> spray from the dancing waves,
> lapping at their base.
> Those surging waves!
> What beautiful mysteries they brought,
> unmuffled, to my ears.

And further on:

> Your shimmering trees,
> reaching up into the sun, tell me
> that you are eternal; the force in you
> is everlasting.
> Your waters whisper the longings
> of my soul. They speak that secret
> which I can never express.

Time passed, but my love and desire for the waters of Lake Geneva never diminished, and I always returned to it. Its role in my life grew and evolved. In August 1973, while I was at Lake Geneva for a week, at Conference Point Camp, during the first of my two trips there as a counselor for the group from my church in my home town, there happened to come into my possession a book entitled *Wychwood,* written by Frances Kinsley Hutchinson (Chicago: The Lakeside Press, 1928). The work is subtitled *The History of an Idea* and is divided into three major parts: "Our Country Home," "Our Country Life," and "Our Final Aim." This charming work describes the conception and realization of a country estate on Lake Geneva, which came to be named Wychwood, and which became a kind of botanical paradise and wildlife sanctuary. Within its delightful and entertaining pages, the scope of the book is a description of the history of Wychwood; the purpose of the estate, the landscaping and development and gardening, whose aim was always to preserve the natural and wild beauty which existed there, descriptions of the peaceful and fulfilling lifestyle which was pursued there, and the purposes and goals of the Wychwood estate.

Of particular interest were some of the passages I came across that described the Hutchinson couple's feelings about Lake Geneva. The words strongly conveyed the fact that their author, like me, had experienced a deep love for the lake, and when I read them I entertained the possibility of some profound implications.

Last to blossom of all the flowers, we found the strange wych-hazel. It met us just within the gate, it followed with its wands of gold our wanderings in blurry glens, it led us to the water's edge. The old myth came into my mind: "Wherever points the hazel-rod, there dig, for water ye shall find." We did not have to even dig, for water indeed was here, in alluring expanse spread out before us. What was there about that particular little lake which so captivated us? Why was it that after looking at and admiring the innumerable small lakes with which our woodland State is dotted, we always returned to this one with a sigh of content?

It was a friendly bit of water, with friendly fish in its cool depths only waiting to be caught,—black bass and perch and pickerel; a lake just big enough to temper the hot prairie winds of midsummer and to reflect its thunder-caps and brilliant sunsets, a long lake with deeply dented shores that sloped into its shining waters so that every pretty point had the coolest breezes and the most extended view! But where was its peculiar charm? To be sure it had the feminine quality of changefulness: it was never twice alike. Did our imagination, even then, leap to its cool touch on August mornings and show us its mirror-like reflections on still September dawns? Did its refreshing breezes tell us of the wondrous moonlit nights before us?—those nights, yes, they must have held the secret, the last exquisite touch. Surely nowhere else did the shimmering water dance under the golden rays in so gladsome a fashion. Floating over its glassy surface, down those paths of light, suspended between earth and sky, a sweet voice making melody and all one's senses lulled to rest,—could happiness go further?

"Surely nowhere else did the shimmering water dance under the golden rays in so gladsome a fashion." What then was the secret of the lake? Its haunting, enchanting presence is alluded to in these words. "Floating over its glassy surface, down those paths of light, a sweet voice making melody and all one's senses lulled to rest,—could happiness go further?"

The following passage movingly portrays the author's feeling of wonder and her love for her surroundings, and her sense of harmony and oneness with the living world and all that it contains.

This shall be our home and our refuge and a refuge for our friends. Can life ever grow monotonous, or the days bore us, with such wonders unfolding before our newly opened eyes? To have a new sensation of genuine pleasure when one has passed the fortieth milestone is something not to be despised, and here was a whole world of new sensations, a daily new discovery to feast upon. To take possession of the sunrises and the starlit nights, to feel the earth full of promise beneath one, to say to each winged creature and trembling being, "You are my brother and sister, let us enjoy all this together!"—what a heavenly outlook!

I surely understand the feelings of wonder of Frances Kinsley Hutchinson as she surveyed the lake, its waters, and its surrounding country. Part of her sensed that there was something special and mysterious there, within the being of the lake and manifested in its waters, which could be detected, "floating over its glassy surface, down those paths of light, suspended between earth and sky, a sweet voice making melody..."

I always recognized a force in the waters of Lake Geneva, a power that compelled and altered my consciousness. It was an energy I fed upon, and a part of me always went hungry until I was able to go to the lake. When I was there, I drank deeply of its incorruptible nature. Within the vast framework of creation, the lake was a gem, gracious and passionate. It was easy and natural for me to hear the thoughts of the lake. It beckoned to me with an unearthly and compelling voice, and if I was fit to receive it, it offered me a depthless spring of joyous life. Perpetually dancing and celebrating the joy of its being, mirroring the inscrutable and indefinable source of its creation and existence, the lake spoke to me ceaselessly of the foundation of the universe, of the Loving Consciousness behind it.

In my eyes, the lake was unquestionably a living being. Its waters expressed a form of life which was different from what most people would understand as living, but that was because their definitions of life were limited, and because their viewpoints were restricted by their perceptions, which ordinarily permitted only the most constricted view of the world. However, impaired perceptions do not change facts. The lake's rocks and trees and hills were alive. Everything there was bathed in a psychic energy. That life was overwhelmingly apparent, and it had been so ever since Negoya appeared to me there and accelerated my consciousness and my perceptions, and ushered me into the dramatic visions that revealed the soul of that world.

I have contemplated the waters of Lake Geneva from many perspectives. But most often I would walk to the Point, where I would sit upon the rocks among the birches at the edge of the water, or upon the granite boulder a short distance away. I almost always approached the Point from the shore path which led there from the west. I could either stay upon this path which would lead directly to the grassy opening, or I could veer off a few hundred feet before that and take a route which would lead me upward to the top of the high hill above the Point. Upon arriving at the spacious, wooded grounds that covered this hill, I could approach the Point from above and, coming upon the long series of concrete steps that led down to the shore, I could look upon the rocks and trees, and beyond to the surface of the water.

I invariably paused at the top of the hill to look at the water before descending. I would stand at the top of the steps, or descend a few feet to the small brick alcove built into the side of the hill. When I paused above the Point on that hill to look down at the surface of the lake, my attention would become powerfully engaged by something I detected with particular clarity. What I invariably saw from that spot was a certain distinct aspect of the psychic life of the water.

Before me lay the firmness and solidity of land, of rocks and trees. I have always had a profound sense of depth and dimensionality, and looking down at those forms from above, I experienced heightened awareness; I embraced the inner, noumenal nature and meaning of form, form projected into spatiality, pregnant, laden with meaning. I had come to the verge of perceiving in higher dimensions, and form acquired a dramatic new aspect. Beyond the forms of land and rocks and trees was the movement of the water. But what I saw upon the surface of the lake was not the movement of something inanimate. The water had become an infinitely responsive field of motion and energy, and yet it was far more than just a mirror for the play of energy that danced in its waves. It was the movement, the life process, of a form of being; a mode of joyous, surging consciousness; an elemental purity, which lay beyond the accepted and impaired concept of life; a form of evolution that men became blind to when they forgot that the world was a living being.

Within the lake, upon its surface, was manifested a living hieroglyph that was enigmatic and elusive, and yet clearly readable to one who could intuit its meaning. But coexistent with that reality, there was another; namely, the unmistakable presence of a personality. Clearly, there was an entity there, a knowing, which drew love from me. I loved the consciousness within that enchanted water just as surely as I had ever loved anything. It was voluptuous and beautiful; it was passionate, and its spirit was pure and happy.

I often sat among the rocks at the Point, by the edge of the water, where I found that, within a few feet of me, there seemed to be enough to fill a lifetime of meditation. Every moment of passing time saw the play of new phenomena. And although they expressed a unity that was totally harmonious, they also embodied a duality to contemplate. The processes in nature were eternally repeating themselves, as days and nights flowed into thousands of years, and yet that repetition never grew monotonous. I could never get too much of it, and I thought many times about the fact that, within a small radius of me, there was an incalculable variety and number of phenomena; there was a joyful and limitless play, overflowing with eternal happiness, perpetually unfolding, which ceaselessly filled me with serenity and delight. Yet, even if I were to multiply what I witnessed there by countless billions of times, I could not encompass what existed there, in the manifold world, or in the infinity of worlds evolving within the gigantic megacosm that embraced them. Ultimately, there was One from which everything had originated. Within that utter unknowable Essence, the world found its existence. To think that I could know such fullness and joy from such a small corner of that world!

When I sat among the rocks and birches, within reach of the water, I could say to myself, "This is everything. What else could I possibly want? I have no more desires; they are all fulfilled here." The world bestowed a peace that, while I remained there, made me unaware of any other desires or needs. My sense of being an entity constricted within one personality ceased. My immersion in the living perpetuality of the lake smoothed my mind. It erased my false identity and restored me to what I really was: a being within another mysterious and far greater being, the world.

A few feet in front of me was a sparkling and transparent surface which was in continuous motion. As the waves rolled in toward the rocks, it swelled toward me, covering many of the glistening, moss-covered boulders, rearranging the sopping green strands. The waves would make their impact upon the rocks and then recoil sharply, covering the grass and tree trunks near me with a fine spray. As the waves dissipated, the bobbing surface would swiftly recede and drop, clarifying the pebbles and rocks on the bottom, allowing me to focus for an instant on their shining forms, submerged in a bath of green, clear water, suffused with yellow light. Overlaying this surging pattern of flowing images, the leafy shadows of the birch trees, whose trunks and limbs reached out over the water, moved soundlessly over the swells of sunlight and green. Rays of sunlight filtered through their leaves here and there, for an instant, to disappear or shift, sliding up and down the rippling bodies of waves. The surface rose and fell. At various intervals, the leaves of the birches hissed and rippled in the gentle gusts of wind which blew off the lake. The wind refreshed my body as it traveled across my skin. It felt cool and clean, and it carried the wonderful smell of water. The boulders around my feet were round and smooth, and they had the vibration of great age. Their forms were ancient. They had known endless expanses of time, and had been formed through thousands of years of erosion and washing. They had endured until this day, to tell me of the past aeons of the world, and they would yet endure for ages to come. What was a thousand years to this world, or even ten thousand, but a mere breath?

My mind was clear and still. Upon its screen danced the images of sun and water, pebbled bottom and undulating branches of white birches. Through the hours I witnessed this elemental life, and through it I looked upon the passing of ages. Ten thousand years before me the melodious voice of the lake sang, whispering along the shores, as she gurgled her thoughts and secrets, and clapped her hands against the boulders. Long after I have gone, perhaps to hear her lovely, sweet song no more, her gentle spirit will yet lift its voice. My self-awareness is lost as I am carried into her world. My thoughts are gone, and I become the lake. Her primordial spirit speaks to my heart now, fills it. I hear only her voice. My mind is washed clean and absorbed in the rushing of her waters. The length of my existence is nothing as compared to hers, yet she is so young, and always renewed.

In the fullness of day, the energetic wind blew over the lake from the tops of the tall, green hills which plunged into its waters, and brought the surface of the lake to life. From the rocks, I surveyed that unending procession of approaching waves; the swells of cool, deep green water, rippling in the gusts of afternoon winds; a sea of glittering movement, accented by the spontaneous appearance of whitecaps where the crests of the waves broke into white foam. And over that melodious sea of greenish blue danced millions of pinpoints of sunlight, instantaneously, soundlessly, bursting forth and disappearing, moving in countless myriads of coruscating shoals, up and down the sliding, rolling planes of water. My consciousness reached out for thousands of yards over that busy, shifting floor of aquamarine which commingled with the downpour of sunny radiance. My mind swept over the rejoicing body of the lake, hovering at one spot and then another, listening with gladness to the talk of the water, drinking in, eagerly, its life, and the beauty of its ever changing emerald form.

At times, I would focus my awareness exclusively upon the myriad atoms of scintillating light which danced in infinite configurations over the surface of the waves. By partially closing my eyes and squinting at the expansive surface of the lake, I could focus solely upon that flashing, soundless play of speckled iridescence. I experienced the silence of light. It penetrated my squinting eyes and quivered upon the dark mirror inside of me. Within the soundless depths of my being, my consciousness became that play of light. For a few moments, perhaps, I was aware of nothing else. All my thoughts, my whole consciousness, was the light. There was something about turning my attention totally upon those points of light which created the sensation that they existed upon an independent plane, by themselves, apart from the rest of the phenomena which I was seeing. They came into being and lived and were extinguished in an instant of time, within a shining realm which, unlike the world of wind and water and rocks, was utterly soundless; an eternally silent vacuum, filled with an infinite number of points of independent light. The aspect of that light, dancing upon the waves, was particularly eminent when I looked in the direction of the sun as it began to set over the water. At those times, those moving points of dazzling light converged into a shining path of radiant, golden-silver luminosity, an intensely fiery, undulating ribbon, whose brightness and intensity blinded me to all else and stretched across the water to merge into the rich, mellowing orb of the sinking sun. I would return from that voiceless world of light to the commingling sounds of wind and water and rocks, to merge again with that outpouring and blending of elemental utterances, to fill my hours with nature's perpetual voice.

At night, the lake was very different. It was the same body of water throughout the perpetual alternation of day and night, yet, there was something about the lake in darkness that caused it to assume a fundamentally different character. My experience has made me deeply aware that, in places of power where one encounters the manifestation of a unique presence, night mysteriously transforms things so that one who is sensitive to that environment apprehends it differently. I cannot say how much of this, if any, is subjective, but when I am open to the environment of the lake, my identification with it becomes so strong that the borderline between myself and it becomes blurred.

There are forces that have more power at night and that become more active then. They eclipse the powers in ascendancy during the day. These forces exist beyond the traditional, impaired concepts of consciousness and life, and they move upon evolutionary paths hidden from all but a few.

At night, the enormous variety and influx of visual stimuli with which one is inundated during the daylight hours is less. This allows one's mind to direct more attention to other facets of perception, and to become more open to the less obvious, but nevertheless real, things that exist within the world. The darkness thus inclines one to use one's eyes differently than during the day, without necessarily being aware of it.

When I first went to Lake Geneva as a youth, my world view changed radically. I found a new world of beauty and light. But I was confronted by a duality there, for virtually overnight I also acquired a set of perceptions that opened an awareness within me to a mysterious side of the world; not evil, but dark and awesome. But light or dark, I had not known any such perceptions before my first visit to Lake Geneva. Since my decisive reading with Robert the psychic, I had become strongly inclined to believe that the set of perceptions into which I had been initiated at the lake were tied to some kind of psychic contact I had experienced between me and certain former American Indian cultures which had once been located around the Lake Geneva area. I had theorized that perhaps I might even have been in psychic contact with specific individuals who had been part of those cultures. My feelings had become strengthened during my various subsequent research efforts, particularly when I began looking into the Potawatomi culture that had once flourished around the lake, and they were eventually confirmed in a dramatic manner when I learned through Shupshe Wahnah that Negoya had been an Ojibwa Medawinne.

It appeared as if I had come to look at the world much more in the manner of an Indian than as a member of the culture in which I functioned. I wish to avoid appearing so presumptuous as to speak for all Indians, or for Indians in general. But I felt I saw eye to eye with Shupshe on everything that was important, particularly my experiences at Lake Geneva.

There were a number of factors that contributed to the character of my nighttime experiences at Lake Geneva. I have known reluctance and even apprehension about being close to the water at night. Various possible explanations for this include undefined forces to which I was psychically sensitive; perceptions and feelings that were related to Indian cultures which had once flourished around the area; and, a fear of wandering off, of being pulled away, into realms from which I might not be able to return, possibly the world from which Negoya had come. Shupshe had explained that when one performed an act such as Negoya had, of crossing from one world to another, they were temporarily engulfed in an abyss of astral darkness, a kind of negative world in which one could become hopelessly lost, unless they possessed the requisite knowledge or a qualified guide.

All these factors have played a part in my need for caution on certain occasions. I was often conscious of an elemental life there at night, particularly within the waters of the lake, and, because of my reluctance to make myself too available to such things, I have had, at least until the present, far less experience with the contemplation of the water and other aspects of the lake area at night than I have had in the daylight. This is something which I am destined to explore more fully, as I grow stronger and more prepared. But I have shied away from such powers, and it has not been possible to experience them as unrestrictedly as I have the phenomena of the day. Yet, without seeking them, I have acutely sensed their presence, and I clearly perceived that the waters of the lake and the hills that surround it are permeated with mystery.

Even on dark, moonless nights, when it was not possible to see for any distance out over the surface of the lake, the melodious sounds of the lake were always present. The darkness made it all the more possible to focus my attention upon the sounds of the water, and except for tree frogs, crickets, and other insects, there was only the whispering of the waves. On occasions, there was the movement of the wind through the trees, but nights were often still. As evening drew on, the number of motorboats dwindled until the lake was empty and quiet.

At the approach of evening twilight, the deep green surface of the lake mellowed in the haze. The strong winds of afternoon had departed, and as the earth cooled, a gentle, cool movement of air from the lake touched the shores. The vibrating wavelets that covered the surface of the lake absorbed the blues and pinks of the sky, and as darkness engulfed the quietude which had settled over the world, the waves of the lake were also covered with the night, and became a murmuring blackness, sloshing melodiously over the rocks along the shore.

On the nights when I went down to the edge of the lake, I sat in the darkness among the boulders, or perhaps at the base of the birch trees, and, my senses deeply soothed and quieted by the restfulness and tranquility there, I listened with delight and reverence to the nocturnal voice of the lake. I was particularly aware of the dark waves as they slid around the boulders along the shore. The water quietly rushed in and out of the narrow channels between the rocks, sometimes washing over them, and slipping down into the grooves and crevices to merge again with the gently purling water. The gentle surging of the waves and the eddies of swirling water, streaming over the rocks and boulders and trickling down into the flow, gurgled and murmured; an eloquent and incomparably beautiful voice which sang sweetly along the shores, whose melodious call floated over the waters and softly invaded the darkness of the surrounding hills.

When the moon was full, the lake was illumined, the expanses of its glittering waters clearly visible. The bright moonlight streamed down upon the lake and made its surface shine; it flooded the hills, and filled the night sky, irradiating its starry depths so that one might think it was day. What an awesome world!

Even some distance from the shore I could hear the lake, and, depending upon where I stayed when I visited the lake, its sounds could often reach within my quarters. I was sometimes able to listen as I fell asleep. Its sounds always accompanied my walks along the shore, and even when I was in the hills above the lake I could frequently detect its voice. I listened intently to the waves below me as I moved along the paved roads at the Point, and on the nights when I chose not to sit at the edge of the lake, I sometimes sat in the brick alcove to one side of the concrete steps at the Point, instead of sitting among the rocks and birches at the water's edge.

There I was nestled in the side of the hill that sloped down to the flat, grassy expanse along the shore. I felt secure in the earth's bosom. The psychic current was profoundly quieting. At eye level was open grass which descended gently to a line of thick vegetation and trees. This dense growth covered the rest of the hill, which fell away more steeply down to the shore path. From the alcove, I could peer through the vegetation and trees, or down the concrete steps and across the open expanse of grass, to where the dark waters, which were filled with silver on moonlit nights, gently rolled in toward the Point. Above me was a clear view of the open sky. The twinkling stars in its silent depths seemed close. Gently, an exquisite breeze from the lake moved over the hill. The crickets chirped softly in the high grass. My thoughts ceased. My mind was still. Not the slightest ripple of thought disturbed the smooth plane of my consciousness. My being became unencumbered, flawless perception. Lifted by its song, the essence of the lake permeated the night and infiltrated the hills like a pure and subtle incense. As if to possess me, it drew me with its murmuring, enveloping me quietly, softly uttering to me its strange and wonderful elemental thoughts.

The Sky

The sky, with its expressive, infinite, and ever-changing aspects, has presented me with a limitless repertory of perceptions. To merge with its sweeping form is to embrace new and endless and dimensionless modes of thought and being. As it is true with the water, so it is true with the sky, that to comprehend it is to experience the sublimely balanced interrelationship between expansiveness and intimacy. For within the aspect of the gigantic heavens lies the possibility for the mind to take flight, to expand and to coalesce with measureless spaces. And yet this is not at all an absorption of self into some great nothingness. Rather, it is the flowing out of self into an immeasurable abode, the geometrical progression of mind into a vast and imperturbable identity. It is the dissolution of inner boundaries that affix and defend the self, a falling away of the barriers that bar entrance into the dark chambers of the mind. It is an interfusion of the depthless, crystalline blue sky with the mind, an infinite dilation of being that quietly soars into the silence of space and fills it.

Thus, the sky offers the mind the possibility of unrestricted outreach. But further still, through the innumerable facets and subtleties of its ever-changing countenance, this boundless and omnipresent aspect of nature offers a continuous communication of knowledge to us, a continuum of messages that express to us, ironically, the most inexpressible and untranslatable things. It is, therefore, a dynamic and harmonious identity of the infinite with the intimate.

To me, one of the most astonishingly expressive and descriptive orchestral pieces ever written is "Nuages" (Clouds) by Claude Debussy. It is the first of three pieces which comprise the symphonic triptych entitled *Nocturnes.* The second and third pieces of this set, "Fêtes" and "Sirènes," depict respectively a festival atmosphere and the sea, with its manifold rhythms and the mysterious song and laughter of sirens. With reference to the *Nocturnes* and to "Nuages," Debussy himself has made the following comments.

> The title "Nocturnes" is meant to be perceived in a general and, more particularly, in a decorative sense. It is not at all meant to designate the established musical form of the nocturne. Rather it is intended to suggest the whole range of impressions and special effects of light and shadow that the word itself calls to mind.
>
> "Nuages" would evoke the unchanging aspect of the sky, with the slow and solemn procession of the clouds dissolving in a grayish vagueness tinged with white.

I refer here to "Nuages" because to me it is much more than a descriptive tone poem. "Nuages" is not a description of the sky. It "is" the sky. Every motive and harmonic progression and timbre is the embodiment and essence of some aspect of the sky; the silent processions of grey clouds, spanning horizon to horizon, their opaque forms tinged with glowing silver-white; the glimmering, vibrant depths of the atmosphere; and the enigmatic duality of the almost oppressive weight of the clouds juxtaposed with their immateriality, which transcends gravity. Every awesome, electrifying aspect of such a tableau is in this music. The true art of "Nuages" lies in this: that it has become that which it is describing. The sky becomes an experience, rather than an object.

Works of art do exist, in this case a piece of music, that transcend the techniques and disciplines of their respective mediums and embody, even become, the essence of that which they seek to express. "Nuages" is such a work. It not only depicts, by means of a brilliant craftsmanship, the phenomenal side of a particular aspect of the world, but it becomes one with, and therefore mirrors, the noumenal, or inner reality behind the phenomena. I feel that Debussy ranks foremost among composers in terms of this ability. Through his music, his art, Debussy has communicated a reality, a perception that was first his. He has accomplished this in other works as well, most notably in *La Mer* (The Sea), a work comprised of three symphonic sketches which deal with various aspects of the sea in a superbly masterful way. These three sketches are entitled respectively, "De l'aube à midi sur lar mer" (From dawn to noon on the sea), "Jeux de vagues" (Play of the waves), and "Dialogue du vent et de la mer" (Dialogue of the wind and the sea). As "Nuages" is the essence of clouds and the sky, *La Mer* is the essence of the sea; the infinite rhythms and voices of the waves, the interplay of the wind and the water, the play of light in the atmosphere and upon the undulating surface of the water. Debussy demonstrated his genius in many of his piano works; in his sets of Preludes, in the *Estampes,* and in the *Images.* There are numerous pieces of programmatic music which deal with an abundant variety of aspects of nature, as well as with many other subjects, and which are noteworthy in their own respects; for example, "Ce qu'on entend sur la montagne" (What one hears on the mountain) by Liszt, the *Grand Canyon* Suite by Grofé, the *Pines of Rome* by Respighi, and *Gaspard de la Nuit* by Ravel, to name a few. But Debussy stands out in my mind because, through the medium of music, he has depicted not only the sensory aspects of the phenomenal side of nature, but he has communicated the essence behind the phenomena, capturing the most refined subtleties and nuances of those living aspects of the world.

In all of the time I have spent at Lake Geneva, I would say that a significant portion of it has been filled studying the water and the sky. Whereas with the water I became deeply engaged in its visual and auditory aspects, I was, where the sky was concerned, dealing exclusively with visual phenomena. However, rather than considering this a limitation, I would describe it as an opportunity to center and concentrate my will and being totally upon one area of my perceptual powers, and I was thus able to accomplish a number of fulfilling and beneficial things which contributed to my perceptual evolution. First, to focus the totality of my attention upon one primary sensory aspect contributed significantly to a remarkable and profound purity of perception. I was all the more able to identify completely with that which I sought to contemplate, and to merge with it totally. Second, through focusing my attention upon one perceptual medium, namely, the visual, I came progressively to experience deeper and more expansive sensations that are not normally associated with visual perceptions. I began to use my eyes for more than just looking at things. Carlos Castaneda has touched upon this subject numerous times. He has asserted that it is possible to use the eyes to "feel" the world, a statement with which I am in complete agreement.

For one who has truly touched the world with his eyes, no explanation is necessary. For those who have not, it is extremely difficult to articulate my thoughts in such a way that I can communicate the beauty and subtlety of the sensations associated with such experiences. It is extremely frustrating to try to do so, because I know that, in light of the utter inadequacy of language, I will never be completely satisfied with what I have said. Such experiences are ultimately incommunicable. Second, in attempting to communicate them in some meaningful fashion, I cannot avoid sounding poetic or otherworldly. Such experiences are characterized by an aspect of transcendental mystery. And yet, I usually do not like to think of them in terms of being religious or mystical or otherworldly. I view them as moments of intensely expanded and sharpened perception. One touches the world in nonordinary ways, and the world acts upon one within deep levels of one's being. This is a state of uncommon lucidity.

Thus, through my eyes I touched many aspects of the world in extraordinary ways, and through the portals of my eyes the sky diffused itself throughout my being, infiltrating me with its power and serenity. Like a chameleon, my being took on its placidity; my consciousness assimilated every exquisite hue. What imperturbable stillness, what flawless tranquility! What absence of care, and what fulfillment of longing those blue spaces enveloping the world gave to me! From the coming of morning through the full brilliance of day, along the dreamlike paths of twilight and into the glimmering blackness of night, my spirit wandered with a light and joyous heart. In the heavens, my mind realized its capacity for an unfettered state of being. As day became night and day again, through an inexorable yet almost imperceptible gradual movement, my mind fed upon a metabolism of cosmic dimensions. The perpetual breathing of day and night became my own immovably tranquil inhalation and expiration, like a great, sublime yoga. My consciousness became celestial movement; the eternal diastole and systole of the megacosm.

There is something unique about the sky over a clear and sparkling body of water. On brilliant, sunny days at Lake Geneva, the sky was intense and vibrant, almost electric. Its blue was sometimes so rich and deep that it appeared almost as violet or indigo, yet luminous. This phenomenon created spectacular contrast for the shining mountains of clouds that often sailed across the midafternoon sky. The images of such days were reflected in the poem which I wrote at Lake Geneva on July 19, 1972:

> In Whose waters, here, I lie,
> In Lake Geneva's deep blue realms,
> Where willow fronds bend down to touch
> The wavering reflections of the sky—
> Its silent, meditative heights, where
> Great vaulted walls of vibrant cyanine
> Arch, to make a roof, for floors
> Of moving waters.

I have always been taken with the interplay of light and sky and water. I grew acutely aware of it when I first began to sail on the lake where I lifeguarded near my home town. Although that lake was considerably smaller than Lake Geneva, I had many memorable experiences there.

Scorching, shimmering sun, beating
down on the sparkling water, a dancing sea of broken glass, its brightness piercing my eyes...

The unbearably bright billowy white
clouds racing across the sun in the
blazing azure of the wide sky, above
the deep green of the whitecapped
lake...

The smell of water, the sound of
waves lapping along the frying
sandy beach...there is a sailboat
in the bay, its white, rippling
sail flapping back and forth in
the hot wind...

I worked and sailed for three summers on that little lake. Afterward, during the summers of 1971 and 1972, I lived on Lake Geneva, where I gave sailing lessons and rides. Some days I sailed for six or seven hours, alighting on land at the end of the day, scorched by the sun and nearly seasick, but totally and inexpressibly happy from having spent my day out upon the shining surface of that lake. I will never forget the first day at Lake Geneva in 1971, when I stepped into a beautiful old wooden Lightning for the first time. I sailed all summer and the next, enveloped in a world of light and movement and joy. After that summer, I wrote a poem that dealt with sailing at Lake Geneva.

I

Jubilant day, exhilarating,
     animate radiance...
Emerald waves, crests of
     alabaster form,
Toss and pitch
     in the dazzling sunshine.
Dance beneath the deep

wide sky, bright
depthless canopy of
vaulted blue.

Piercing the flaming
ivory clouds,
Afloat, in the glowing
firmament,
Transplendent shafts
of sunlight pour
Down into billows of
sparkling jade.

II

White sails bulge,
with gusts of rushing wind,
Spread full in draughts
of summer breezes.
Swinging, the boom draws
taut the lines,
Tugging, wrenching fast
and firm.
Pitching, heaving, the sailboat
ploughs through the tossing,
dancing wallow.

Near the rocky shores,
sunny aquamarine resolves
Transparent, lucid;
transmutes to pebbly brown,
As the bottom rushes
to the flashing surface.
Passing back and forth I sail,
flanking the rockbound banks,
Enthralled in the shimmering
drama of light, and wind
in the rustling birches.

III

The rocks and waves
thunder in dialogue,
Their mysterious
roaring colloquy.

Hurling themselves at
  the glistening boulders,
The waves are dashed
  into frothing foam.

With sudden puffs of
  rushing wind, lashing
    over the rippling swells,
The shores loom near,
  then stretch away,
Receding swiftly
  under each fresh tack.
Out on the undulating sea
  of water and light, from afar
I see the dark green bluffs,
  standing out, against the tableau
    of water and sky.

Planing on deep green swells,
  in the cool blue shadows
    of the verdant hills,
I come about, and glide
  away, out again into
    brilliant sunshine.
But always, I return.

When I have driven to Lake Geneva, it has usually been from the south. And as I drove north through Illinois and into Wisconsin, I would experience a mounting anticipation for my first glimpse. The road led me into the wooded hills encircling the lake, and I watched eagerly for that first flash of water through the trees. My joy and expectation always grew as I neared those waters, and upon making that first sighting, something inside me jumped to life; some part of me which knew a great longing would quicken to attention. Then I would enter the town of Lake Geneva, and driving down a hill and turning, I would suddenly behold the mysterious lake.

Sometimes I would plan my trips so as to arrive during midmorning, but I have also gotten there shortly before sunset. At such times, viewing the lake lengthwise from its eastern end, I was possessed by what was the most glorious phenomenon. When I looked out over the lake in twilight, toward the west, all my desires came to rest. I experienced an immediate inner silence, and my entire being fed upon that alluring mystery. My body drank in an immaculate power after what were often many months of longing for that moment.

Above me, the sky was darkening to indigo, and as it stretched away toward the western horizon, it glowed above the hills with the most perfect and translucent and subtle beauty: a flawless, radiant confluence of orange and rose and delicate, luminous blue. Those matchless hues delicately permeated and transformed the entire atmosphere, enveloping the earth in an almost imperceptible haze of glowing light. They were reflected in the waters of the lake, whose fragmented, undulating surface caught the delicate shades of the sky and liquefied its dreamlike pastels, sliding them up and down the quivering forms of the waves. Even the darkening hills seemed to bathe in that aura of breathing color.

There was something else there too, a mysterious power. I could see it, but not in the commonly understood sense. I could feel it with my eyes. It seeped into me and filled me. Some knowledge within my physical being quickened, and my body became alert. It seemed to grow younger and stronger in moments, and yet it was more than that. My body seemed to respond to that environment by operating on a higher and different level of consciousness.

I peered with awe at the power oozing from the lake and sky and hills, and I was filled with a new kind of knowing. The world was not the same. It was a different world. I had come home. I had rediscovered an ultimate sanity, solidity, inner harmony, and cohesion. I had returned to a living world. What I "saw" out there in the hills, and filling the sky told me that I was alive again. I had come out of a land of death and reentered the living universe. I had found ultimate rationality and order.

There was always power at the lake. However, there were certain days or specific times of the day when I felt especially aware of it. But that power seemed at its fullest in twilight, when the sun descended toward the western hills. I liked to arrive around early evening, and I always considered it a good omen, a sign of propitious circumstances, when I did so, especially when the sky was clear. There was something about arriving at that time of day which seemed absolutely right, and in harmony with things. I felt enveloped and protected by the fading light— that I was completely safe, that I could not be harmed in any way, and that all my actions would be the right ones. Any circumstances which I might encounter would be auspicious. I was in harmony with the world.

My sensations must have been akin to those of Hesse when he wrote the following words.

> In shadowy caverns
> Long I dreamed
> Of your trees, your cloudless skies,
> Your fragrance, the song of your birds.
> Now you lie before me
> In all your glory.
> A world of light,

Yerkes Observatory

A world of wonder.
Yes, and you know me,
And sweetly tempt me.
My limbs tremble
At your sweet presence.

                                        Spring

He was speaking not of a place, but of Spring. And yet how harmonious my feelings must have been with his.

There is a plateau atop the high hills on the north side of Lake Geneva, above the George Williams College Camp and just west of Williams Bay. This is the site of the Yerkes Observatory, with its beautiful architecture, its imposing domes and magnificent telescopes. Shortly after my visit to the lake in August 1974, when I had been there for a week at Conference Point Camp, I wrote down many of my impressions from that experience, among which were the following.

It is really true that, as the soul awakens to itself, its surroundings become more and more unreal and unbelievable and dreamlike. And I grow increasingly aware of the infiltration of this kind of consciousness into my life...

At Yerkes, too, I have found mystery and power; a dynamic and vibrant breathing. The sensation of the movement of a psychic force whose great body intersects the three-dimensional world, whose deep and dark volition is keenly and excitingly, even disturbingly, sensed. I have known deep satisfaction and peace from sitting and walking on the top of that great hill, meditating on the life there; the noble fir trees, the plateau, and the Observatory itself, with its inscriptions and its watchful gargoyles...

Even the Yerkes Observatory and its grounds have held an unusual power and beauty for me on many occasions, because of their nearness to Lake Geneva. The observatory seemed close to the sky, and the openness of the surrounding grounds permitted a sweeping view of the heavens. How beautiful it was as day expired into evening; the great dome, reflecting the fire of the sunset, as the blackness of night gradually enveloped the hills. I remember one summer night when I walked around the grounds, peering up into that starry vault. The cool brightness of the moon illumined the darkness of space and bathed the grass, bushes, and trees in an eerie pale light that was enchanting and somehow alluring. The American astronauts were walking upon the surface of the moon for the first time.

One night in the summer of 1972, I was inside the observatory, standing underneath the enormous dome, which had been opened so that one could look up into the starry night. Nancy was standing by my side with her hand in mine. What perfect happiness, what pure and transcendent romance to be so close to her, and so close to that glimmering eternity above us. Happiness could go no further. It was complete fulfillment. If only that moment could have lasted forever.

During the winter preceding that experience, I wrote a poem which had been inspired by the observatory, and by the strikingly beautiful aspect of the sky as I had often viewed it.

> Below the soft green verdant plateau,
> lies the Lake in deep blue haze....
> Your mammoth dome is flaming gold
> in the glowing dusk; your Eye
> reaches out to probe the sky.
> You must comprehend it all,
> from here; Heaven is spread
> below you and above.
> Here, I stand enveloped in the depths
> of indigo, inhaling the draughts
> of starry infinity, contemplating
> this deep, dark peace.
>
> from a July evening
> at Yerkes Observatory
> December, 1971

During the summers of 1971 and 1972, while living on the lake, I was able to do some night sailing. I have done so under the bright moon and also in its absence, when there was a giant blackness, pinpointed with stars. On such dark nights, there was no shore or horizon, only an unbroken sphere of darkness. And only a moderate distance from the boat, it was impossible to distinguish the point at which sky ended and water began. Perhaps a number of sailboats would go out, and they would loom suddenly and startlingly into view only a short distance from my boat, to be swallowed up again by the night as quickly as they had appeared. To encounter the night under such circumstances, in a sailboat out on the lake, was to experience it in its most mysterious aspect. The darkness seemed to amplify the sounds of the water. I was aware of the waves thumping against the bottom of my boat. I could listen to their gurgling and whispering as I looked beyond the pale, looming forms of the sails into the shining sky.

There were many nights when I walked along the shore path to Conference Point, where I often sat near the edge of the water and surveyed the night sky. There was a brotherhood among the stars, between them and the earth, and the trees and rocks and water. One could sense a harmony that permeated the universe and embraced everything within it. The pale, golden light of the moon, which on some nights seemed almost warm because of its extraordinary brightness, illumined and unified the landscape, creating an unearthly effect that evoked the impression of a strange nocturnal daylight. The sky was sometimes delicately veiled with an exquisitely beautiful lacework of clouds that spanned the horizons of hills around me. On some nights, the ocean of deep, clear sky would perhaps be occupied only by the splendid presence of a solitary, ominous cloud, its form gilded with the luminosity of the moon, floating soundlessly, imperceptibly, over the landscape. Such nights were pregnant with meaning. Below are some lines from a poem I began in February 1973, which convey my longing for those nights at the lake.

> O, dark, sighing Mystery!
> Night, heavy with the weight
>   of Eternity!
> Sparkling moonlight on
>   the introspective surface,
> Gold and silver, pale
>   under the processions of feathery,
> Glowing, eerie silent clouds,
>   veiling sister Luna;   ·
> Pierced through, by icy stars,
>   brothers of the distant lights,
>   here and there, on
>   imagined shores...
>
> O, intoxicating Mystery!
> How your dark and subtle fire
>   igniteth the brooding depths
>   of my soul!

My sleep is thrown here
and there, twisting, in its fever,
for that Union.

When I arrived at the Point before nightfall, I felt a power in this. It was then possible for me to merge with the growing darkness, sealed in its protective power. When I came upon that area after the darkness had fallen, I often felt I was not in harmony with it, that I was alien to it and outside of it, and that my spirit was not properly aligned with a certain element that part of me clearly sensed. On frequent occasions I avoided going to the Point if it had already grown dark. Something inside clearly warned me about doing so. I have never as yet ignored that feeling, but rather have obeyed it. On the other hand, if I arrived before or during twilight, I felt in harmony with the forces there. I did not always have feelings of apprehension about approaching the Point after darkness had set in, and on such occasions I sometimes went there after dark, but not frequently. There were also times that I was there when I felt that it was better to move on after darkness had set in, even though I had arrived there before twilight. I always obeyed those feelings.

A thousand people might go to that place and never be influenced by the feelings I have just described or even experience them in the slightest degree. The same thing could justifiably be said about hearing a Beethoven symphony, reading a poem by Hesse, or viewing a Stravinksy ballet. Different people have different sensitivities to different things. Whatever I experienced along the shores of Lake Geneva, it was deeply real. Although it was a mystery, it was characterized by sober rationality and the highest sanity.

Those evening twilights held a magnificent and sublime power for me. In the dusk was something awesome, indefinable, alluring, which revealed itself at that magical hour and changed the earth into something mysterious. That exquisite power could be felt in the dying light at the edge of the world, between the deepening darkness of the sky and the earth. Its power was pure and incorruptible. Whatever was out there in that light was eternal. It filled my emptiness and gave me peace. It answered my deepest longing, and yet made me yearn to know what it was.

When I think of that inscrutable power which manifested itself at the end of the day and permeated the lake and hills, I call to mind the words of don Juan, from a passage in Castaneda's *Tales of Power.*

"The twilight is the crack between the worlds," don Juan said. "It is the door to the unknown.... Beyond, there is an abyss and beyond that abyss is the unknown."

I underwent a number of extraordinary inner experiences during the summer of 1980 that set the tone for the visit I made to Lake Geneva for five days in August. That trip had been especially significant because I returned from it with a kind of final conviction; a certainty from thenceforth that, outside of myself and my own mind and consciousness, there was a power and mystery at the lake that had always been there and always would be. That force had been there before I came to know the lake, and it would await me there for the rest of my life, pulling me, drawing me to it. It permeated everything there, but I had known it most deeply in the glittering twilight, as each successive night I sat upon the granite boulder near the Point and looked with wonder into the west.

After that trip, I happened to become more aware of that great symphonic work by Mahler, *Das Lied von der Erde* (The Song of the Earth). I was particularly interested in the musical material of the sixth and final movement, entitled, "Der Abschied" (The Farewell), because I had once seen the film of an incredible solo dance to that movement, choreographed and performed by the great modern dancer and choreographer, Pauline Koner. I had seen the film during the summer of 1978, while working as a pianist at the American Dance Festival, held that summer for the first time at Duke University in Durham, North Carolina, after having been based previously for many years in Connecticut. Pauliner Koner was also in residence at the festival that summer with her dance company, and I will always consider it a real privilege to have met her and to have been able to spend some time with her.

Although I had been taken with the music of "The Farewell," I did not hear it again until after my trip to Lake Geneva in August 1980, and I had forgotten its source, identifying it only after hearing it again on the radio. I immediately acquired a recording of *Das Lied von der Erde,* and for the first time became aware of the words upon which the music was based. The music is inspired. It is expressive and brilliantly orchestrated, and its motives are haunting and unforgettable. The ideas embodied in the text are transformed and set forth in the music in such a manner that one cannot fail to perceive the purity of Mahler's genius and insight.

The text upon which "The Farewell" is based is taken from a work entitled *The Chinese Flute*. This collection of old Chinese poems, which was translated into German by Hans Bethge, forms the textual basis for the entire symphonic song cycle. "The Farewell," which reminds me powerfully of my evenings at the lake, speaks of the beauty and power of nature, and a love and longing for its mysteries and secrets. It depicts a farewell between two friends in the evening twilight. The moon is rising, and there is the melodious singing of a stream in the darkness. A cool breeze is stirring, as the flowers turn pale in the twilight. The lushness and opulence of the earth are portrayed in the following lines.

> I wander to and fro with my lute
> on paths swollen with soft grass.
> O beauty! Flush with love, with life unending—O drunken world!

There is an intense, mystical sensuality in these words, an indulgence in the sensory delights of nature. There is a quietude, a serenity, a coming to rest in these lines:

The stream sings melodiously through the darkness.
The flowers turn pale in the twilight.
The earth breathes a deep tranquility;
now all longing wants to dream.
Weary people make their way home,
to learn once more in sleep
forgotten happiness and youth!
The birds perch quietly on the branches.
The world falls asleep!

Two friends are saying good-bye. The one is going away, to wander in the mountains, to seek peace for his lonely heart; to wander to his homeland, to his abode. His heart is quiet and awaits its hour, as the earth turns to spring. There is an exquisite power calling to him. It permeates the whole earth. But the purest, most alluring and fatal magic is in the sky, in glowing twilight. The final two lines of the poem hold the secret.

Everywhere, forever, distant spaces shine light blue!
Forever... forever...

The Land

The waters of Lake Geneva were a great and beautiful living power, an exquisite consciousness, whose pure, sweet voice rose into the air and pervaded the hills; whose strange and wonderful elemental thoughts were articulated by the whispering waves and carried by the wind to fill the surrounding world. Above the lake loomed the vibrant, shining, blue canopy of sky which stretched over the earth and poured down its light upon the sparkling waters, where surging waves mirrored it back again into the radiance of the atmosphere. The communion and interplay between the powers of water and sky generated a great field of elemental energy that permeated the surrounding land and hills and commingled with the psychic energies that moved within the earth there. That living confluence of elemental powers, with the electromagnetic, cosmic, and solar forces that flowed through the area, created a unique power center in that locale. The land and everything in it was permeated with power. There was a special presence in the woods and hills. It was a life, a consciousness, that oozed from the earth and from everything that was a part of it; the rocks and trees, the shady, sloping expanses of grass, and the bright flowers and vegetation.

It transformed all my thoughts and actions into something more meaningful than what they were anywhere else. The paths and roadways, and even the buildings, were imbued with the superior vibrations of that place, although the men who had created those things were probably unaware of that unique energy. I occasionally found myself wondering if what I perceived was some elaborate hallucination I had invented and was playing out in my own mind. This was probably an inescapable consequence of my seeing other people who were apparently, to my amazement, oblivious to that marvelous world. Because the life there was so real to me, it seemed incongruous to see other people moving about there in a state of unconsciousness, completely cut off from an awareness of the forces there. However, in spite of my periodic doubts, I knew that what I perceived was incomparably more real than the delusions I had come to regard as worthy of occupying my thoughts and energies in my existence away from there. I came to regard my perceptions at the lake, and the life which was manifested there, as real, and to view the vast majority of things which I apparently had to do in order to function within my culture as relatively meaningless and unreal by comparison.

I loved to walk along the sunny shore path that followed the edge of the lake. As I pursued its happy, wandering course, my hungry senses soaked up the wondrous repertory of perceptions that it revealed to me. Winding among tall trees, past bluffs covered with lush green vegetation and bright yellow and red wild flowers, across the flickering play of light and shadow that moved soundlessly over the spacious expanses of dreaming grass, the path led me through rich and inexhaustible spectrums of color and sound. And always nearby, flanking the shore path, the water talked to me as it accompanied my walks. I studied the motions upon its surface when it captured my attention, and the focus of my perception shifted between it and the life upon the shore path and in the hills. I have often thought of that day when Nancy and I followed the shore path around the entire perimeter of the lake during the summer of 1972. The distance was about thirty miles, and we had done it comfortably in one day. It had been a magical experience to tread those miles of beauty and power. At the end of the day, after we had returned to the George Williams College camp, I experienced an extremely pleasurable exhaustion, which came from knowing that, in one day, I had experienced every foot of shoreline on that beautiful lake.

Although there is no land along the perimeter of the lake that is still wilderness, there are several fairly natural areas, including church camps and conference centers, and many beautiful private estates. In general, the entire area that skirts the lake is well kept and protected, and much of its natural beauty has been left relatively intact. Even though that locale is thoroughly inhabited, it is remarkably beautiful. The presence of man there has bothered me more than it used to, especially after I learned of the Indian civilizations that once flourished there. I have often thought of how the lake must have been before white civilization encroached upon it—its primeval forests and its unbroken line of hills against the sky; its shoreline, unblemished by docks and piers; and the purity of quiet which must have existed there. How polluted the land has become with noise! My culture had poisoned the minds of its people with noise to the point that they could not endure true quiet even for a short time. Their nervous systems had become addicted to being constantly agitated with the most trivial garbage. But I could still find a profound quiet and a deep peace at the lake, especially in the early morning and from evening twilight into the night. Particularly at those times, the serenity of that world cleansed my mind and sharpened my perceptions. Sometimes when I sat at the Point at night, listening to the quiet of evening, I was confronted by one of the large touring boats that occasionally passed by. They would often be heavily loaded with laughing, screaming people, who were accompanied by a deafening and mindless racket of nauseating music. At such times I often felt a certain hopelessness about my culture, and I was glad when those people had floated beyond my range of perception. I wished to forget they were there and return to the elemental silence that was the natural state of the lake and the hills.

A certain amount of contact with other people was unavoidable. Still, I wanted to speak as little as possible, since to converse meant expending psychic energy and clouding my thoughts, so I rarely initiated conversation with others. By remaining silent, I had learned that I ordinarily dissipated tremendous energy through trivial conversation and churned up a mountain of garbage upon the screen of my consciousness. This would severely impair my receptivity to the marvelous things around me. I sought out areas where I could go and be alone, and since there were many such places at the lake, I was able to find the isolation which I needed. I had learned that it was absolutely necessary for me to make my trips to Lake Geneva alone and, once I had become convinced of this, I found a wonderful sanity and restfulness. Thus, during my stays at the lake, whatever communion I had with the world outside my own mind was, as much as possible, nonhuman. I sought to tune my thoughts to move with the sweeping forces that operated there; I opened myself to embrace those elemental modes of consciousness that were evolving within the world of nature, and which were not readily accessible. I was able to escape, for a time, from the way of perceiving and thinking that was considered normal and acceptable, but which I found empty and bleak.

For the most part, I stayed out of the towns and close to the shores of the lake. And although I was fairly familiar with a good deal of the area, there were only a few spots to which I went regularly. Thus, my movements were, voluntarily, fairly restricted and predictable. Although I have had thoughts about exploring other areas around the lake more fully, and although I feel that it would be good to do so, I have not done much of it because the areas I do frequent are so beautiful and full of power that I have no desire to go anywhere else. To explore other areas would take time, something precious to me when I am at the lake, and I have to use the limited time I do have in the most productive and efficient way I can. But whenever I have explored around the lake, I have found everything to be amazingly alive, and during my visit to the lake in August 1981, while looking for old sites connected with my Indian research, I explored several new areas. Without exception, I found them consistent

Trail near Conference Point

with the general character of that locale, and expressive of the power there. I drove over many back roads that surround the lake and encountered a profusion of enchanting sights. I was particularly drawn by the sparsely inhabited areas, where the roads led me along the edges of dense natural forests. The branches of the towering trees met above the gravel roadbed to form wavering arches through which golden streaks of sunlight fell to the road and to the floor of the forest, where they played softly over the flowers and fallen leaves, blurs of mellow luminosity that shifted soundlessly in melting, kaleidoscopic patterns over the ground.

But I was usually within the area that occupies a mile of the northern shoreline, bounded by Conference Point on the east, and by the George Williams College camp on the west, directly above which, on a high plateau, sits the Yerkes Observatory and its spacious grounds. I frequently stayed at the George Williams College camp, the organization where I had given sailing lessons during the summers of 1971 and 1972. Much of my time was spent at Conference Point. It was the heart of the lake. Not only was it typical of that locale in terms of its beauty and power and enchantment, but it expressed those qualities to an exceptional degree, possessing a unique magnetism and power.

I found the shoreline between George Williams and Conference Point particularly magnetic, and I often walked that segment of the shore several times each day. I also frequently walked up the road or climbed the steep path through the trees that led to Yerkes Observatory. The grounds were spacious and sufficiently removed from the road to be undisturbed by noise from automobiles. Here and there were lovely shade trees, and a few pines. I have always found pine trees extremely inviting. Their scent is pure and refreshing, and for a long time I have regarded them to be very spiritual. Whenever I was near them, I sensed something highly refined and profoundly soothing in the quality of the vibrations they emitted. The steep trail I often used to reach the plateau of the observatory ascended through woods that bordered part of the open grounds. At the top, the trail abruptly ended where the expansive lawn met the neatly defined edge of the woods. Only a few yards from where the woods opened onto the grass, there was a small stand of pines, underneath which was a soft, attractive bed of needles. It was comfortable there even in the hot summer, and it was calming to sit in that spot, especially in late afternoon or early evening. It seemed an ideal place to meditate, a place where one could allow the subtle emanations from the pine trees to stroke the mind and cure its nervousness.

There was an excellent view of the western sky, and the sunsets were striking. The horizontal rays of the sinking sun flooded the open plateau and kindled the dome of the observatory with a gleaming, mellow golden light. There is a difference between the consciousness of that area and that which is closer to the water. This is quite understandable, since it has always been my experience that there is nothing else in nature as alive as water. It is extremely conductive to psychic forces. Even though the observatory grounds were attractive, there was nothing that could compare with the lake. Its charm and magnetism were fatal, and nothing else could even approximate the effect it had on me.

Nevertheless, there was much to be experienced in the hills surrounding the lake. The body of the earth embraces a hierarchy of forces. There are many energies that flow through the earth, and it is the dwelling place for numerous elemental entities, whose abodes are within the ground and rocks. I call to mind here the *nampé-shiu* or *nampéshi-k* of the Potawatomis. This water panther spirit was considered to be an evil power that traveled through the earth as well as the water. I also cite the Seven Sacred Springs in Fontana, which were once surrounded by forest and which were an important council site for the Indians, where they propitiated the spirits that lived within the pools and the earth there. Likewise the spirit stones of Cedar Point, which I never located, were once a site for the invocation and propitiation of the spirits that dwelt in them.

Although there are billions of entities upon the earth who fall within the boundaries of definition which designate them as human beings, each is different in some way from all the others. Each one manifests a different degree and quality of light, magnetism, intelligence, and sensitivity; and there are such enormous differences among various individuals in terms of development of consciousness and modes of perception that it is hardly accurate even to place all of these beings upon the same evolutionary path. The directions and emphases of development are so divergent that it is difficult to identify all men within the same species, culture, or even within the same family.

Likewise, every locale manifests differences from all others, and each expresses its own individuality. Many places are benevolent and inviting, while others are hostile and even uninhabitable. Furthermore, certain locales clearly manifest vibrations that are more refined and spiritually evolved than those of other areas. There are many forces which contribute to the identity and psychic character of a given geographic region, including the influence of men.

Thus to walk upon the earth at the lake, under the towering, gracious trees, and to sit upon its eloquent stones, was to communicate with the subtle and shining thoughts of a special part of the world. When my feet were upon that ground, when I felt the soft earth and the silent grass, and experienced the vibrant energy in the atmosphere, in whose spaces of vibrating light stood the dark, massive trunks of the oak trees, the spaces within my own being became permeated with that mystical silence, and I felt a serenity and a quiet strength. I felt firm and immovable, like the great trees around me. And yet I was buoyant and weightless. I listened quietly to the earth. My body grew strong and energetic when it saw the anticipation and delight which the clear light of each new morning held. There was a mystery in all of this, so that each pebble upon the ground, each twig and fragment of bark, and every fallen acorn, became a talisman. The light lived in everything; under each stone and log, and within the spaces among the blades of grass. Each tree knew its share, and it commingled with the fiery leaves that moved in the distant treetops. Out upon the surface of the lake, it became a molten consciousness whose gleaming body set fire to the surging waves and danced silently over the open plane of water that stretched away to the distant shores.

There have been many times when I have sat near the lake, perhaps along the shore at the Point, and studied the rows of hills on the other side of the water. Depending on the direction in which I looked, they were anywhere from a half mile to two miles away. Particularly on days when there was sunlight, the contours of the distant hills created many contrasting areas of light and shadow, and within that visual texture, it was possible to perceive a category of visual phenomena that I might describe as pockets of power. In spite of the fact that I perceived them visually, it is impossible to say what they looked like. This apparent contradiction is reflective of the true nature of such types of perception. It points to their very essence, and is relevant to many of the perceptual experiences that I have described in this book. There is no way to describe what I saw because there was nothing there to look at, except the hills and the light and shadow that anyone could see if they looked. And yet there truly was something there, which I clearly perceived.

Through my eyes, it was possible to detect the presence of a power within those pockets of light and shadow. And although it might not be accurate to describe what I detected there as an entity, or a force, or a presence, neither would it be entirely inaccurate to do so.

One might ask how I came to perceive such things and what benefit there might be in doing so. No one taught me to perceive the world in the manner I have described. My perceptions were the result of natural, or instinctive techniques. They seemed to arise through certain innate, or intuitive tendencies, although at various times in my life certain ideas of other people have served as cues. For example, I recall the influence Margaret Patton had upon me when I became acquainted with her during my first visit to Lake Geneva. Her remarks concerning the idea of God in nature, which I happened to overhear, had a tremendous impact, and it was Margaret who had subsequently suggested that I might find some quiet place along the shores of the lake where I could open myself and meditate in order to find the answers to my questions. As I have explained previously, the writings of Carlos Castaneda have also been influential and have provided me with various techniques of perception that I have experimented with and found valuable and effective. The clue to accessing that world of perceptions lies in being truly fluid, flexible, and curious enough to realize that there is much more within the world than what we are ordinarily aware of. Desire has been an important factor in my experiences, for I have been intensely motivated to seek new and expanded perceptions. Thus, I have been willing to experiment with my own consciousness to realize new modes of perception and experience. There is an extraordinarily powerful key in the realization that not only is our view and definition of the world inadequate, but it is cripplingly constrictive, and indicative of deep inner poverty. We are encumbered with this view because we have lost our sense of awe. In our glibness and conceit, we have made a costly sacrifice. We have forgotten that the world is an incredible and insoluble mystery. In our blindness, we have come to regard the world only as an object. We have forgotten that it is a living consciousness.

To truly realize these things, to actually embrace them as part of one's personal knowledge, is to find power. There are techniques one can employ to alter one's consciousness in various ways, but how can one maximally benefit from their value and power unless one's inner efforts are permeated with the desire to go to the very heart of things and effect a fundamental change in the way one views the world? That is where the answer lies; it is the real key—to discover that our repertory of perceptions is incomplete and that our modes of perception are extraordinarily finite, and to want to know and experience more. I do not know what combination of forces and circumstances drives one to bring about such changes in one's life, but perhaps, at least in part, the answer lies outside our control.

My contact with Negoya somehow effected a profound change in my consciousness and crucially influenced the way in which I perceived things. His role in my experiences was unforeseen and beyond my control. He was a force from another world that touched my life in a dramatic way, and his identity remained a complete mystery for over seventeen years. I may never know more about him than I do at present, and with reference to the ultimate design that caused our paths to cross in such an incredible manner, I have remained in darkness. Nevertheless, my encounter with him brought great light into my life.

As I look at the culture around me, I know that it is missing something vital, and that its people are suffering from spiritual starvation. They have turned their backs on the beautiful, living mystery within the world, and have lost access to incredible facets of their own minds. They have accepted the fate of living with a cramped and limited view of the world, and have become imprisoned by their own defective perceptions. The culture is sick because it has forgotten how to relate to life, and because those who live within it cannot even perceive many of the wondrous modes of being that surround them as living and conscious. They look upon the living universe as inanimate, and rather than knowing communion with the marvelous, living world which they inhabit, they exploit it and rape it and trample it.

Many of the experiences my culture offered me—bars and drugs and the unending stream of garbage and brainwashing from the television—only numbed me and made me unhappy. They blurred the truth I had found at the lake and made me feel as if I were dying. Undeniably, there were certain aspects of my culture, such as music, in which I found great beauty and joy. And yet, without the world of the lake, my life could not be complete. Eventually, I accepted this fact and set about to fulfill my true needs by focusing my energies in the proper direction. I looked within my own spirit and within the realm of perceptions the lake had revealed to me.

Whatever was in those hills fed some part of my inner being. It imbued me with a kind of inner strength. My physical being acquired vital knowledge from it. And yet, although that is exactly what I experienced as I watched the hills, I know of no way to convey what it was that my body shared with that power, or what that power expressed to it.

Our bodies, as well as our mental and spiritual aspects, derive sustenance from that kind of perceptual food. Thus, it is not only our poor diets that are making us old and fat and sick, and forcing us to resort to artificial exercise, and finally killing us. We have starved our bodies, as well as our spirits, of the perceptual food that they need, and which exists within the being of the world. Rather than allowing our bodies to become permeated with that energizing power, we have inundated them, along with our minds, with the avalanche of perceptual poisons which our culture continues to generate with unabating momentum. I am uncomfortable about portraying my perceptions and experiences at the lake in such a way that will give them the connotation of loftiness or otherworldliness. My physical body, with its own level of knowledge and mode of perception, is an integral component in the body of experiences which I have encountered at the lake. Those experiences are a communion between myself and the corporeal body of the living earth, and the living universe within which it moves.

My awareness of power was achieved through looking at things softly, allowing them to act upon my inner perceptual faculty. Rather than arresting the impressions of an object or phenomenon with my eyes by aggressively staring at it, I changed the way I focused on it visually so that whatever was there, beyond the ordinary visual stimuli it was sending me, would be able to permeate the censoring tendency of my eyes and affect me on some deeper level. I was, therefore, looking beyond the surface texture of the world which the eye is normally content with seeing. People sometimes receive impressions from things in this manner and experience certain feelings about them, although they may not understand why or how, since the process is not a conscious one and operates only on a subliminal level.

The technique I used in detecting those concentrations of power in the hills was one I employed in experiencing many aspects of the world, and particularly those of the natural world in the setting of the lake. When I looked at a particular object, such as a rock or a tree, or a row of distant hills, I did not focus upon any small area, but rather allowed my eyes to absorb everything within a large field of vision. At the same time, I emptied my mind of all thoughts, interrupting the automatic mechanism that constantly reinforced the inadequate view of the world that had been systematically pounded into me since the time I was born, and which I had perpetuated by thinking of the world only in terms of the meaningless labels and empty words and fallacious concepts which had shored up that view. By suspending my thoughts, I freed myself to become open to a world of pure, uncensored perception. I developed new sensitivities and began to relate to the world differently. I achieved a perspective from which I could understand the meaning of certain ideas; for example, those lessons don Juan Matus had tried to convey to Carlos Castaneda concerning the noumenal realities behind the various physical phenomena of nature.

Although my awareness of the power within the hills was related to my other perceptions at the lake, it seemed to have a particular affinity to those modes of awareness in which I experienced an acute sense of spatiality and exercised my depth perception. Thus, in my perceptions of the power within the hills, there seemed to be a profound sense of depth involved, an experience of space, which somehow related to other perceptions I encountered when, for instance, I contemplated the forms of the trees and rocks as they were manifested in three-dimensional space, or the vast, expansive plane of the lake as it stretched away to the distant shores, or the aspect of the moving surface of the water as I looked down at it from above, atop the bluff which overlooked the Point.

Thus, as I came to perceive the world in a different manner, I also came to apprehend space differently and to expand my perceptions beyond the limits of three-dimensional space. It was thus that I felt certain forces whose sphere of movement intersected with three-dimensional space, and yet also transcended it. And as I got in touch with those components of my mind capable of apprehending a dimensionality not altogether restricted to three dimensions, I began to sense more clearly the existence of other things within the world, things that were alive in some sense, and which acted upon those unseen parts of me that were opening up to heightened perceptions and which were being stimulated and fed by the realities of that new world. As my consciousness evolved, I comprehended the physical world in a higher sense, so that within the context of that expanded spatiality I found new perceptions; what I was seeing were sections of greater modes of consciousness whose forms moved through higher space. And it was dramatically clear to me that those forces were fully alive. I acquired new insights into the meaning of the term, "living," for I had encountered a whole new spectrum of living forces. Within that expanded dimensionality was possibly the key to the nature of all the marvelous things I had witnessed at the lake and hills. From somewhere within those spaces Negoya had appeared to me and shown me a new world.

Other phenomena, such as the currents of psychic energy within the earth itself, reached me by a means I understand so incompletely that I can offer little comment. With respect to the wind, I do not understand the mechanism that made me aware of its power. Yet the wind produced a distinct sensation that betrayed an elemental consciousness behind its movements. Obviously, the wind generated or participated in an unnumerable variety of phenomena within the world of nature that could be detected directly by the senses and which, when viewed from an expanded state of consciousness, revealed an underlying aspect of consciousness; for example, the motions and sounds of the waves, the shimmering trees and vegetation, and the passage of clouds. It was a force that blended intimately with all other aspects of nature. But just as the water was alive in its own way, as were the skies and hills, the wind was also capable of expressing an identity. When Negoya appeared to me and exerted his influence, the wind had displayed a powerful and responsive force. It was the instrument of expression for many of nature's varied manifestations of consciousness. But aside from the evidence of its effects in nature, what alerted me to the fact that it was more than it appeared to be, and how did I perceive this?

Just as I had wondered how it was possible to sense the consciousness within the earth, I had also sought to understand how the volition in the wind could communicate. How did I acquire the knowledge of its power, and why was it so apparent? When I rejected the accepted view of the world, I had to do so unconditionally. Everything became something other than what it had been, including the wind. One reason the wind gave me a knowledge of itself was that I had allowed it to. And in casting off many ideas, I came to see the tragedy of the religion I had grown up with, and the nature of the conflict it had created in my life. Admittedly, that religion had acknowledged a living God, even though in an emasculating, comfortable and anthropomorphic way. But it had denied life to the universe; it had denied me the deepest desire of my heart, which was to embrace and commune with the living world and to learn from the endless and unnumerable rivers of consciousness that flowed within it. Indeed, the religion of my youth conceded that God had made the world, although through their eyes He had apparently done so much in the same fashion, I suppose, as one would bake a cake or build a garage. But they had not extended the concept beyond that, and the universe was therefore, in essence, perceived only as an object, as something made rather than as a living force. As a result, operating under the excuse of having dominion over the world and everything in it, men have undertaken to perpetuate a mindless exploitation of it.

This explains why my philosophical outlook "permitted" the wind to speak to me. But to explain that communication on another level, it is necessary to make it clear that, regardless of which aspect of nature I was focusing my consciousness on, and whether I received the sensory impressions of those various phenomena by sight, or by hearing, or through feeling them with my body, all the phenomena of Lake Geneva and the manner in which they acted upon me shared a certain commonality. Through each of them, I experienced a noumenal aspect of the world. Each spoke to the same being within me, to the being whom I felt I really was, and who came fully to life only when I was there. And the being I became perceived the world in a special way. I did so through some inner mechanism I did not understand, and whose manner of operation was unknown. Nevertheless, it was quite clear that these things were so. The manner in which my perception reached out and grasped the world was not limited to working specifically through vision, nor through any other particular mode of sensory awareness. This knowing brought matchless peace, inner integrity, sobriety, and clarity. It enabled me to meet the world as a wondrous, beautiful being instead of an inanimate lump. It brought me to a state of realization that the world was a living continuum of exquisite and mysterious power in which was embodied a shining reality, an expression of mystical, primordial love. How can the word, "love," ever convey the drive for expression that is so unimaginably potent that it engendered entire galaxies? Yet through some knowing I could contemplate that power, and through it, it was possible to be a conscious part of it and breathe the same energy that animated the world; that energy which to me was, in the most absolute sense, the breath of life.

Many of the sounds in nature were capable of arousing certain states of awareness within me, and perhaps they did so by affecting certain psychic or astral centers much as the nervous system could be influenced by the use of mantras, or by various Eastern and Oriental musical instruments. Thus, in various occult and religious contexts one could find many sense-directed devices that were used for the purpose of inducing desired states of consciousness. My awareness of the power of sound has been deeply enhanced through my many years of experience as a musician, and through my study of yoga and other occult paths. Thus, the momentum of those experiences, coupled with whatever psychic sensitivities I possessed and with the unique power in the area of the lake, contributed to my being extremely open to the influences of sound there. After all, when one considers the profound effects which art and music can have upon the consciousness of an individual, and the meaning and knowledge which they can convey, what then is so improbable about my assertions that the sensory phenomena in nature were vehicles through which I perceived a whole spectrum of metaphysical realities?

With respect to this, I can make a strong analogy here between music and the aspect of sound in nature. For example, how could I ever convey the nature of the beauty and power which I might perceive in a piano concerto of Mozart, or an etude of Chopin, to someone who was indifferent to classical music? Their insensitivity to it and their inability to be nourished by it denies its realities only to them, and in no way changes the fact that within the music there lives a noumenal reality which only waits to be apprehended and understood by the ones who are capable of doing so. Indeed, the same may be said of the world of power which awaited me at the lake. The fact that others went there and were blind to its lovely consciousness denied the reality only to them.

I detected a great expressiveness and potency in the sounds of the insects and other small creatures that lived in the hills surrounding the water. There was an abundance of animal life there. Squirrels were everywhere, darting across the lawns and running through the trees. Elusive chipmunks flashed momentarily across the shore path, only to dart from view and disappear among the vegetation and fallen leaves. There were rabbits and raccoons, and an occasional opossum, and a muskrat now and then along the banks of the lake. There were many birds, but, given my focus on other parts of the environment, I did not often notice them, and I do not recall hearing many songbirds. The lake supported the usual characteristic waterfowl, and I occasionally sighted a kingfisher perched in the branches of the trees along the shores.

But despite the beauty in all of this, the creatures that fully arrested my attention were the ones that were rarely visible. These were the various insects, particularly the cicadas and crickets, and the tree frogs. I was always very alert to the sounds which they made, and they seemed to be an integral aspect of the great fabric of life surrounding the lake. In the late mornings and through the fullness of the hot summer afternoons I was called to attention by the electric sounds of the cicadas that issued from the shimmering heights of the trees and drifted across the vibrant, deep blue skies. In the early evening, the crickets and tree frogs came to life and, far into the night, they called from the trees and bushes and other dark places. Their voices seemed to be the very embodiment of the awesome and mysterious volition which breathed in the darkness. Perhaps it was because they were so seductive that I detected an ominousness in them. Or perhaps there was something unnerving in the fact that I could hear them and yet never see them nor define their exact location. But whatever it was, that faculty of knowing inside me apprehended something about them that, although I do not think it was actually evil, was nevertheless dark and frightening, and when I heard them I often became alert and cautious.

I have endeavored to discuss the psychology of this kind of experience in terms of my own perceptions and my reactions. I have analyzed it in terms of its possible relationship to Indian perceptions and beliefs, and have attempted to pinpoint various factors that might possibly engender such experiences, such as the intuitive fear of becoming too close to an astral world and its accompanying dangers, or the psychic awareness of other forces that existed in the world there, both those that possessed a conscious volition and those that did not. There was something very powerful in the voices of the nocturnal creatures that made me feel as if they were the very voice itself, the very embodiment and expression of whatever it was in the night there that aroused my feelings of apprehension and made me feel a need for caution.

The feelings of apprehension that I sometimes experienced during my nights at the lake have also been described at length in the chapter entitled "Negoya" (see pages 101–103). When I had my vision of Negoya, although that night was one of realization and beauty, I was apprehensive and filled with anxiety, and the sounds of the night expressed my emotions (described on page 1 of this book).

There were various causes at the root of those experiences, and I have discussed them extensively, but it was often through the mysterious sounds of little night creatures that I became acutely aware of those undefined and unsettling forces that existed within the world of the lake.

The sounds of the cicadas that filled the skies during the warm and sunny days affected me very differently from the tree frogs and other insects I was aware of during the nighttime. Not only was the emotional aspect of these phenomena entirely different, but I felt that they were linked respectively with two different levels of consciousness within my being. Despite the coherence and unity of my perceptions at the lake that, together, comprised the overall character of my experiences there, those somewhat eerie nocturnal sounds aroused one area of sensitivity in my mind, and the noise of the cicadas stimulated another. The nocturnal sounds gripped me on a feeling level and seemed to speak to my body itself, to the mind that controlled it and signalled that primeval instinct, or consciousness that registered such sensations as alarm or caution, desire or exhilaration, or other powerful, emotion-backed states including the age-old awe and fear of the supernatural, which is particularly relevant. It would be misleading to imply that those nocturnal sounds always produced such sensations, for on many occasions they were simply beautiful and mysterious, and nothing more. And even on the occasions when they were frightening, they were at the same time provocatively alluring. It was undoubtedly true that their enticing quality enhanced their sometimes sinister character. I am not certain why this was so.

The sound of the cicadas immediately evoked a lucid and meditative frame of mind. They enabled me to focus my attention and cleared the screen of my consciousness of its cobweb of meandering thoughts. The noise of the cicadas was quite similar in its effect to that which the sounds of the waters of the lake often produced in me, in that to focus my awareness on either of those sounds for even a short period of time was to achieve the state of mind which I would realize if I were to sit and meditate, and do yoga.

The sounds of the cicadas and the water produced effects much like practices that employ various sense-directed trappings. There many such devices, including icons, incense, Gregorian chant and many other kinds of music and musical instruments, other kinds of chants, mantras, drums, tom-toms, a wealth of garments and apparel, talismans and other such instruments, magical words and diagrams, and a host of other things that might produce this state. However, with reference to my comments about the water and the cicadas, I am primarily interested in the science of sound and the manner in which it is related to consciousness.

When I studied yoga and other occult practices, I acquired a knowledge of chakras and learned that each center was related to particular states of consciousness and to specific abilities and powers. The energies within those centers could be aroused in various ways. A common method was to meditate on a particular chakra by envisioning it in its correct location inside the body while at the same time employing certain techniques of concentration, one of which was to focus upon the color and sound specifically associated with that chakra. There are seven main chakras located along the spinal column and in certain areas of the brain. Although there are specific phenomena that accompany the operation of each chakra, including certain characteristic colors and sounds, I have observed what is apparently a wide range of discrepancy among various occult schools as to what those colors and sounds are. I do not know how to account for this, except to speculate that it may be the result of anything from sheer ignorance to the possibility that techniques may vary according to the nature of the desired end. I really am not certain of the reasons behind these variations.

In my own personal training, however, my spiritual teacher, Swami Nirmalananda Giri, gave me a particular color and sound to employ for each chakra when I meditated. To one chakra he attributed a kind of buzzing or electric sound quite similar to that made by a bumblebee, or to the sound of a cicada, which is produced by the plate-like organs on the thorax of the males. To another chakra he attributed a sound similar to that of water, perhaps like a waterfall or the rushing of waves. The goal of this technique is to enable the practitioner to attune himself with the correct astral colors of the chakras and to hear the sounds they actually make in the astral nervous system. One result is that one acquires a steadiness of mind characterized by calmness and the ability to sustain focused concentration. I was able to achieve a similar state of mind at the lake, in which I knew a deep inner calm and a profound lucidity, and in the quietness of which I was able to intuitively understand many of the messages of nature. There was something about the character of certain natural phenomena that was instrumental in evoking those states of consciousness, and I found it an interesting coincidence that two of the sounds that affected me the most profoundly, those of the water and the cicadas, resembled very closely those sounds produced by certain chakras in the astral nervous system. There are many other sounds in nature related to the astral physiology of man, but the water and particularly the cicadas held special significance for me. These natural phenomena helped me to become attuned to power centers within my inner being. My consciousness was purified, and I was able to open myself even more to the forces around me, which I sought to know ever more fully.

Thus, within the hills that encircled the lake, I embraced a rich and beautiful spectrum of wonders. I encountered what one might describe as an entire hierarchy of forces and powers that moved within the consciousness of nature and acted upon my being. At times, my fears had prevented me from being too available to realms that seemed dark to me and that I did not understand. Perhaps in time I would understand those fears more clearly and overcome them, and find the power to venture where I had previously felt that I could not go. Some of the forces there were awesome and frightening, and yet they were all beautiful, and they all fed me and taught me what it was to feel truly alive. The only true understanding I could have of those forces would come from opening my perceptions and merging with them, and with that great unifying field of consciousness that pervaded them. It was my deep longing to embrace that reality which expressed itself so fully there that brought me back to the lake again and again, to the place whose power pulled me across time and distance, which lived in the sparkling waters and shone in the soft twilight, and permeated the lush green hills.

The Point

Conference Point, located on the northern shoreline of Lake Geneva about a mile east along the shore path from the town of Fontana, forms a prominent feature of the landscape. The shoreline, which follows an easterly course from Fontana to the Point, abruptly changes direction there and heads north into the town of Williams Bay, before angling east and then south toward Cedar Point. The shoreline forms the U-shaped inlet known as Williams Bay, the access to which is marked by Conference Point at its western tip and by Cedar Point at its eastern tip, where the shoreline then turns east and eventually reaches the town of Lake Geneva at the eastern end of the lake. Conference Point, like Cedar Point, is characterized by steep bluffs that level off to form sites from which one can command an excellent view of a considerable portion of Lake Geneva.

Among all places on earth, it is unique for me. It is a place of profound experiences and incredible memories. It is a living mystery whose relevance to my life has maintained a powerful influence. In fact, that influence has grown and evolved dramatically. My relationship with that area was further strengthened and greatly clarified by the remarkable series of events that began in December 1980, when I learned through my reading with Robert, the psychic, that Negoya was an American Indian word, and that my experiences at the lake were somehow related to some past American Indian influence there. After months of sporadic research, I had visited the lake during August 1981, to investigate American Indian cultures which had flourished there in the past, and during the following month of September I had come to know Shupshe Wahnah and finally arrived at some answers.

Conference Point

According to Indian history and legend, a thunderbird, a spirit being, is said to have alighted on Conference Point. This supported the idea that this was a place of power. And my vision of Negoya had also occurred at Conference Point, over the waters just beyond the shore.

My subsequent meeting with Shupshe Wahnah in September 1981 had resolved some perplexing mysteries. I identified the spirit being I had encountered as Negoya. I learned who Negoya was and how he had appeared to me, and that he had heightened my perceptions. I also received independent information from Shupshe that Lake Geneva was indeed a place of power, and I gained some insights as to why this was so.

I have lived in many places, engaged in many pursuits, and walked among diverse groups of people. But the influence of the lake and the Point is a thread that has been woven in and out of those changing circumstances and vicissitudes, enduring through the years, submerged sometimes beneath the affairs of my life, and surfacing at other times to exert a powerful influence upon my thoughts and actions. Whether or not I have always recognized it, that wonderful place has never released me, nor I it, and it has always drawn me back.

At the Point, each hour of the day was different. The quiet mornings, the exuberant afternoons, the gradually expiring light of the dusks, each revealed new moods. The twilight held the greatest secret in its mysterious, dying colors. From early to middle afternoon, the world was most fully awake, a kaleidoscope of movement and play. But when I went to the Point during the quiet hours of the morning, it always seemed to me, more than at any other time, the most evident face that God had made the world.

It was there especially that I was filled with feelings that were profoundly religious. There, in the stillness of morning, as the light of the new sun caught the lake and brightened the hills, as I looked toward the east, I felt like falling to my knees and bowing my head to worship the power whose love had created that world. At that quiet hour, the lake was calm and undisturbed. A gentle morning wind blew steadily across the water, lightly ruffling the surface and creating successive, unbroken rows of small waves that glided serenely toward shore. The sound of the waves quietly smacking against the boulders was clear and melodious. From time to time a light breeze would gently stir the birch trees that reached out over the water, faintly rustling and shaking their leaves.

When I looked at the wet, glistening boulders along the shore, their shining forms covered with bright green moss; the soft grass glowing in the warm light; the white birch trees, their roots clinging to the banks and reaching out here and there into the grass; the yellow flowers and bright vegetation that covered the bluffs; the flight of an occasional insect, its iridescent body and wings catching the sunlight, I knew I was treading upon hallowed ground. It aroused in me a profound and quiet reverence. The waters of the lake and the haze that floated over it shone brightly in the morning light, as if the shining body of some radiant spirit being were moving across the waves.

There have been many times in my life when some outer sensory stimulus has caused powerful memories to surge into my consciousness from the past, often with enormous emotional impact. Such memories may have been aroused by a piece of music or some other sound, by a familiar object or a particular view, perhaps by a fragrance, or even by some momentary, fleeting thought. At such moments, I have found myself flooded, sometimes overwhelmingly, with feelings and images from the past that may range from intensely pleasurable and nostalgic to extremely painful and sad, depending upon the nature of my original experience. I may have thought mistakenly that those things were long dead, but such experiences have helped to convince me that the events that have filled our lives continue to live after they have happened, and I believe that it is possible for one to tap those past experiences, consciously or unconsciously, and find oneself suddenly re-experiencing them with the full impact and vivid reality of the original event.

It seems as if the memory of certain times actually releases more energy into one's being and consciousness than did the events themselves. The content of the memory can seem even richer than the content of the original experience. The easy explanation for this is that one's memory can become colored as time goes on. This is sometimes the case. However, I am really not talking about those cases in which one simply romanticizes about a past event or even embellishes it. I am not speaking about situations in which the original reality is distorted. Rather, I am referring to those memories whose contents release even more energy within the mind than did the original event. I suspect that, in actuality, this is not what really happens. But it can appear so, and I believe that it does for the following reason. A sequence of events linked together by some common emotional thread may have taken place. The overall impact of these events was formed by separate experiences that transpired over an extended period. All of the experiences may each have contained great energy and may have been intense and meaningful. But since they did in fact take place one at a time, in succession, rather than simultaneously, they did not totally overwhelm the one who experienced them because they did not converge upon him in one single moment of time.

But one's memory has a way of compressing such periods of time. Thus, reflecting back over the past, a person might say, "It was a good year," or "It was a difficult week," or "I had a beautiful summer!" In effect, one has compressed a series of happenings into a simultaneous whole. Although such a visualization is meant to be nothing more than a tool, it is useful to imagine that the passage of time is a continuous line upon which one moves through the succession of events that comprise one's life. But when one looks back through one's memory at a particular segment of events upon that line, especially a segment that is unified in some way into an emotional whole, one tends to look back down that line of time from a point upon the line itself, rather than from one above it, and one tends to see, instead of the broad sequence of original circumstances, those events compressed into one overall, general image, condensed into one unified moment. Thus, the intensity and energy of many separate and successive moments is seen, or remembered as a whole, and is therefore magnified.

During my absences from the lake, which have often been months long, even three years in one case, I have been suddenly confronted with disturbingly powerful memories of the lake and the Point. My mind would become flooded with recollections and longings. Sometimes I would be deeply involved in some activity and would find myself suddenly aware of the lake. To be transported abruptly into such perceptions was often an emotional jolt; I would unexpectedly realize myself to be cut off from that marvelous place. Yet, even in that isolation, I would also experience an inseverable tie with the lake, which I knew that nothing could break.

There were many things in the outer world that might have the power to arouse such feelings and memories. Chief among them were various phenomena of nature; some aspect of the sky, as a formation of clouds; the cicadas and tree frogs; the perception of water, particularly as it sparkled in the sunlight; and the sounds of the waves. And yet, even when those various aspects of nature aroused feelings about the lake and the Point, I perceived a profound difference between them and the real thing; that is, they could never affect my consciousness in the same way that similar phenomena did at the lake and the Point. They were not the same. The exquisite power was not there, and I knew it. Thus I longed for the lake even more.

Lake Geneva exercised an enormous influence upon my relationship to music, for although I had started studying the piano shortly after my tenth birthday, having shown an interest in it from an early age, and although I was quite serious about it by the age of twelve, it was at the age of fifteen, after my first trip to Lake Geneva and the Point during August 1964, when I encountered my initial experiences and visions there, that I discovered a new reason for playing the piano and studying music. Music was a vibrant and fluid psychic medium through which I could express what I had found at the lake. By playing the piano, I could creatively release the energies and articulate the perceptions and feelings that had been born out of my contact with that incredible world. Although the chief avenue for the expression of my feelings was music, I also began to direct some of my creative energies to writing about my experiences, and I wrote my first poem in February 1966, which was about Lake Geneva.

Because of its passionate character, filled with intensely mystical overtones, the piano music of the Russian composer Alexander Scriabin has always been special to me, particularly his piano preludes. And even more so than the music of certain other composers that has had a similar influence upon me, Scriabin's music has possessed a deep affinity with many of my experiences at the lake, particularly those that took place during my early years there. Thus, I have always been deeply interested in Scriabin's piano music. I have felt close to it, and have played much of it on the piano over the years. There is an ecstatic joy, a surging beauty, that shines in this music, and whenever I have heard it I have found myself flooded with intense memories of my early experiences. Because of the energy the music released in me, those experiences haunted me and I sought to rediscover them. These feelings made me identify all the more with Scriabin because there is an intense longing in his music, particularly in his early preludes, as if for some shining, beautiful light that, once seen, has become obscured. One of his early preludes, Opus 11, Number 1, seemed to embody and epitomize these feelings, and I invariably experienced an intense reaction whenever I listened to it. The words I wrote in August 1971 captured this longing.

> How swiftly passed,
>   the Summer dream,
> This radiant vernal somnolence!
> Summer's evanescent vision,
> Sun-filled realm
>   of Soul's lost Silence...
>
> In memory's echoing changers,
> Through imagination's filter,
> Glows the spirit
>   of a memory,

Lost somewhere in
Time's vast ocean.

In Scriabin's younger music, I found the same elements which predominated within my own inner nature during the years following my first experiences at the lake and the Point—an intense mysticism and longing, fused with the sensuality and erotic passion of youth. From my earliest experiences through the present, the lake has been my beloved. I have known an ultimately inextinguishable passion for it. I have also loved women, and I have had many intense involvements and relationships with them. But the being who has never released me and whom I have never forgotten is the lake.

It was only after I had begun to experience a conflict with the church and to sense its criticism of my ideas that I acknowledged explicitly religious sentiments less and less. After many years of frustration and struggle I turned my back on the organized church. But even though I gradually came to express my perceptions in terms of concepts other than those that were exclusively religious, for example, through the use of such terms as "beauty," "power," "force," "being," "consciousness," I never lost the awareness of a loving presence within the natural world, a shining being that was the creative force behind all I saw. I believe that in freeing myself from those words and concepts that were attached to various religious dogmas and carried preestablished religious connotations, I was casting off burdensome dead weight that only impeded me from soaring into realms of purer, unobstructed perception. I therefore see my relationship with Lake Geneva as part of a plan, ideally suited to my personal nature, for within the environment of the lake, I was able to encounter a reality unencumbered by dogmas or definitions. The lovely consciousness within the world revealed itself through Negoya and through the visions given to me at the Point.

I have spoken of the power music held for me, and of my feelings of reverence at the Point, particularly in the quiet of the mornings. Despite the fact that my experiences during my early years at the lake had nothing to do with the religious activities of the people with whom I had gone there, I found certain music they used to be deeply meaningful. In spite of its simplicity, or indeed, perhaps because of it, there was one song that spoke clearly to me and aroused the feelings I experienced during those quiet mornings:

Let us break bread together,
on our knees, on our knees.
Let us break bread together,
on our knees, on our knees.
When I fall on my knees,
with my face to the rising sun,
O Lord, have mercy on me.

> Let us drink wine together,
> on our knees, on our knees.
> Let us drink wine together,
> on our knees, on our knees.
> When I fall on my knees,
> with my face to the rising sun,
> O Lord, have mercy on me.
>
> Let us praise God together,
> on our knees, on our knees.
> Let us praise God together,
> on our knees, on our knees.
> When I fall on my knees,
> with my face to the rising sun,
> O Lord, have mercy on me.

"When I fall on my knees, with my face to the rising sun..." These were the words that gripped me. For I had stood with my face toward the rising sun, filled with awe for the being whose love had manifested such beauty. Removed from any explicitly Christian implications, it was those few words that set into motion a powerful, empathetic vibration within me, and which, during my separations from the lake, aroused a tremendous longing to stand upon the Point and survey the lake in the morning light. Even in the glistening rocks and the breathing grass, there was an indwelling consciousness. And the light from that consciousness kindled everything there and permeated all things.

There was another song I knew that brought home certain feelings to me much as did the song about which I have already spoken:

> All night, all day,
>   angels watchin' over me, my Lord.
> All night, all day,
>   angels watchin' over me.
>
> Day is dyin' in the west,
>   angels watchin' over me, my Lord.
> Sleep, my child, and take your rest,
>   angels watchin' over me.
> Now I lay me down to sleep,
>   angels watchin' over me, my Lord.
> Pray the Lord my soul to keep,
>   angels watchin' over me.

Thy love stay with me through the night,
   angels watchin' over me, my Lord.
And wake me with the morning light,
   angels watchin' over me.

All night, all day,
   angels watchin' over me, my Lord.
All night, all day,
   angels watchin' over me.

Neither this song nor the others were great musical compositions by my standards, nor by anyone else's; nor were the words great poetry. But such is frequently the case with things to which one attaches great emotional value or which are capable of engendering powerful emotional responses. What is important is that these things represent experiences that profoundly affected one. For under certain circumstances, these things can evoke those dormant experiences and emotional energies that accompanied them. Thus, because the songs I am speaking about became part of my life during my early encounters with the lake and the Point, whenever I heard them, my consciousness became flooded with the states of mind that had been engendered by those experiences.

There was something in the gently repetitious and lyrical refrain, "All night, all day," which brought to mind the eternal nature of the primordial power behind the lake, and the almost endless expanse of time during which its unfathomable consciousness had manifested its creative energies through the vehicle of this enormous world. Even the shining rocks along the shores told me of the great age of the world; of the passing of day into night and back again into day throughout innumerable centuries; of the countless revolutions of planets around their suns. I had contemplated the metabolism and respiration of the living universe; a cycle of cosmic life so vast that men could not begin to measure it in their minds. As I went to the Point daily to fill myself with its life and perceived there the expression of the perpetual cycles of nature, I considered all these things, and I pondered the gloriously imponderable dimensions of the world's creator, whose existence has reached from before the beginning of time and whose thoughts will continue after time has ceased to be.

Thus, when I heard the refrain, "All night, all day," I remembered the things about which I have spoken, just as they were called to mind whenever I reflected upon the following words from Psalm 8.

O Lord, our Lord,
How majestic is Thy name in all the earth,
Who hast displayed Thy splendor above the heavens...

When I consider Thy heavens, the work of Thy fingers,
The moon and the stars, which Thou hast ordained;
What is man, that Thou dost take thought of him?
And the son of man, that Thous dost care for him?

I do not recall ever feeling that I was being watched over by angels, but I can remember times when I have experienced feelings that must have been as wonderful. How many times, particularly at twilight, I have sat at the Point and felt protected by the power there! Everything was as it should be. I was the being which I was supposed to be; I was balanced and whole, and tuned to the mysterious and wonderful forces around me. In all things I perceived an ultimate order and sanity, which at such times also pervaded my thoughts and circumstances.

But of all the evenings I have spent at the Point, and all the evenings I have spent on earth, there was one which, above all others, made a unique impact. That was the evening in August 1964, when I encountered Negoya. After my vision of him, I had left the Point and walked back to the cabin where I was staying. As I stood in the cabin, among the other individuals who were there, I felt an immeasurable distance between myself and them, as if I were actually on a totally different plane. My surroundings, including the presence and conversation of my peers, seemed vague and remote. And yet within myself, I was experiencing a state of unparalleled and crystalline lucidity. At that moment I perceived the subtle presence of roses encompassing me. Within that ethereal garden, which seemed to isolate me from my physical surroundings, it was as if for a period of time I was being protected, so that the incredible energy through which my vision at the Point had manifested itself would be sustained for a while longer. Surely I was being watched over by the lovely power which had guided my steps to that unique moment in my life. "All night, all day, angels watchin' over me." In the time to come, when I heard the words to that song or thought of them, I remembered the nights at the Point, and particularly that one special night that had changed my life and set its course in an entirely new direction.

During my yoga training, I had been struck by the significance of roses in many of the ceremonies and initiations connected with it. At those times, I and the others involved had been surrounded by the presence of physical roses, as well as by icons and images of various deities and pictures of some of the great gurus. I had shared my early experiences at the Point with my spiritual teacher, who also felt that there was a noumenal tie between the phenomena of roses at the lake and their use in the yoga ceremonies. When I recalled that wondrous night at the Point when I had seen Negoya and then the roses, I thought of the beautiful peace that had surrounded me in the cabin, and of the hopes which I had felt then; that is, that I would always be able to live my days in the matchless state of grace which I knew during those fleeting hours. I could not have foreseen the years of searching and spiritual conflict that were before me, and which would truly begin to resolve themselves only after I had entered my early thirties.

But at the lake, I had come to know a perpetual, shining Presence in all things, and to feel an unparalleled joy and mystery in everything I did. I moved through an ocean of Loving Consciousness. I saw the Mind of God in every rock and blade of grass; its power was within every wave on the lake. It was in the sunlight. It was in the buildings, and in the food I ate, and even within the utensils I used to eat. It entered me with every breath. It exuded a Love that endured with me through the nights; and when I awoke, its Presence was the first thought which occupied my mind. In the words of the song, "thy love stay with me through the night, and wake me with the morning light."

The grounds that comprise the Point are fairly extensive, bounded on the south and east by the lake shore, along which extends the shore path. This is the site of Conference Point Camp, upon which there are a number of buildings, including many cabins. Bounded on the east, then, by Williams Bay, and on the west by a private estate, Conference Point Camp extends northward from the north shore of the lake for some distance until it reaches the entrance to the camp, which is located on the northernmost border of the grounds, and beyond which are private residences.

As one enters the grounds from the road, by the entrance along the northern property line, one proceeds south on that road which ascends to the spacious grounds atop a large hill that comprises the southeastern section of the camp. That is the great hill that overlooks the lake, whose southern and eastern sides are defined by steep bluffs that descend through the thick vegetation to the shore path. At that extreme southeastern point, the concrete steps descend from the hilltop, past the brick alcove, down to the flat, grassy opening of the Point itself. There, the shore path forms a ninety-degree bend and heads either west, past the George Williams College Camp and on into Fontana, or north, along Williams Bay and into the town. It was there, where the trail turns sharply and where the birches reach out over the waters of the lake, that I saw Negoya in August 1964.

From the plateau atop that lovely hill overlooking the Point, the land slopes gently down to the north and to the west, across the grounds shaded by towering trees. The extreme western portion of the grounds opens out into a huge field, but if one continues on the road that leads to the top of the hill above the Point, it circles the hilltop and proceeds north, descending gradually through the shaded cabins and inviting lawns, and eventually angles west across the more level portion of ground along the northern extremes of the camp, to return finally to the entrance.

Did it really exist, a locale filled with such extraordinary power? In spite of the intensely reality-oriented consciousness I experienced there, and in spite of the characteristic sobriety and unparalleled feelings of sanity that pervaded all my perceptions, it still sometimes seemed like a dream. At one point in my life, it had seemed that perhaps as one's consciousness became more aware of its own real nature, the world around it appeared to become progressively more dreamlike, almost unreal. It was true that my consciousness became far more alive at the Point, awakened to a clearer quality of knowing. This, then, could perhaps explain why my perceptions and the manner in which I apprehended the world there sometimes seemed dreamlike.

That locale seemed like another universe, separate from the rest of the world I knew. And yet, there was no elaborate voyage involved in getting there. Physically, it was not on some distant world. It was removed only in terms of its uniqueness. There has always been an illusion in my mind that the lake was far away. But for many years I never lived more than a few hundred miles from the lake, and it was within a day's drive.

Even though I planned my trips to the lake well ahead of time, sometimes months in advance, it was generally somewhat of a shock, albeit a positive one, to find myself transposed into a world whose environment was so utterly different from the one in which I spent most of my life. This reaction was due to the fact that I was able to transport myself to the lake in such a short time. My relative accessibility to the lake, geographically speaking, was not accidental. For although there were many opportunities to move to other locales considerably more distant from the lake than the places where I had lived, and although I may have considered such moves if the circumstances would have proven to be favorable enough, I felt that I did not want to live at a great distance from the lake and make it difficult to go there. Yet, ironically, when I was away from the lake and the Point, it seemed as if there was a universe of distance separating that world from the one where I lived. And when I found myself at the lake, looking out over the waters, the reverse was true, even more so. The world beyond the lake and all my involvements and responsibilities seemed not only tremendously far away, but somehow illusory. I found it difficult to think about them at all; and when I did, I could hardly even grasp them as existing. The environment was so wondrous that my thoughts about the rest of the world were simply crowded out.

I have continued to experience a clear and sometimes painful dichotomy between my life at the lake and my life away from it. Over the years, I could not seem to integrate those two contrasting facets of my existence; sometimes I could hardly even reconcile them. I had always had difficulty incorporating the world of the lake and the Point into the rest of my existence. My apparent inability to assimilate the perceptions and experiences of that unique world of power into the rest of my life in a harmonious manner created an inner conflict which, although it has varied in intensity, has lasted for many years. It began almost immediately after my return from my first visit to the Point in August 1964. Because of that feeling, although I had conceived the idea of writing this book during a visit to the lake in August 1980, and had subsequently begun some initial work on it, my efforts had gradually dwindled, and had virtually come to a halt by the time I had my decisive reading with Robert the psychic in December 1980. After meeting Robert, I resumed the project and labored through to its completion.

When I contemplate the future, I feel that there is much waiting for me at the lake and the Point. I have hardly begun to delve into the mysteries they embody. And through the vehicle of that magical locale, I will do as Shupshe Wahnah has urged, and what I have known I must do. I will look more deeply within my own mind for answers to the great mysteries that confront me there. And in doing so, I must resolve that conflict which has been with me for so many years. I must find the knowledge and the courage to fully embrace that matchless power which exists there; to assimilate it, totally and wholly, into my being; to fuse it irreversibly and forever, through some inner chemistry, with the totality of my nature, and give to my life a wholeness that expresses the happiness I have found at the Point; looking into the pure and incorruptible Truth, the inexhaustible and loving Consciousness that shines there, within the lake and hills.

> light and shadow on the old brick
>   washing the bunches of flowers in
> afternoon ancient Yellow sunlight
>   oh, primeval light   soft diffusion of gold
>   through the foliage...
>   negoya...
>   shining threadlike Beam hallowing
> the cathedral of the mind
>   the mind's searchlight spiraling, om.
>   its Beacon diving down
>   and down...
>   The light in one leaf   all the leaves of eternity,
> oh, Negoya you who make things to live in all times at once,
>   Glory be to the Father
>   Oh, silent cathedral in me...
>   light filtering through the
>   stained glass windows of my eyes...
>   And to the Son,
>   Joy, joy,
>   this happy, winding singing rocky path
>   flowing into Dimension in all direction...
>   and to the Holy Ghost...
> (oh, wandering in the ocean of sunshine dancing
>   on the bark
>   through the trees)
>   melting now...
>   surging waves dancing, dancing,
>   around the rocks
>   drenched with spray
>   sing for a thousand thousand years...

As it was in the beginning,
  oh, this aching freedom
  bursting forth measureless Expansion
   riding the wave of the future...
     eternal now,
Is now and ever shall be...
  angels watching over me,
   sing forever and ever
  World without end, amen,
melting in one and all breathing forth joy...
  free, free, dancing in time
  stripped away to Eternity
   World without End,
    Amen...

   Amen.

        Fall 1969

Epilogue

I finished *Darkness Is Light Enough* in March 1982 and remained in Louisville, Kentucky, with my wife Suzanne until a move to Los Angeles, California, in 1985. My friendships with Jerry Alber and Shupshe Wahnah grew, and I took Jenny to Fort Wayne, Indiana, to meet Shupshe in November 1982. During the years between my completion of the book and the present, I have been to Lake Geneva many times and have had extraordinary experiences which perhaps I will write about one day. But there is one event of such import that I include it here, because it was a milestone in my coming to understand the lake's meaning for me and its impact upon my life.

The following conversation regarding Lake Geneva and Negoya is an excerpt from a more extensive telephone reading I had with Lazaris* on July 2, 1983. Lazaris is a nonphysical entity who channels only through Jach Pursel. In our conversation, Lazaris and I explored and discussed many areas of my life, but the following material contains all the information pertaining to Lake Geneva and Negoya.

Lishka: I would like to ask you, first of all, if you have anything to tell me about Lake Geneva; that is, perhaps, its character, or my relationship with it, and its role in my life, past and future. I would like to know if I have ever lived there in the past and who I was, and if perhaps I was an American Indian there.

Lazaris: All right. The main Lake Geneva, the one that everyone thinks of when they think of Lake Geneva?

---

*Lazaris is a nonphysical entity who has been channeling through Jach Pursel since October 1974. Lazaris holds seminars frequently in major American cities, and has released more than two hundred audio and video tapes and books on a vast variety of metaphysical and spiritual issues. Concept: Synergy, which publishes The Lazaris Material, can send you more information. They can be reached at 1–800–678–2356, or by writing PO Box 3285, Palm Beach, FL 33480.

Lishka: I'm speaking of the Lake Geneva in Wisconsin.

Lazaris: Yes. All right. The one in Wisconsin then. There are a couple of them,
          you know. We would suggest here that—all right, the one, yes, all
          right. All right, Gerald, as we look at the vibration we know you've got
          lots of questions, and so we're taping this, of course, and we're going
          to answer very rapidly as we can, so that we can get as much informa-
          tion in this hour as possible.

          Lake Geneva, the connection. Yes, we would suggest you have
          spent two lifetimes there, on or around and about Lake Geneva. One of
          them, you drowned in the lake, and we would suggest here that it was a
          rather interesting lifetime. You were born an Indian in that particular
          lifetime, and we would suggest here you were a young boy. When you
          were, it was discovered that you had a weakness, a physical weakness.
          They didn't know what it was, but it was actually—what happened is,
          is in your growing up as a little boy, etc., it didn't show up. But when
          you became a young man, a young boy, to develop your skills as an
          Indian, etc., with running and trapping and hunting, etc., that you
          became very weak and would often pass out, just collapse. And so, in
          that sensing, the medicine men and all that discovered that there's a
          weakness in your system and that you would never be a strong, war-
          rior-type boy at all. Well, indeed, you were very disappointed and very
          chagrined at this, and your life was ruined as far as you were con-
          cerned. You had a great deal of self-pity and a great deal of victimhood
          going on.

          And we would suggest what happened here is that you had a
          dream one night, a dream very clearly where, indeed, there was a beau-
          tiful woman that came up out of the lake, and she lifted up out of the
          water and came to the shore of the lake and she spoke to you. And this
          very beautiful woman told you that there was very powerful work for
          you to do, work of the mind and work of the spirit, and that, indeed,
          you did not need a healthy body for that. In fact, a healthy body would
          only detract you, and you would spend your time out being like the
          other men and warriors and braves, and this sort of thing, and your
          work was of the mind and of the spirit. And therefore not to dishearten,
          and not be afraid, and to know that that was your work, etc., and to pur-
          sue the spiritual warrior and to pursue the mental warrior. And in that
          particular god, as quickly as she came, she walked back into the lake
          and seemed to disappear into the water.

          And as you woke in the morning from that particular dream, you
          went and talked to the medicine man about it, who indeed asked you
          many very strong and powerful questions, for he knew of the woman of

the lake. He knew of the lady, and, in that particular sensing, knew that for you to have experienced her was a very strong sign.

And so you began studying, and you began studying the mysticisms and the medicine law, and to become the next generation medicine man, etc. And indeed, you studied for a period of time of, oh, maybe six or seven years, until you were very, very good at it, when once again you had a dream, at around, this would have been around age, maybe, eighteen or so, maximally, and we would suggest the lady of the lake came out of the water once again and entered your dream and she came to you. And she said to you, "It's now time for you to come to me." And, in that sensing, in the dream you got up and you walked out over the water of the lake, and you went into the lake with her, etc., and that's all you remember of the dream. But when you awoke in the morning, indeed, you know that something very powerful must have happened while you were under the water with the lady of the lake at that particular point.

And we would suggest, Gerald, that what happened, in that sensing, is that you became very superb at healing. And in that particular way you were doing healing kind of work that was miraculous, much more than the medicine men could ever imagine with their shakers and with their herbs. And in that particular sense you also being very prophetic, in terms of both psychic and prophetic, etc., at this very young age. And indeed, you were doing the work. You were doing the work that was very much needed, etc. And what happened, in this sensing, is that you went on like this for a few more years, they being very gratified, etc., and then again you had a dream.

And in this dream, you saw the future of the Indian tribe to which you belong, and you saw it being wiped out, and you saw it being totally obliterated. And so we would suggest here, in that particular sensing, it caused you to weep very deeply, and upon waking you were very melancholy and very depressed. And you went down to the lake very early in the morning to sit by the lake, to get guidance, to seek guidance, from the waters itself, etc. And, in that particular sensing, what happened you don't know. But you got up and you began to run. You began to run like the Indian brave you thought you were going to grow up to be. And in running, etc., you could feel the pain within your heart, and you could feel the pounding within your chest, etc. But you kept running. You kept running. It's like you could not stop. And you came to a certain point at the lake, etc., a most very special place that you already know of, and you came to a very special place and you stopped running and stood there frozen in your tracks like a statue. (Author's note: This refers, of course, to my special place of power on

Conference Point Camp, where the birch trees stand at the water's edge.) And, in that sensing, fell forward, fell forward into the water. And, in that particular sensing, dead. And we would suggest that you drowned of the water; drowned, that sort of thing, for your work was done, and, in that particular sensing, your life ended.

That lifetime very powerful and important to you in terms of both positively, and unfortunately, some negative influences. But we would suggest here very positively, in terms of your work, in terms of your spirituality, in terms of your direction, to try to reach and to teach and to heal, in different ways in this lifetime than that. But we would suggest, also, it speaks to your melodrama, it speaks to your tendency to extremism, and we would suggest here it also speaks to a certain tragic quality that is threaded in your life. That's one of the lifetimes, Lake Geneva.

Another lifetime, much briefer than that, we would suggest here, is actually earlier. It's before that one that it occurred. Again, well, an Indian, yes, we would suggest so. And we would suggest here that, in that particular sensing, you lived by the lake, and it provided your livelihood and your activity, etc. It was also a place where you got into deeply meditative places, as you'd go out into the water, sometimes very early in the morning, as the mist was still hanging low. And you would sense as though you could hear the lake talking to you, and you would take solace in her words, and, in that particular sensing, you would leave your problems with her. And we would suggest here that you had a very beautiful rapport, no pain, no unhappiness, no distress. A very simple life, most definitely, where you lived much as a hermit, almost, etc. You had, as a young boy, discovered, etc., the very secret places along the banks, etc., and hidden there quite frequently as a young man, retreated from the tribal unit, was not interested in the social life, etc. And just lived almost as a hermit, etc., just you and the lake, and the lake providing you food and solace, and you providing the lake protection. And we would suggest here that there was a very strong sense of that in your vibration. And there's nothing more happened in that lifetime. You lived to be an old man and died. But we would suggest that, plus the other lifetime we mentioned, the two, that speak very strongly of you and Lake Geneva.

Lishka: Will I continue to have a relationship with it?

Lazaris: Most definitely you will. And we would suggest that, well, you won't drown, however. And we would suggest here that it will be much of a relationship with the lake. And the lake, of course, represents in so many beautiful ways a healing spot, not like Lourdes, but a healing spot of the spirit and the mind. Because it is, in a sense; it has within it the feminine energy, the goddess force, and we would suggest here that of a nurturing, healing quality. Not everybody can feel it. Everyone is affected, but not everybody knows it, and we would suggest here that it's one of the very powerful spots. And, oh yes, you will always find yourself returning to her, from time to time in your life, etc., and she'll be very important to you for most of your life, yes.

Lishka: I'm stunned. I've been waiting twenty years to hear that. Can you tell me anything about Negoya; my role with him, if I will ever see him again, if I ever knew him in a past life at the lake?

Lazaris: Right. Now, what was the name? Negoya?

Lishka: Yes.

Lazaris: And who is he, physically?

Lishka: Negoya, according to a Potawatomi medicine man that I know, was an Ojibwa medicine man that lived in that area several hundred years ago, and he believes that Negoya appeared to me in this life and taught me.

Lazaris: All right. The medicine man believes that?

Lishka: Yes.

Lazaris: And that's what you're asking about. All right. And why we ask in terms of that, with names, we often need to have other references to identify the energy, because names shift from lifetime to lifetime, and it's a very unstable point of reference.

We would suggest here that it totally makes sense, Negoya, as an energy. We would suggest here that where we sense it, in this particular sense, is the lifetime that we spoke of first, where indeed the medicine man took you in and asked you very many questions after your dream of the lady of the lake. And, we would suggest here, then taught you very diligently and very swiftly at that particular time. We would suggest here the energies feel to be that that would be the one to whom you are referring, Negoya. And we would suggest here that, in that particular sensing, you knew him then, very clearly.

We would suggest here that your rapport with the lake is so very strong, and with the Indian lore that is there, so very strong, that it would not be at all inappropriate for him to come to you, to talk to you, to teach you. And we would suggest here that there is a very special— oh, let's see, where is it? When you are near the lake, and even you don't have to be near the lake any more, for you can feel the energy of it just by thinking of it. But we would suggest here there seems to be a time when you were earlier in your life, when you were a teenager, fairly young, and then just moving into puberty, and therefore a high energy time, that you were there, by the lake, and that there was a special sort of wind, or special sort of sound. And that's when it occurred that he made his contact with you, and a lot of communication, a lot of teaching, was occurring at that particular time, and has subsequently occurred, though not necessarily with that physiological warning that he is there.

And we would suggest here that he is in many ways like what we would call a counselor, a spiritual guide, as others would call him, but of a very special nature, not one that would be there just at your calling, but one that comes at his decision. And we would suggest here that, as you are now thirty-four, we would suggest here his contact is not as frequent, but it is very powerful when it is there, and we would suggest there will be two times more in your life where you will feel his presence inextricably. There'll be no doubt. Absolutely, you'll know exactly who it is, and you'll know exactly what he looks like, etc. And that doesn't mean there'll only be two more contacts, but there'll be two times yet in your life that will be profoundly important for you, where there will be major shiftings in your life. One of those seems to occur during your thirty-seventh year, the other seems to occur during your forty-third year. And we would suggest here not to again indicate that that's all the contact you'll have, but at those two intervals, there will be a very powerful contact. You will be at the lake again, and we would suggest here that you will hear that same sort of sound and that same sort of wind shift, and it'll be like a déjà vu to when you were a pubescent teenager. And we would suggest here that there will be an aliveness that will be planted in you that will feel like a whole new person, almost. And that's there for you.

For other titles of related interest, write for our free catalog.
Send your request to:

Galde Press, Inc.
PO Box 460
Lakeville, Minnesota 55044

Credit card orders call **1–800–777–3454**